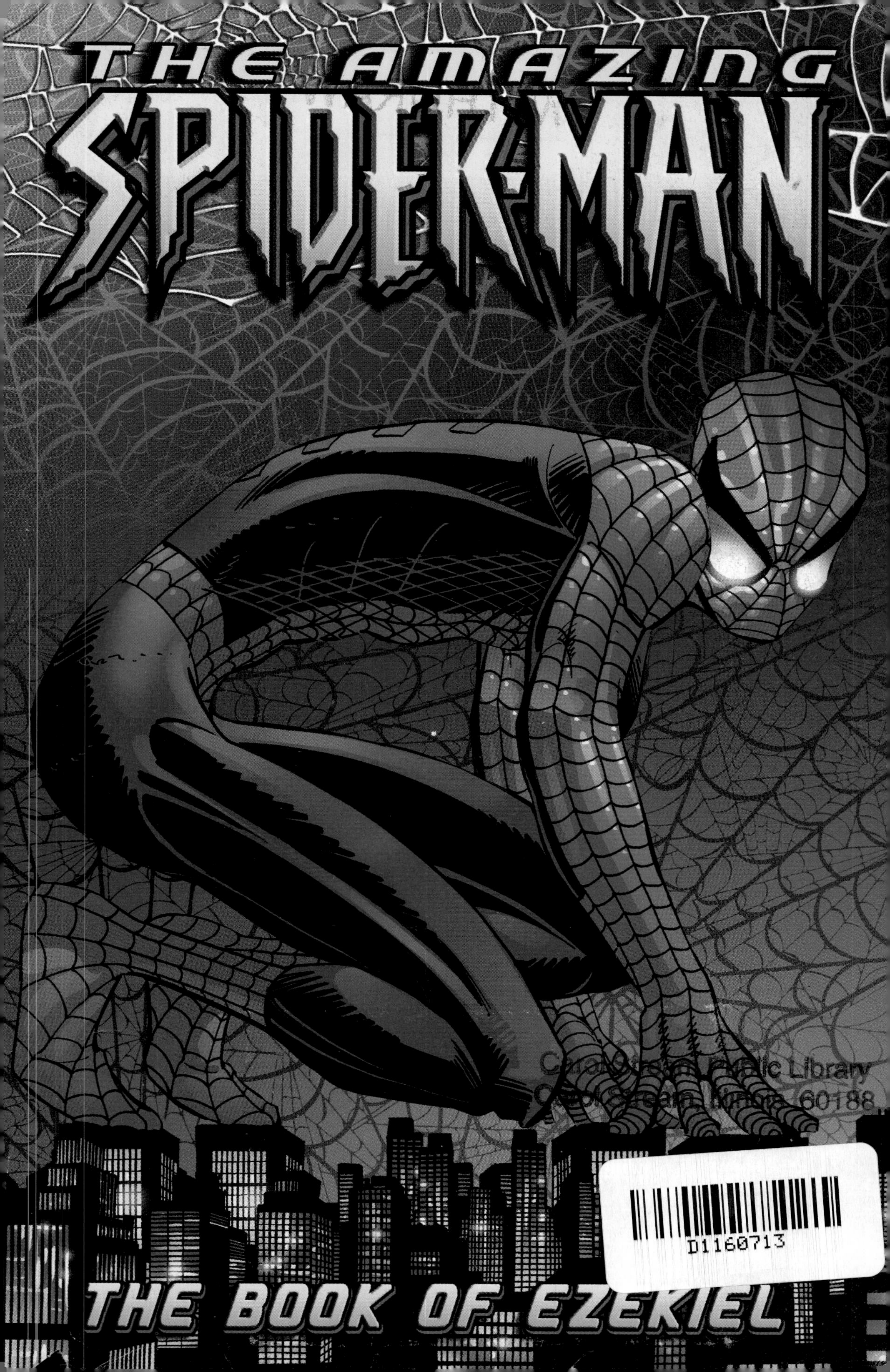
THE AMAZING
SPIDER-MAN
THE BOOK OF EZEKIEL

THE AMAZING SPIDER-MAN

THE BOOK OF EZEKIEL

writers: J. Michael Straczynski
with Fiona Avery
pencils: John Romita Jr.

inks: Scott Hanna with Scott Koblish
colors: Matt Milla
letters: Virtual Calligraphy's Cory Petit
cover art: John Romita Jr.
assistant editor: Warren Simons
editor: Axel Alonso

collections editor: Jeff Youngquist
assistant editor: Jennifer Grünwald
book designer: Carrie Beadle
creative director: Tom Marvelli
editor in chief: Joe Quesada
publisher: Dan Buckley

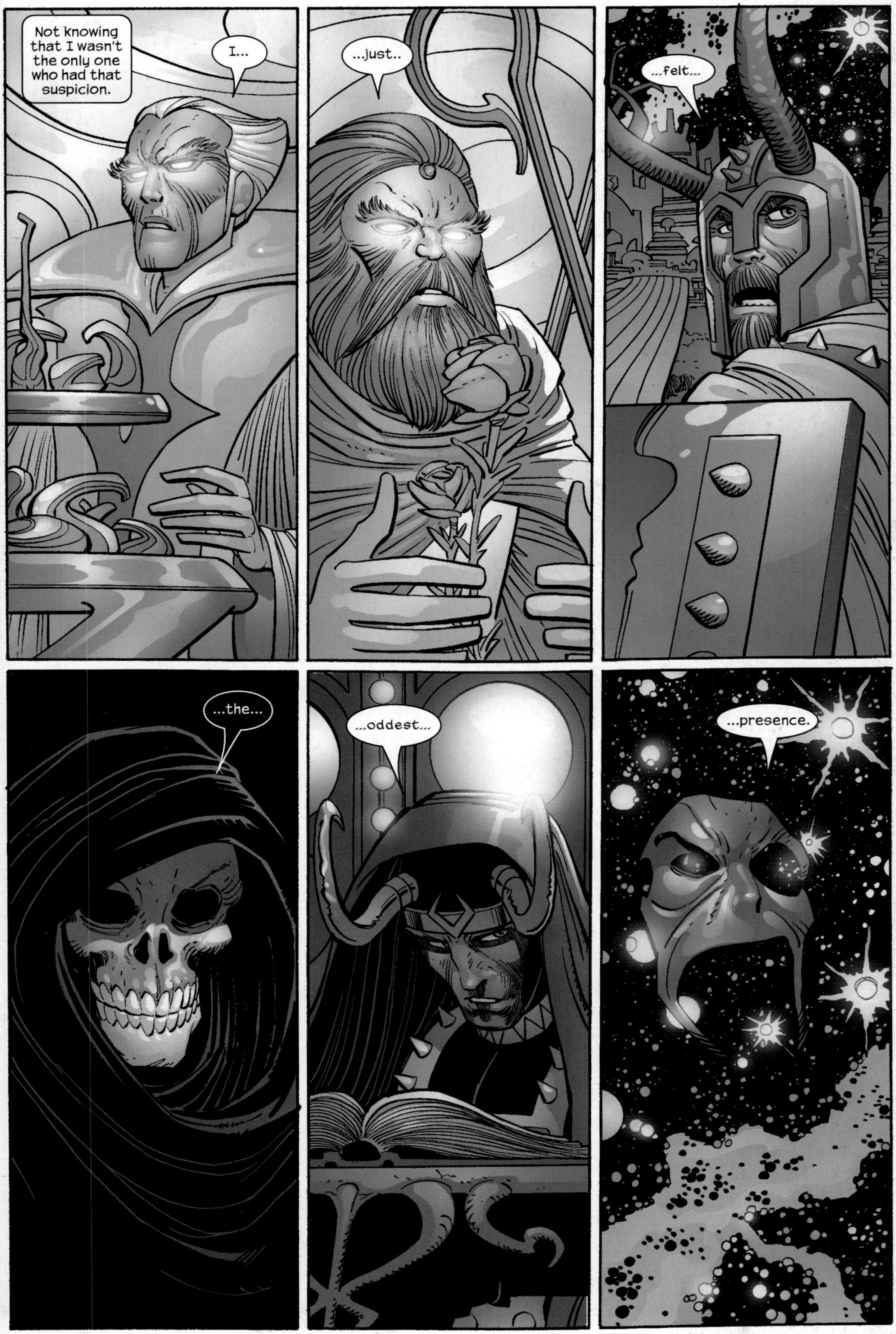

Not knowing that I wasn't the only one who had that suspicion.
I...
...just..
...felt...
...the...
...oddest...
...presence.

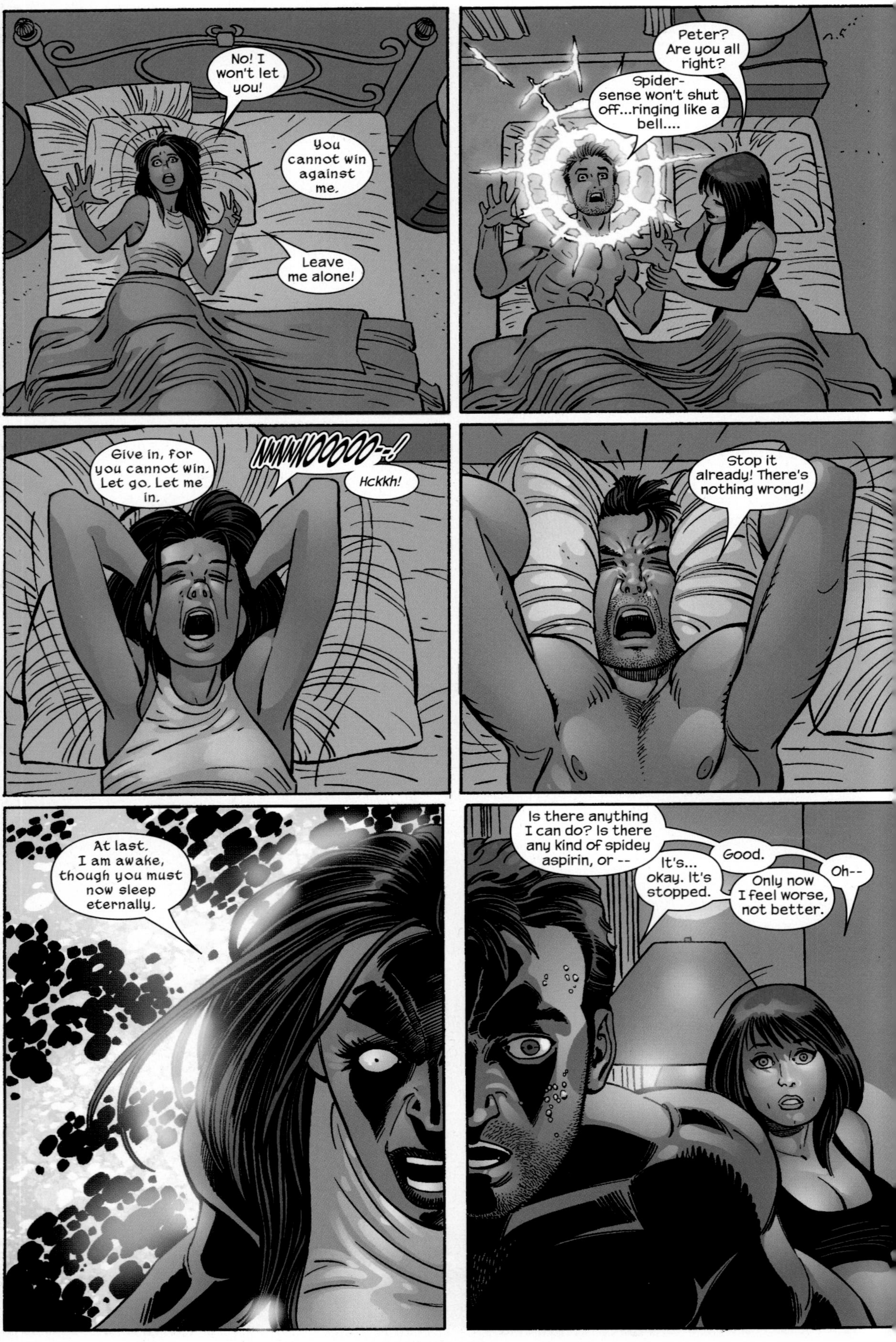
No! I won't let you!
You cannot win against me.
Leave me alone!
Peter? Are you all right?
Spider-sense won't shut off...ringing like a bell....
Give in, for you cannot win. Let go. Let me in.
NNNNOOOOO--!
Hckkh!
Stop it already! There's nothing wrong!
At last. I am awake, though you must now sleep eternally.
Is there anything I can do? Is there any kind of spidey aspirin, or --
It's... okay. It's stopped.
Good.
Only now I feel worse, not better.
Oh--

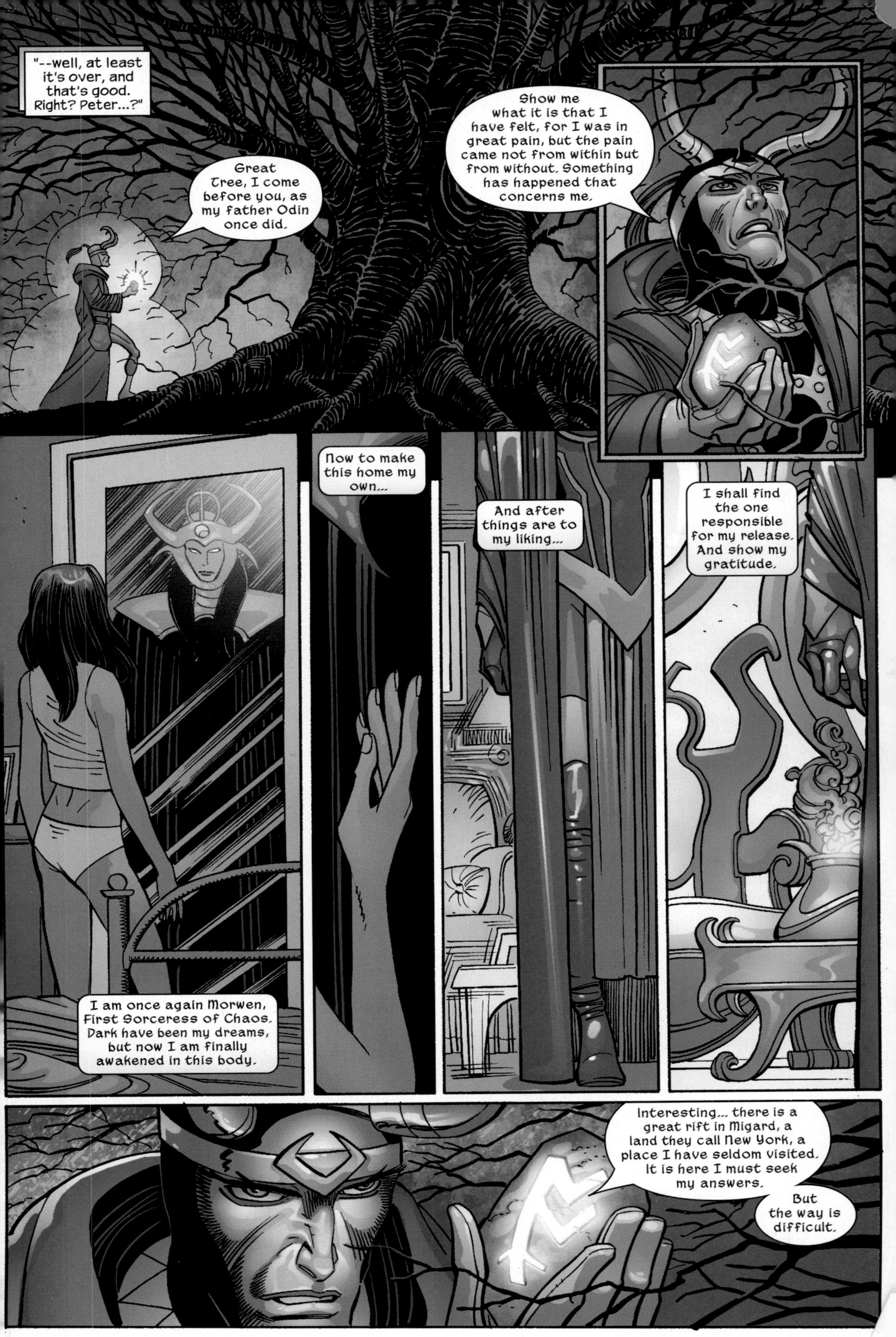
"--well, at least it's over, and that's good. Right? Peter...?"
Great Tree, I come before you, as my father Odin once did.
Show me what it is that I have felt, for I was in great pain, but the pain came not from within but from without. Something has happened that concerns me.
I am once again Morwen, First Sorceress of Chaos. Dark have been my dreams, but now I am finally awakened in this body.
Now to make this home my own...
And after things are to my liking...
I shall find the one responsible for my release. And show my gratitude.
Interesting... there is a great rift in Migard, a land they call New York, a place I have seldom visited. It is here I must seek my answers.
But the way is difficult.

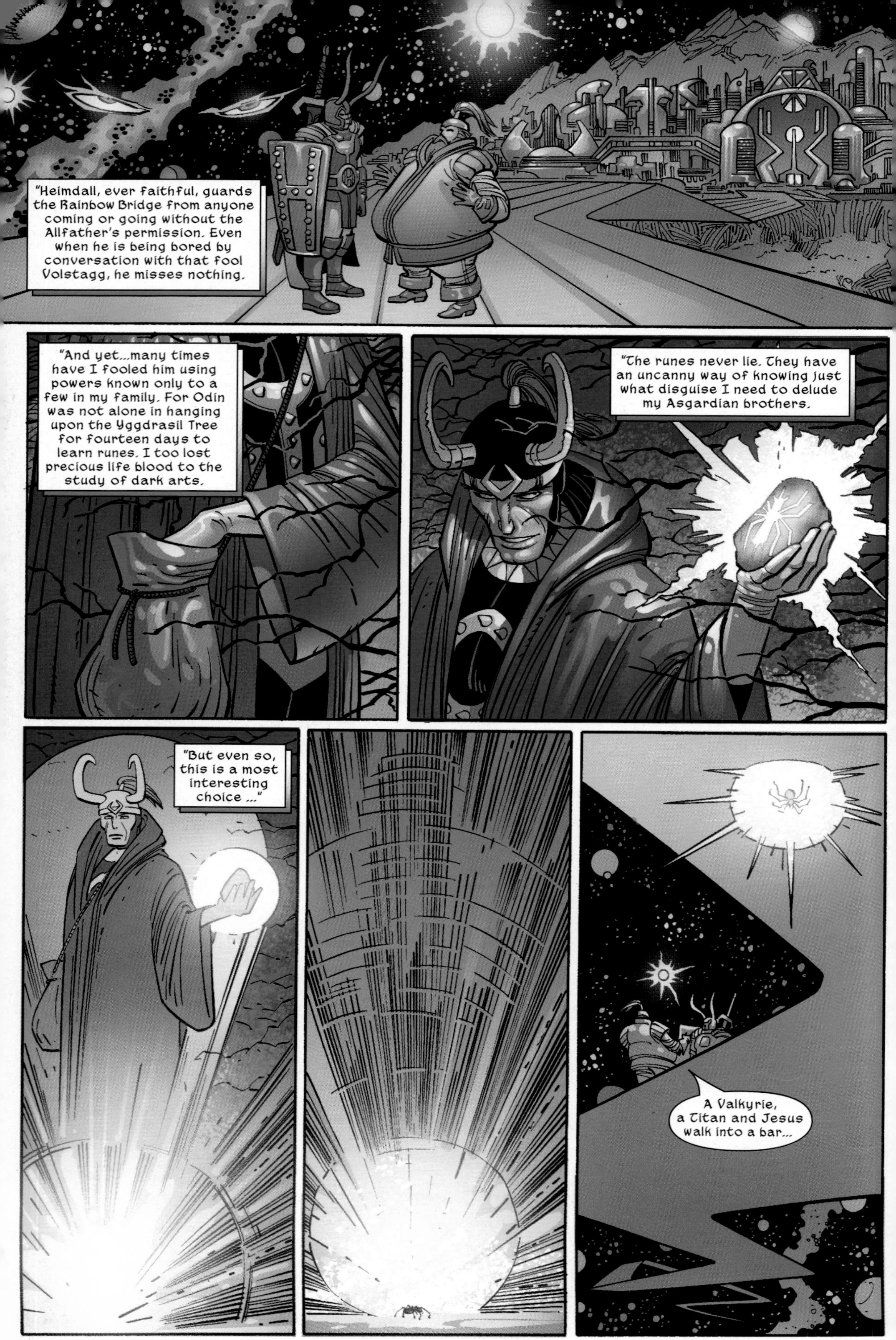
"Heimdall, ever faithful, guards the Rainbow Bridge from anyone coming or going without the Allfather's permission. Even when he is being bored by conversation with that fool Volstagg, he misses nothing.
"And yet...many times have I fooled him using powers known only to a few in my family. For Odin was not alone in hanging upon the Yggdrasil Tree for fourteen days to learn runes. I too lost precious life blood to the study of dark arts.
"The runes never lie. They have an uncanny way of knowing just what disguise I need to delude my Asgardian brothers.
"But even so, this is a most interesting choice ..."
A Valkyrie, a Titan and Jesus walk into a bar...

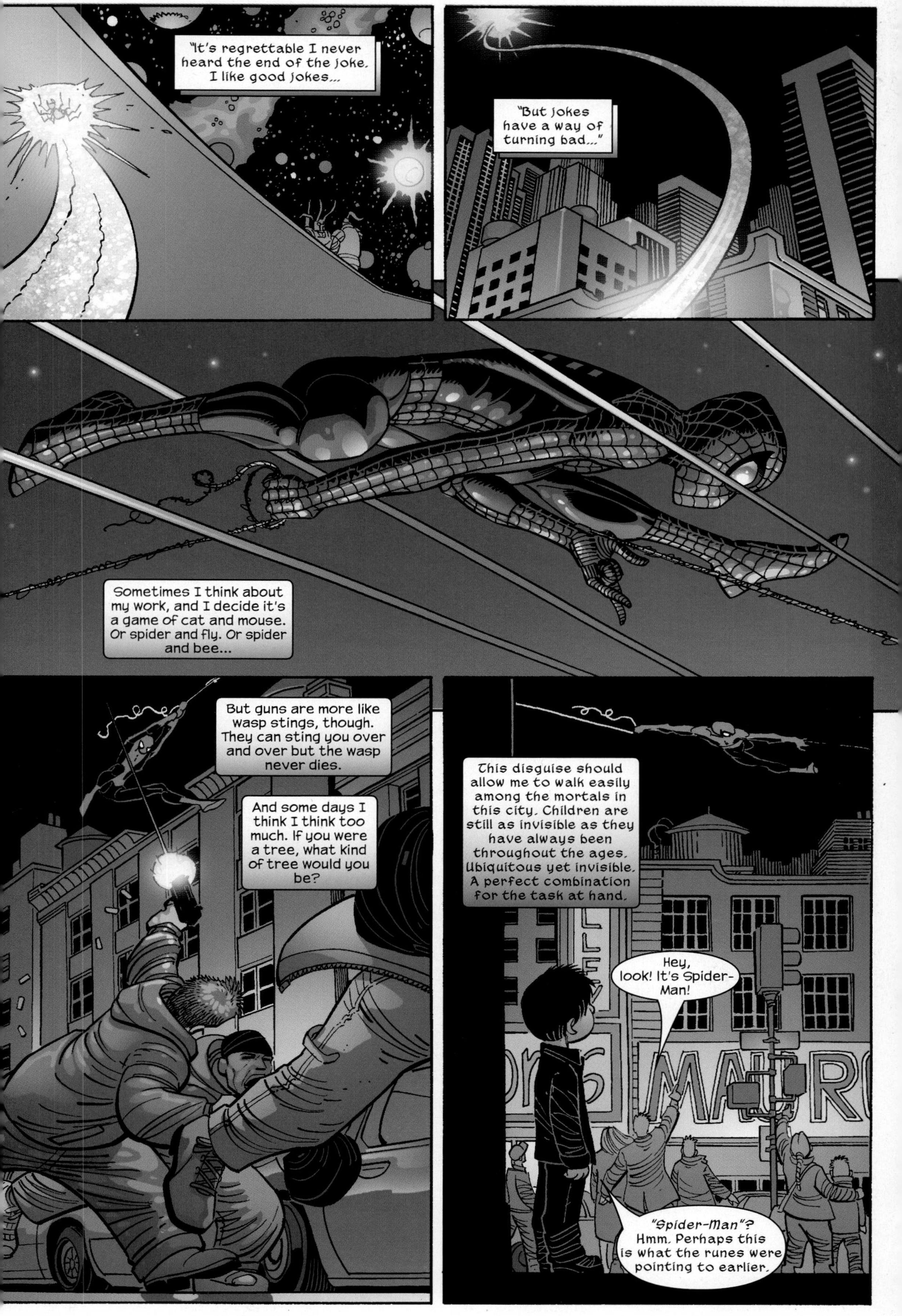
"It's regrettable I never heard the end of the joke. I like good jokes...
"But jokes have a way of turning bad..."
Sometimes I think about my work, and I decide it's a game of cat and mouse. Or spider and fly. Or spider and bee...
But guns are more like wasp stings, though. They can sting you over and over but the wasp never dies.
And some days I think I think too much. If you were a tree, what kind of tree would you be?
This disguise should allow me to walk easily among the mortals in this city. Children are still as invisible as they have always been throughout the ages. Ubiquitous yet invisible. A perfect combination for the task at hand.
Hey, look! It's Spider-Man!
"Spider-Man"? Hmm. Perhaps this is what the runes were pointing to earlier.

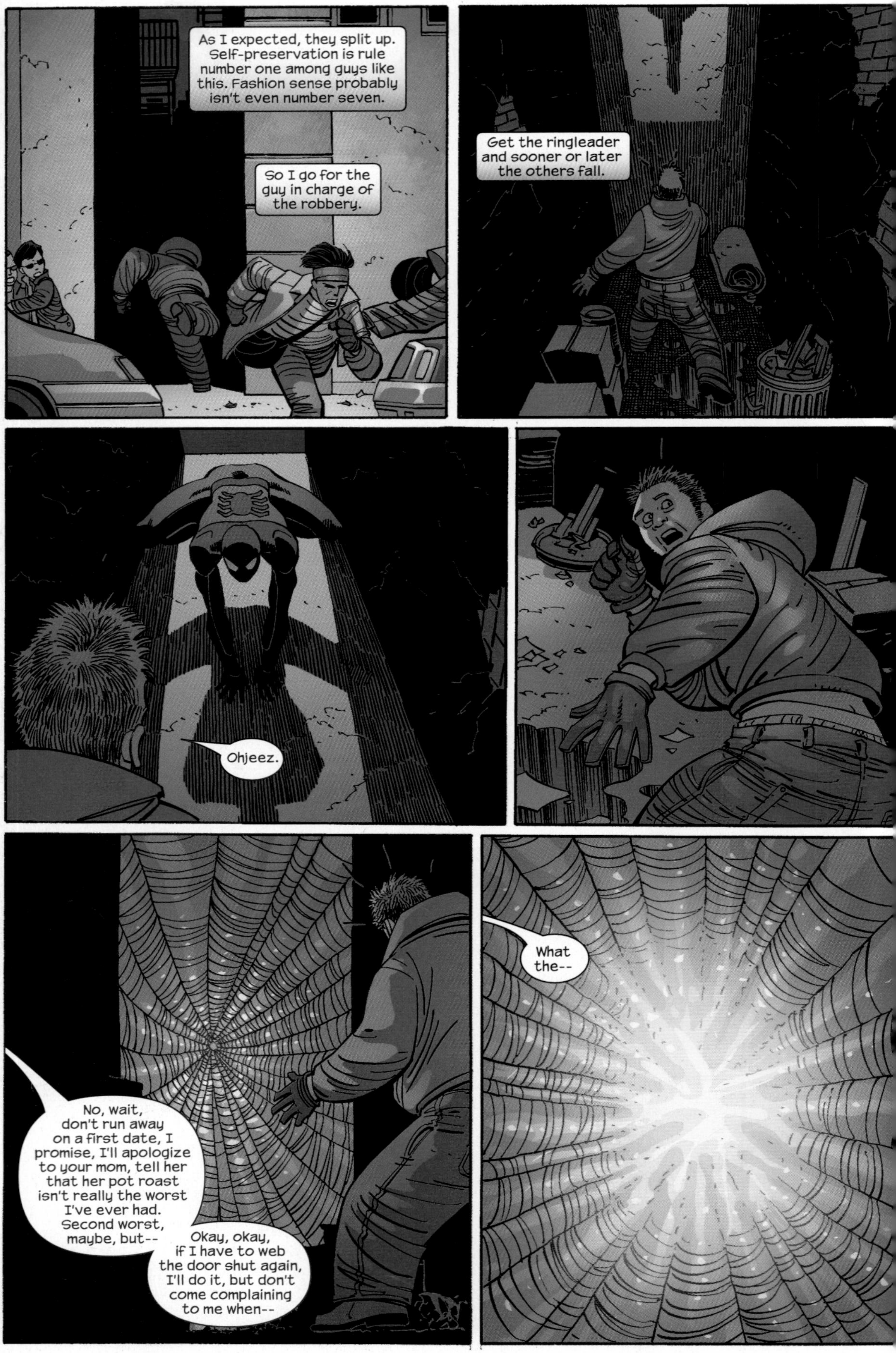
As I expected, they split up. Self-preservation is rule number one among guys like this. Fashion sense probably isn't even number seven.
So I go for the guy in charge of the robbery.
Get the ringleader and sooner or later the others fall.
Ohjeez.
No, wait, don't run away on a first date, I promise, I'll apologize to your mom, tell her that her pot roast isn't really the worst I've ever had. Second worst, maybe, but--
Okay, okay, if I have to web the door shut again, I'll do it, but don't come complaining to me when--
What the--

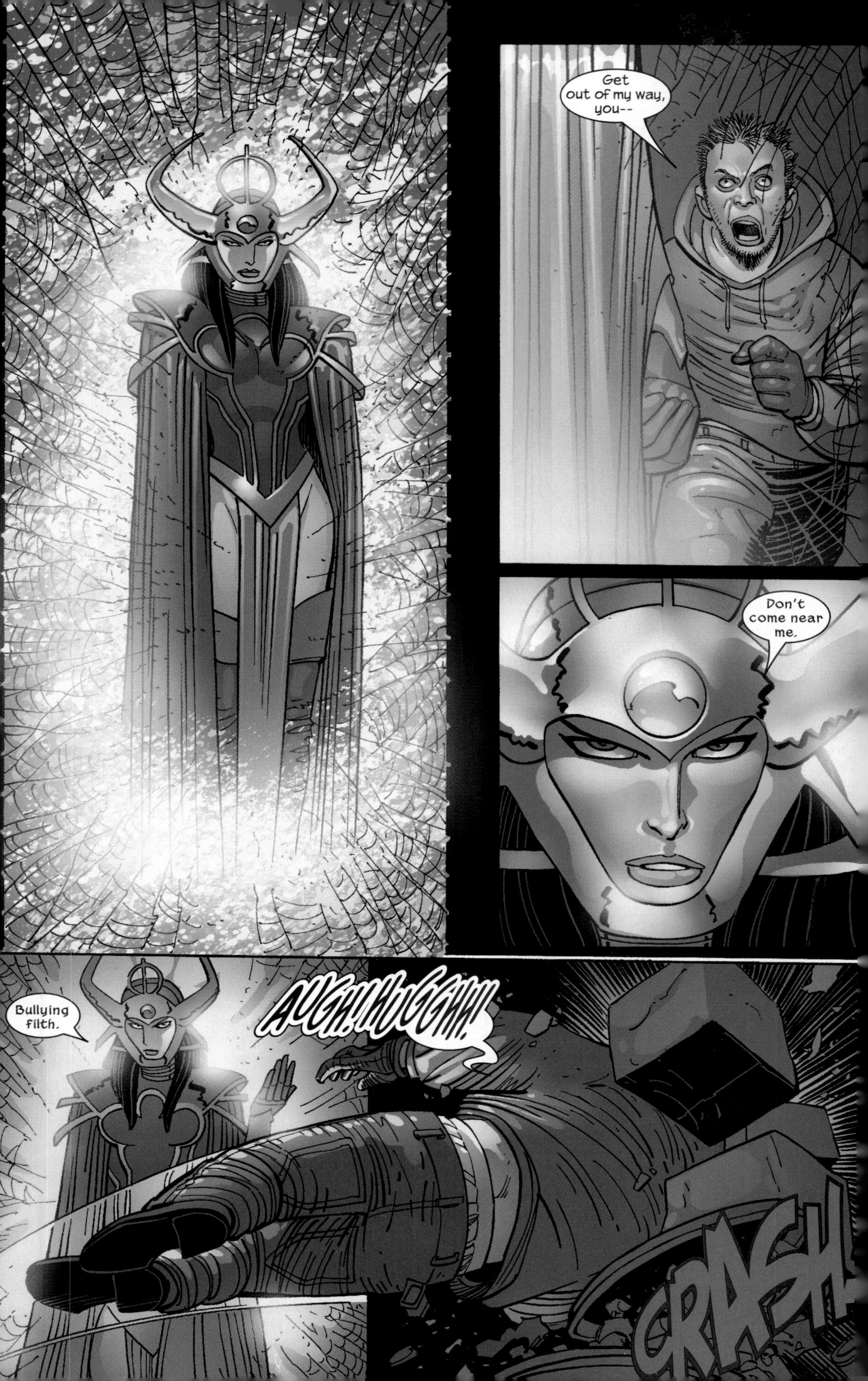
Get out of my way, you--
Don't come near me.
Bullying filth.
AUGH! UUGGHH!
CRASH

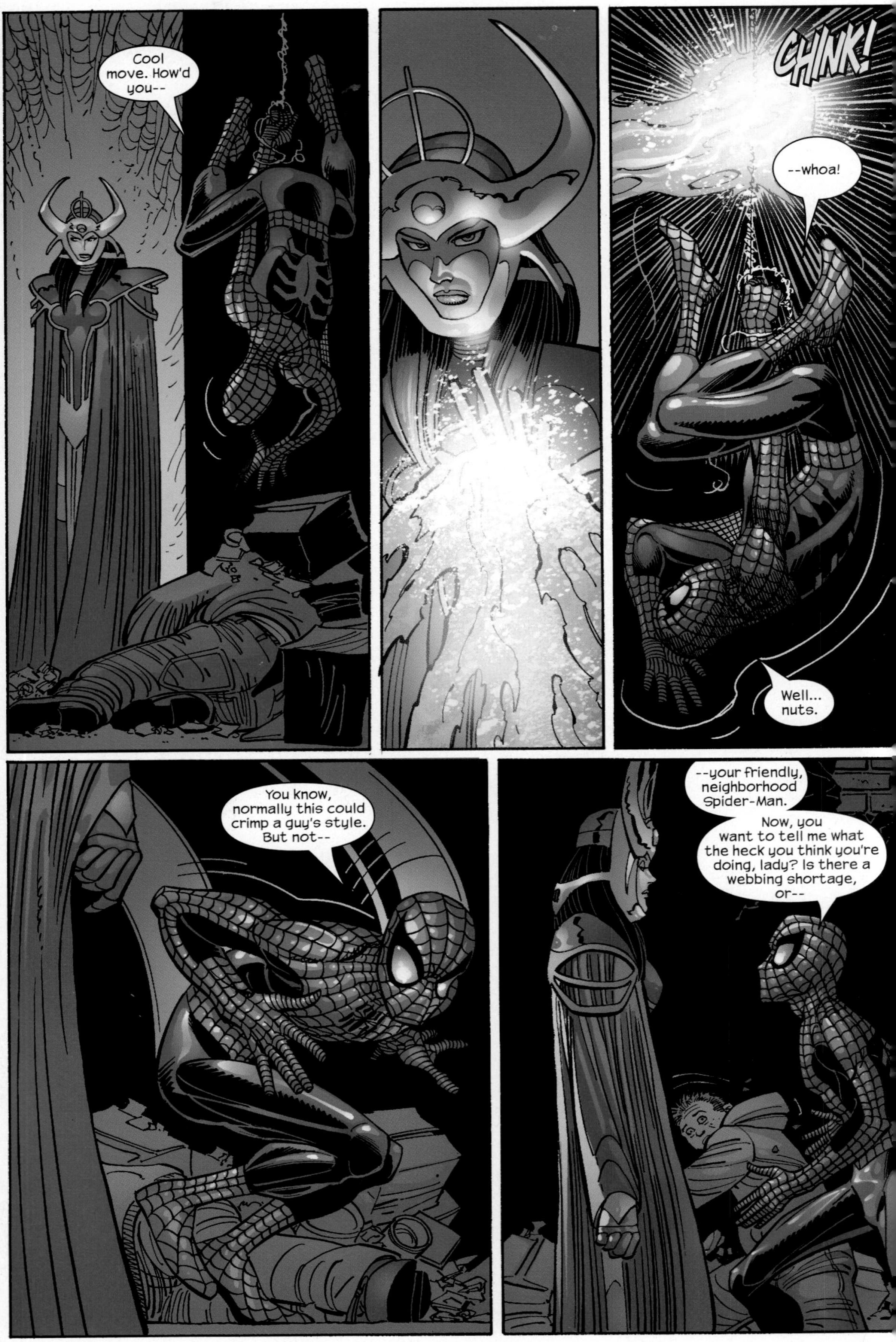
Cool move. How'd you--
CHINK!
--whoa!
Well... nuts.
You know, normally this could crimp a guy's style. But not--
--your friendly, neighborhood Spider-Man.
Now, you want to tell me what the heck you think you're doing, lady? Is there a webbing shortage, or--

Hey! He's getting away.

He is not important.

The Spider-Man is here, I can feel him.

And I feel something more, the same presence I felt before. Is he the key to what I am seeking?

Hey, kid, you know you're talking to yourself, right? Gotta watch that or you'll end up like me, and--

Silence, mortal.

I wish to thank you.

Thank me? Can we back up a second? What part of thanking me is letting one of the bad guys get away? I don't even know you, so how can--

Not long ago, you released me from an ancient bondage that nearly destroyed me.

Look, lady, your lifestyle is none of my business, so--

There was a great battle between worlds. In that battle, you became my savior.

I really don't have time for this. I gotta try and pick up that guy's trail, get something to eat, and my favorite cartoon comes on in half an hour, so--

You fell through time, you and the other, Doctor Strange.

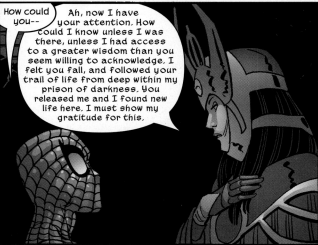

How could you--

Ah, now I have your attention. How could I know unless I was there, unless I had access to a greater wisdom than you seem willing to acknowledge. I felt you fall, and followed your trail of life from deep within my prison of darkness. You released me and I found new life here. I must show my gratitude for this.

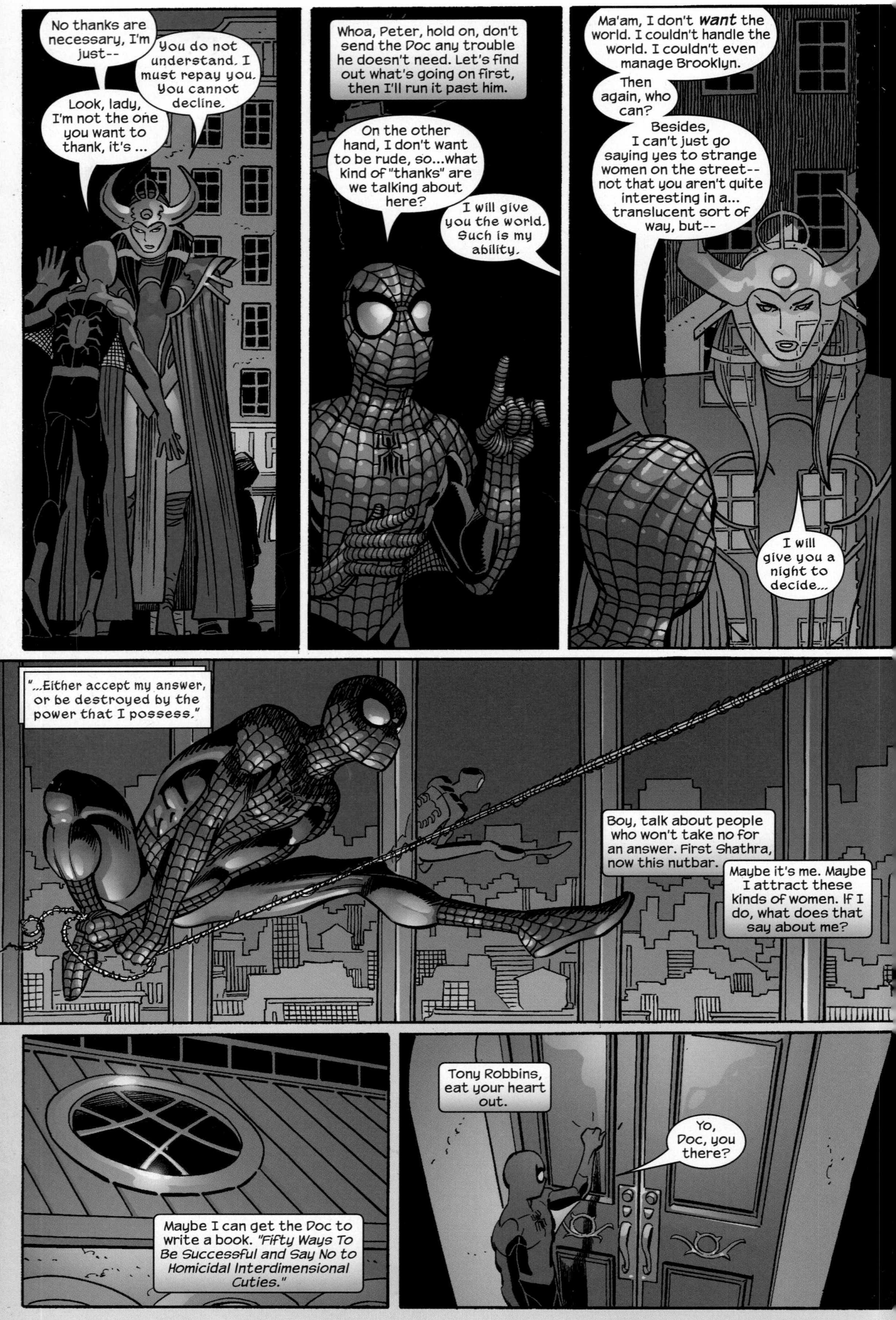

No thanks are necessary, I'm just--
You do not understand. I must repay you. You cannot decline.
Look, lady, I'm not the one you want to thank, it's ...
Whoa, Peter, hold on, don't send the Doc any trouble he doesn't need. Let's find out what's going on first, then I'll run it past him.
On the other hand, I don't want to be rude, so...what kind of "thanks" are we talking about here?
I will give you the world. Such is my ability.
Ma'am, I don't *want* the world. I couldn't handle the world. I couldn't even manage Brooklyn.
Then again, who can?
Besides, I can't just go saying yes to strange women on the street--not that you aren't quite interesting in a... translucent sort of way, but--
I will give you a night to decide...
"...Either accept my answer, or be destroyed by the power that I possess."
Boy, talk about people who won't take no for an answer. First Shathra, now this nutbar.
Maybe it's me. Maybe I attract these kinds of women. If I do, what does that say about me?
Maybe I can get the Doc to write a book. *"Fifty Ways To Be Successful and Say No to Homicidal Interdimensional Cuties."*
Tony Robbins, eat your heart out.
Yo, Doc, you there?

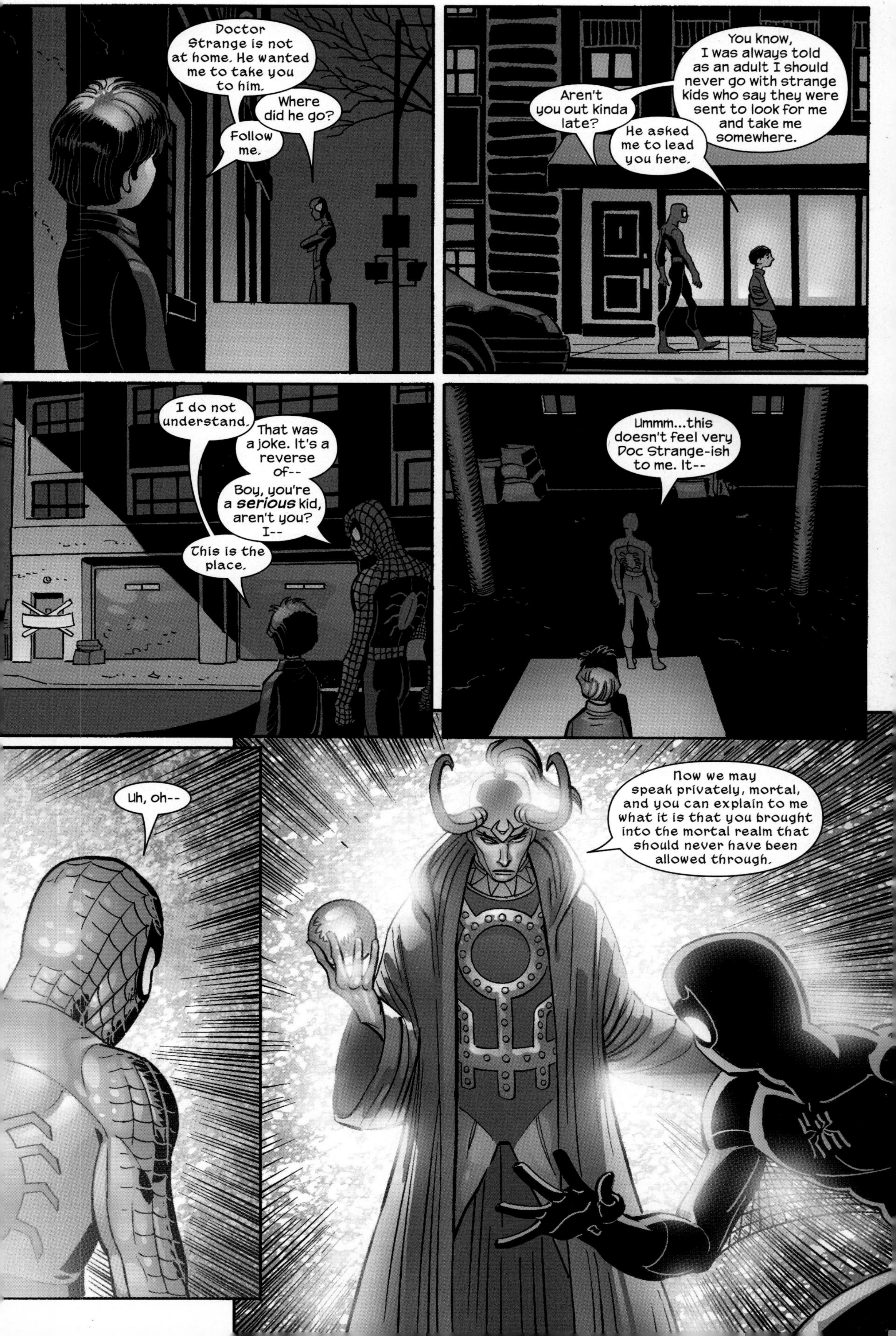

Doctor Strange is not at home. He wanted me to take you to him.
Where did he go?
Follow me.
Aren't you out kinda late?
You know, I was always told as an adult I should never go with strange kids who say they were sent to look for me and take me somewhere.
He asked me to lead you here.
I do not understand.
That was a joke. It's a reverse of--
Boy, you're a **serious** kid, aren't you? I--
This is the place.
Ummm...this doesn't feel very Doc Strange-ish to me. It--
Uh, oh--
Now we may speak privately, mortal, and you can explain to me what it is that you brought into the mortal realm that should never have been allowed through.

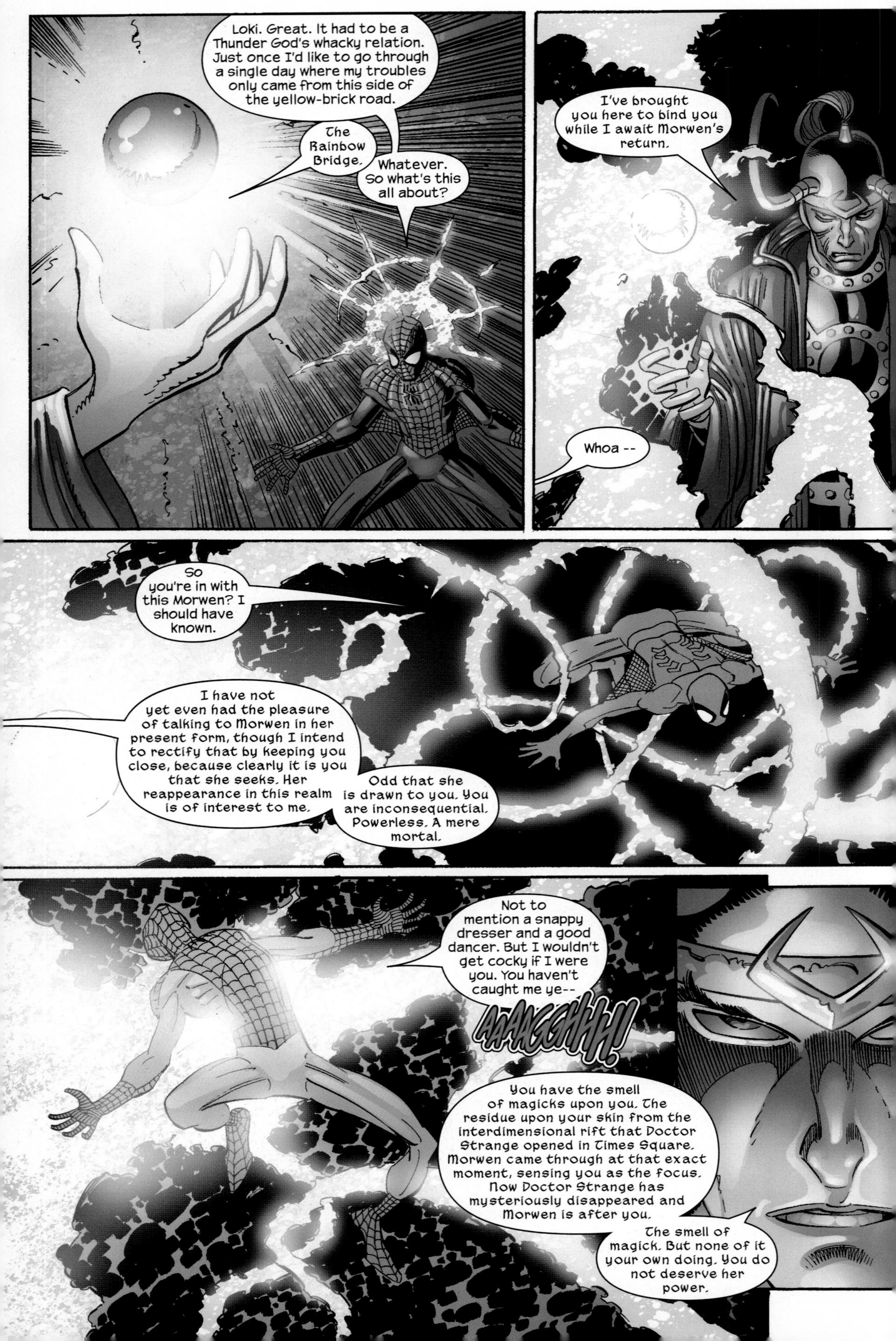
Loki. Great. It had to be a Thunder God's whacky relation. Just once I'd like to go through a single day where my troubles only came from this side of the yellow-brick road.
The Rainbow Bridge.
Whatever. So what's this all about?
I've brought you here to bind you while I await Morwen's return.
Whoa --
So you're in with this Morwen? I should have known.
I have not yet even had the pleasure of talking to Morwen in her present form, though I intend to rectify that by keeping you close, because clearly it is you that she seeks. Her reappearance in this realm is of interest to me.
Odd that she is drawn to you. You are inconsequential. Powerless. A mere mortal.
Not to mention a snappy dresser and a good dancer. But I wouldn't get cocky if I were you. You haven't caught me ye--
AAAAGGHHH!
You have the smell of magicks upon you. The residue upon your skin from the interdimensional rift that Doctor Strange opened in Times Square. Morwen came through at that exact moment, sensing you as the focus. Now Doctor Strange has mysteriously disappeared and Morwen is after you.
The smell of magick. But none of it your own doing. You do not deserve her power.

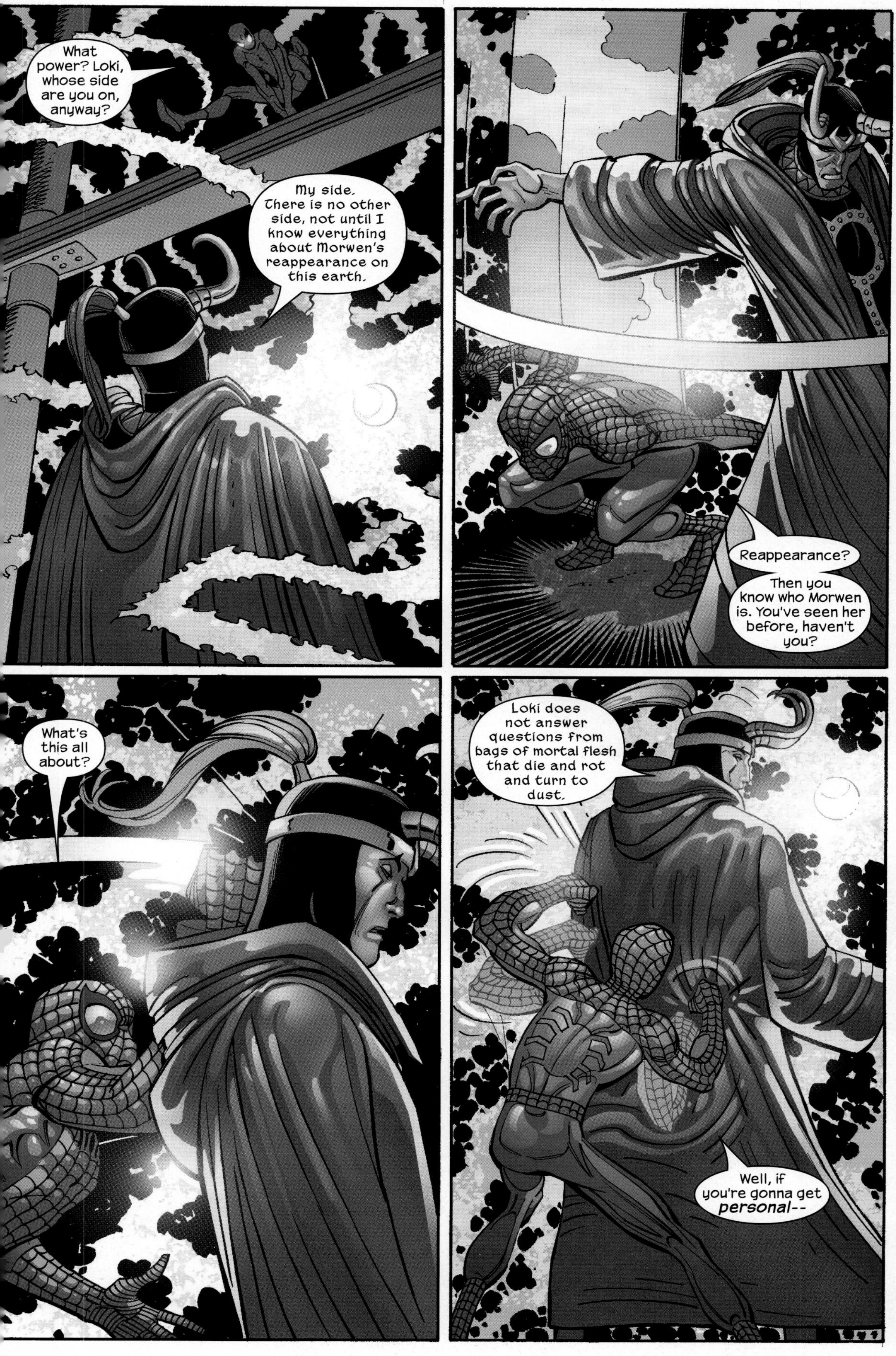

What power? Loki, whose side are you on, anyway?
My side. There is no other side, not until I know everything about Morwen's reappearance on this earth.
Reappearance?
Then you know who Morwen is. You've seen her before, haven't you?
What's this all about?
Loki does not answer questions from bags of mortal flesh that die and rot and turn to dust.
Well, if you're gonna get *personal*--

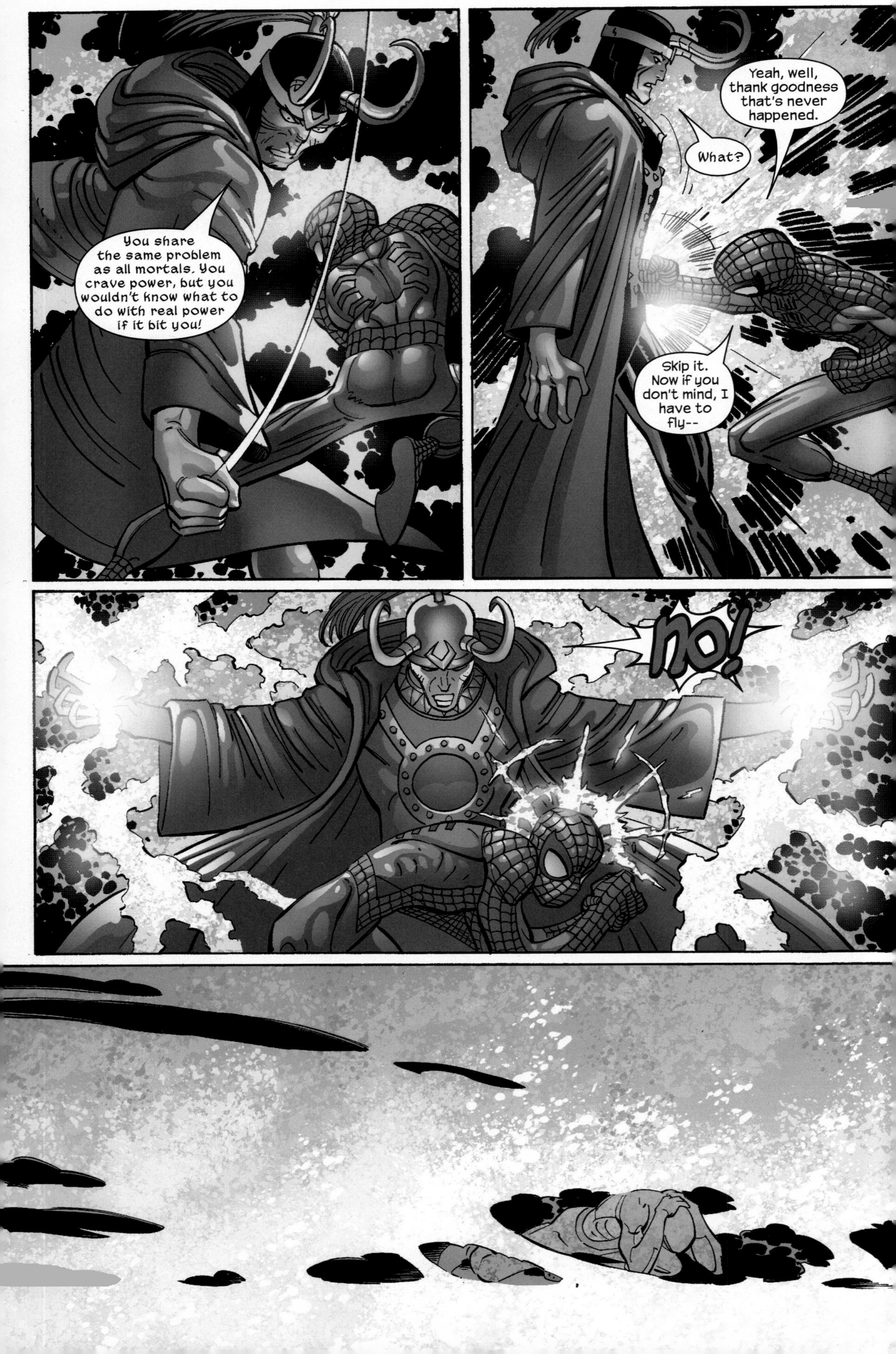
You share the same problem as all mortals. You crave power, but you wouldn't know what to do with real power if it bit you!
What?
Yeah, well, thank goodness that's never happened.
Skip it. Now if you don't mind, I have to fly--
NO!

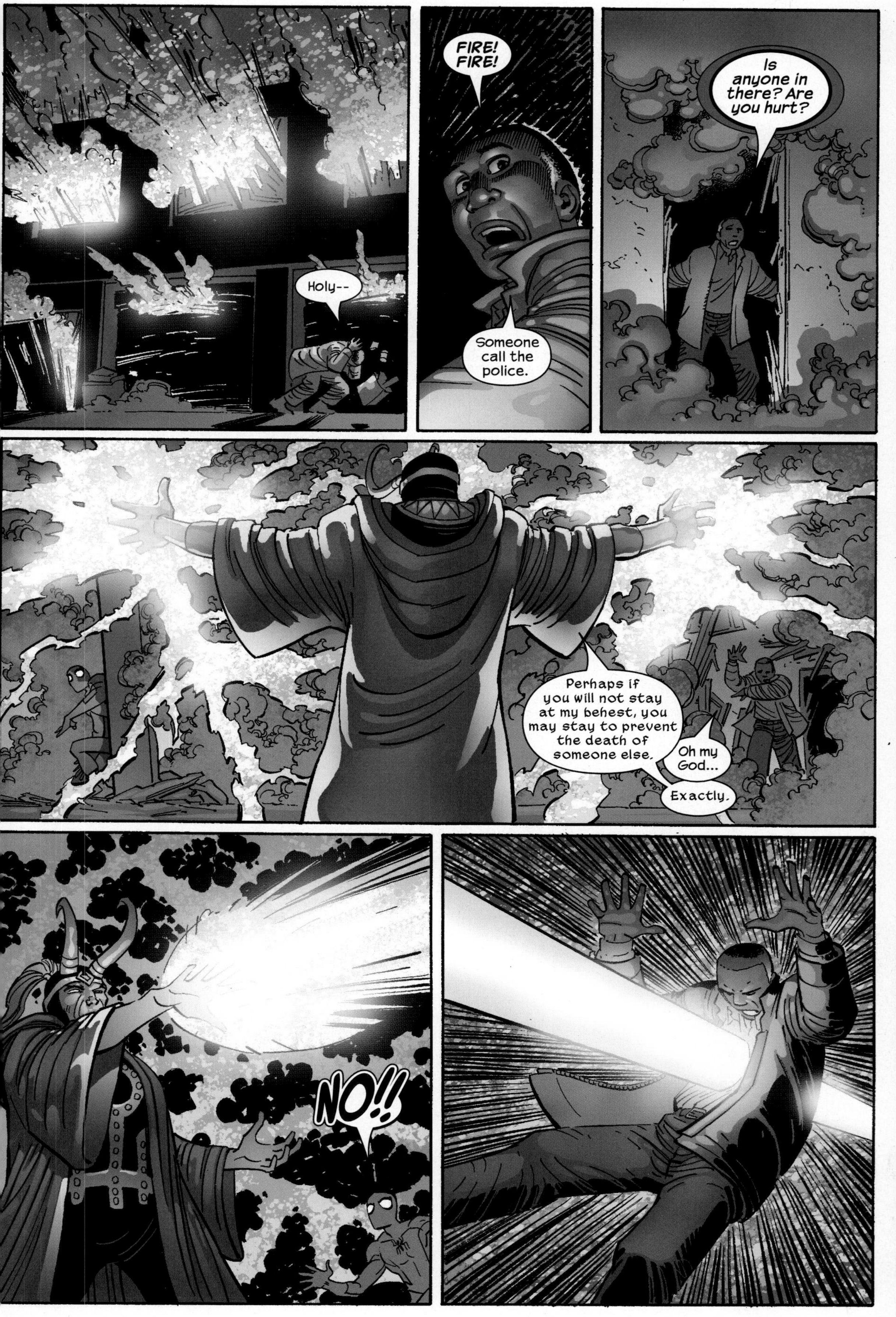
Holy--
FIRE! FIRE!
Someone call the police.
Is anyone in there? Are you hurt?
Perhaps if you will not stay at my behest, you may stay to prevent the death of someone else.
Oh my God...
Exactly.
NO!!

What have you done?! Tell me what I want to know about Morwen and I will spare his life!

Hold on! Hang on!

He only has a matter of minutes left to live. Tell me you will stay with me and I will save him.

You can't just--

Can and will. You may carry him to safety, but give me your word that you will stay by my side, or I will allow him to die.

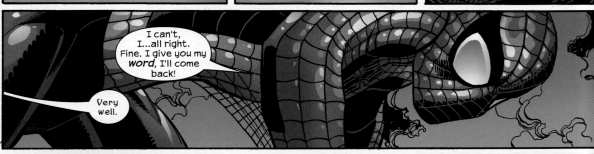

I can't, I...all right. Fine. I give you my word, I'll come back!

Very well.

Runes of life and blood, touch this mortal...

...And restore his life in the name of the All Father and the Sacred Tree.

I almost expected him to weasel out of the deal somehow, but he did as promised. I got the guy as far away from the god as I thought I could.

Even thought about breaking my promise to Loki...but if he kept his side, how could I do less than him?

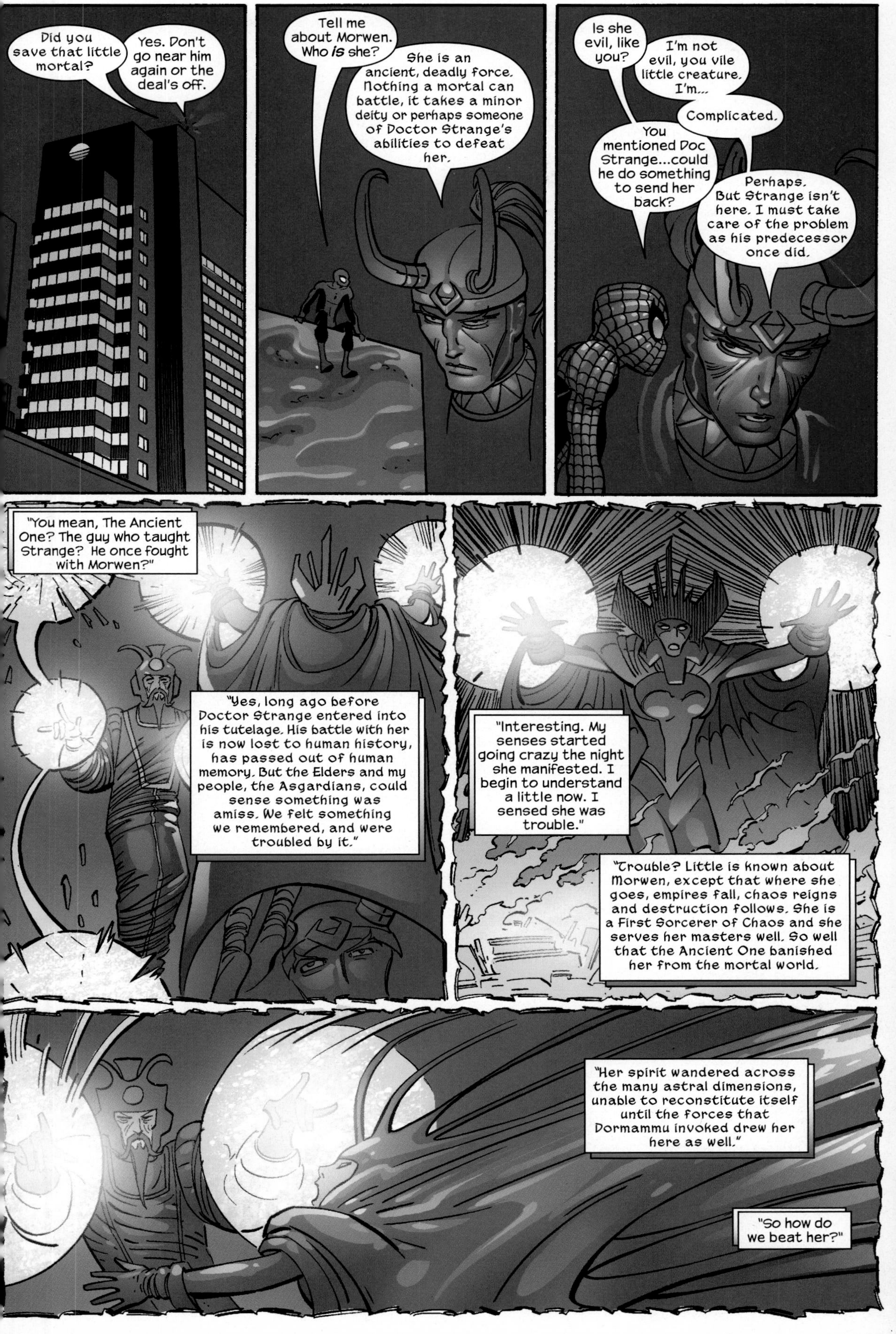
Did you save that little mortal?
Yes. Don't go near him again or the deal's off.
Tell me about Morwen. Who *is* she?
She is an ancient, deadly force. Nothing a mortal can battle, it takes a minor deity or perhaps someone of Doctor Strange's abilities to defeat her.
Is she evil, like you?
I'm not evil, you vile little creature. I'm...
Complicated.
You mentioned Doc Strange...could he do something to send her back?
Perhaps. But Strange isn't here. I must take care of the problem as his predecessor once did.
"You mean, The Ancient One? The guy who taught Strange? He once fought with Morwen?"
"Yes, long ago before Doctor Strange entered into his tutelage. His battle with her is now lost to human history, has passed out of human memory. But the Elders and my people, the Asgardians, could sense something was amiss. We felt something we remembered, and were troubled by it."
"Interesting. My senses started going crazy the night she manifested. I begin to understand a little now. I sensed she was trouble."
"Trouble? Little is known about Morwen, except that where she goes, empires fall, chaos reigns and destruction follows. She is a First Sorcerer of Chaos and she serves her masters well. So well that the Ancient One banished her from the mortal world.
"Her spirit wandered across the many astral dimensions, unable to reconstitute itself until the forces that Dormammu invoked drew her here as well."
"So how do we beat her?"

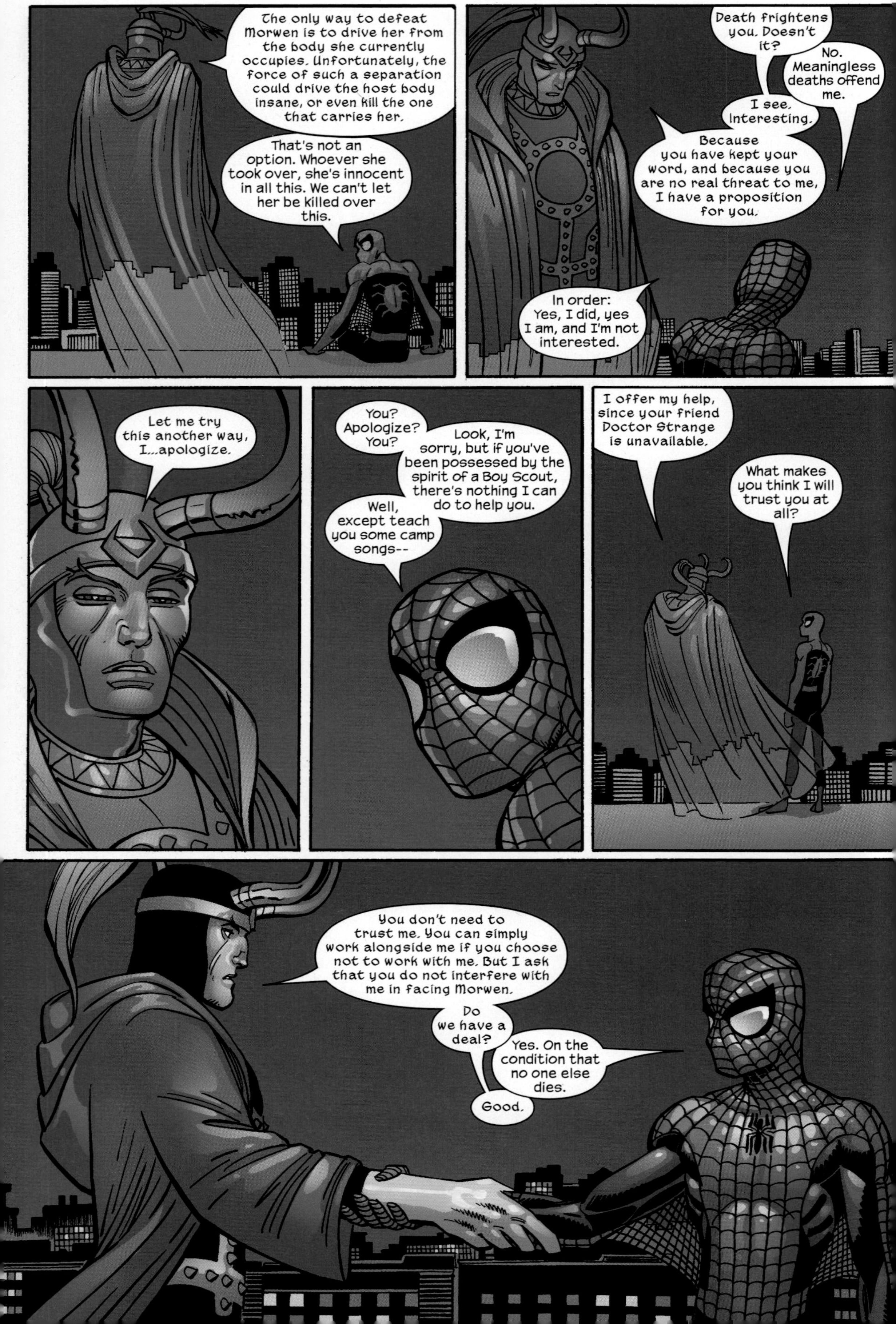
The only way to defeat Morwen is to drive her from the body she currently occupies. Unfortunately, the force of such a separation could drive the host body insane, or even kill the one that carries her.
That's not an option. Whoever she took over, she's innocent in all this. We can't let her be killed over this.
Death frightens you. Doesn't it?
No. Meaningless deaths offend me.
I see. Interesting.
Because you have kept your word, and because you are no real threat to me, I have a proposition for you.
In order: Yes, I did, yes I am, and I'm not interested.
Let me try this another way, I...apologize.
You? Apologize? You?
Look, I'm sorry, but if you've been possessed by the spirit of a Boy Scout, there's nothing I can do to help you.
Well, except teach you some camp songs--
I offer my help, since your friend Doctor Strange is unavailable.
What makes you think I will trust you at all?
You don't need to trust me. You can simply work alongside me if you choose not to work with me. But I ask that you do not interfere with me in facing Morwen.
Do we have a deal?
Yes. On the condition that no one else dies.
Good.

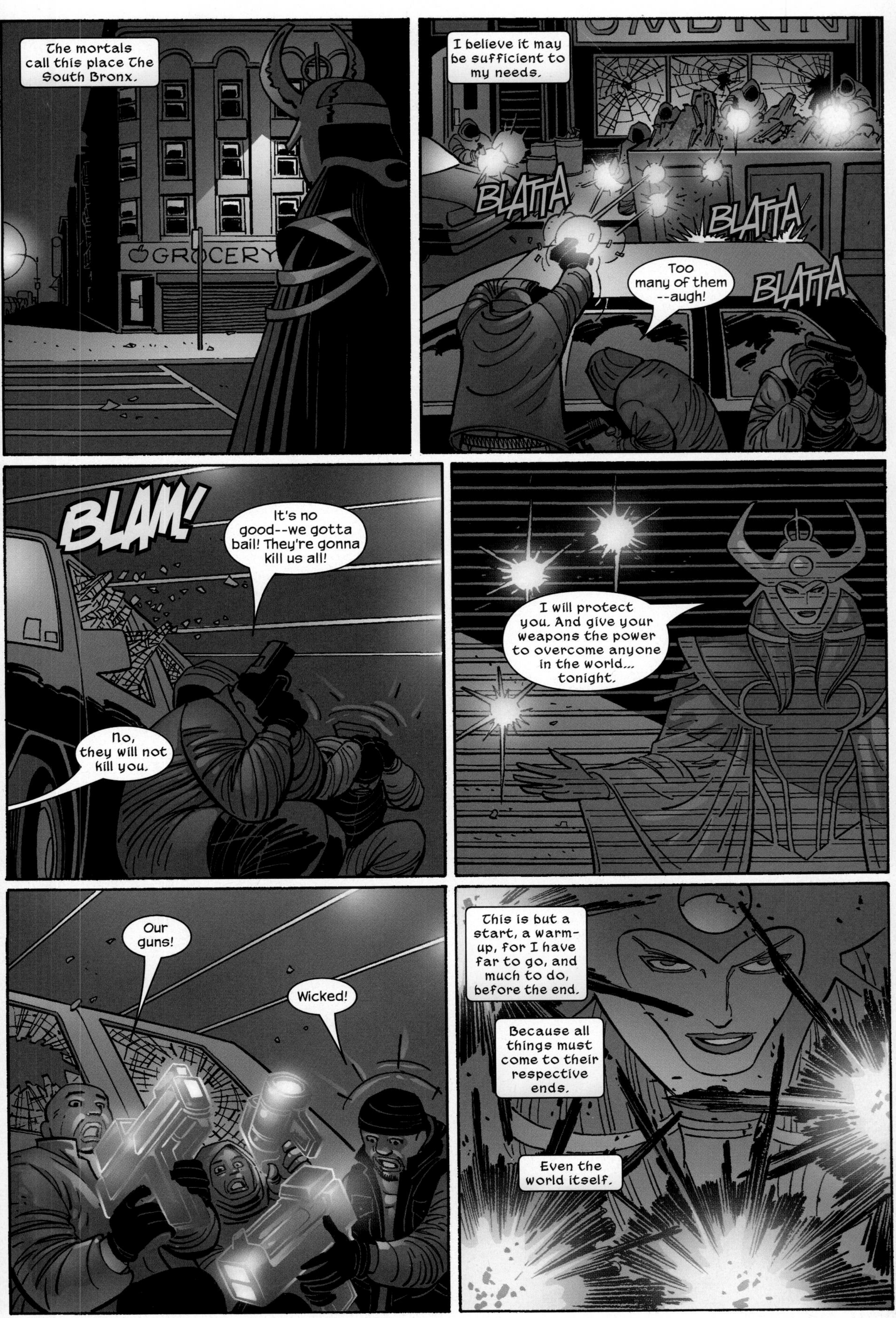
The mortals call this place The South Bronx.
GROCERY
I believe it may be sufficient to my needs.
BLATTA
BLATTA
Too many of them --augh!
BLATTA
BLAM!
It's no good--we gotta bail! They're gonna kill us all!
No, they will not kill you.
I will protect you. And give your weapons the power to overcome anyone in the world... tonight.
Our guns!
Wicked!
This is but a start, a warm-up, for I have far to go, and much to do, before the end.
Because all things must come to their respective ends.
Even the world itself.

#504

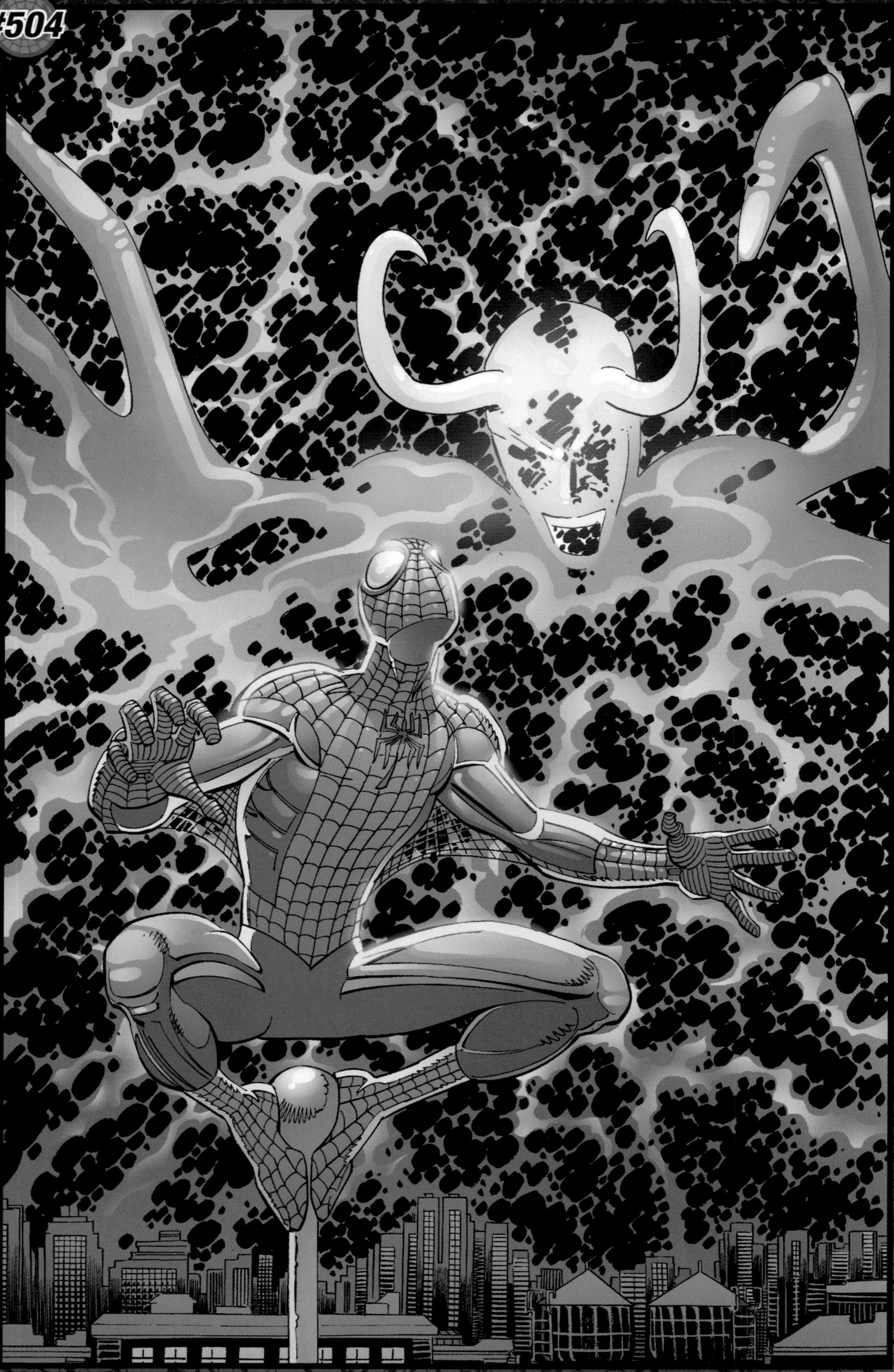

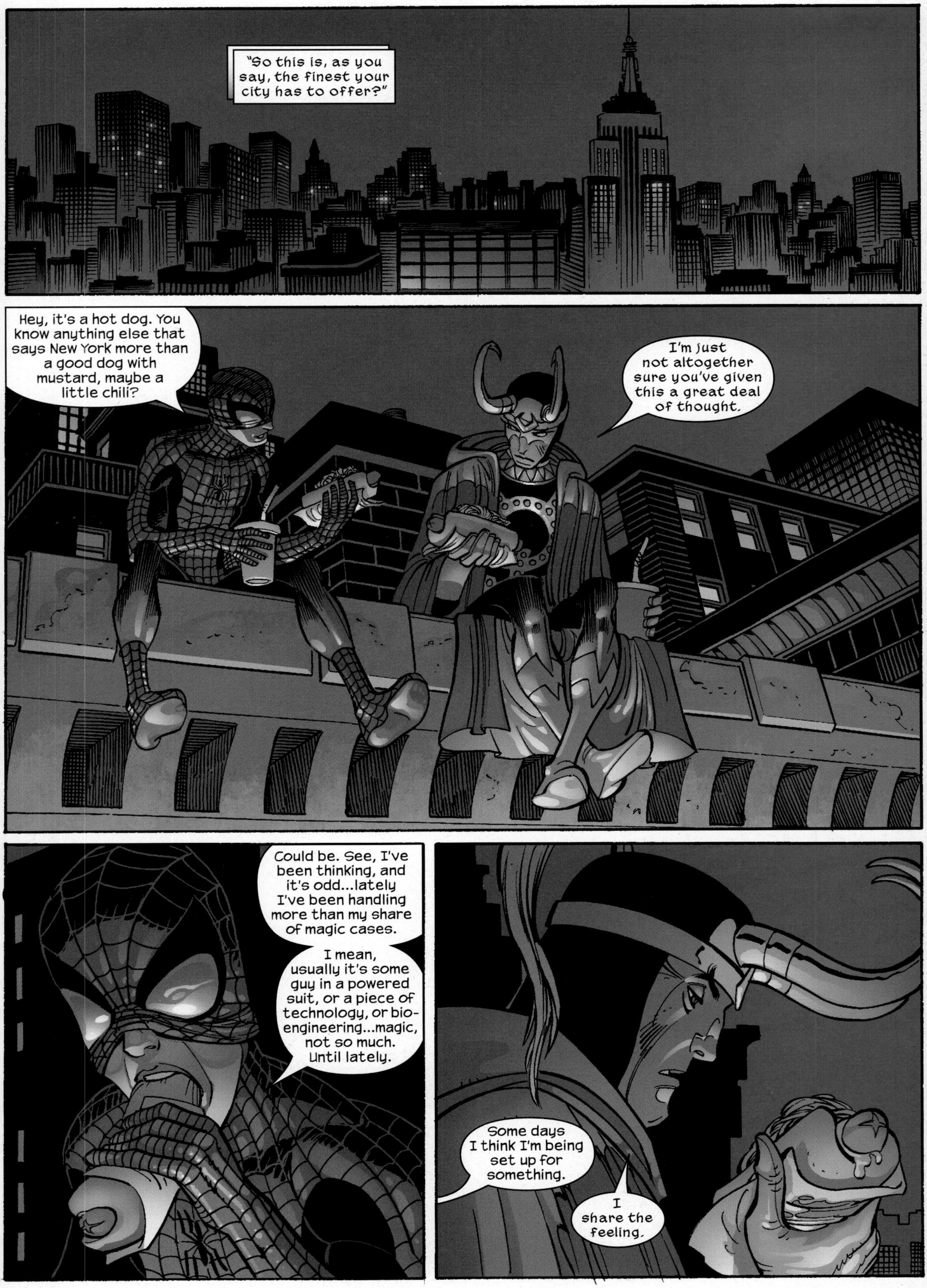
"So this is, as you say, the finest your city has to offer?"
Hey, it's a hot dog. You know anything else that says New York more than a good dog with mustard, maybe a little chili?
I'm just not altogether sure you've given this a great deal of thought.
Could be. See, I've been thinking, and it's odd...lately I've been handling more than my share of magic cases.
I mean, usually it's some guy in a powered suit, or a piece of technology, or bio-engineering...magic, not so much. Until lately.
Some days I think I'm being set up for something.
I share the feeling.

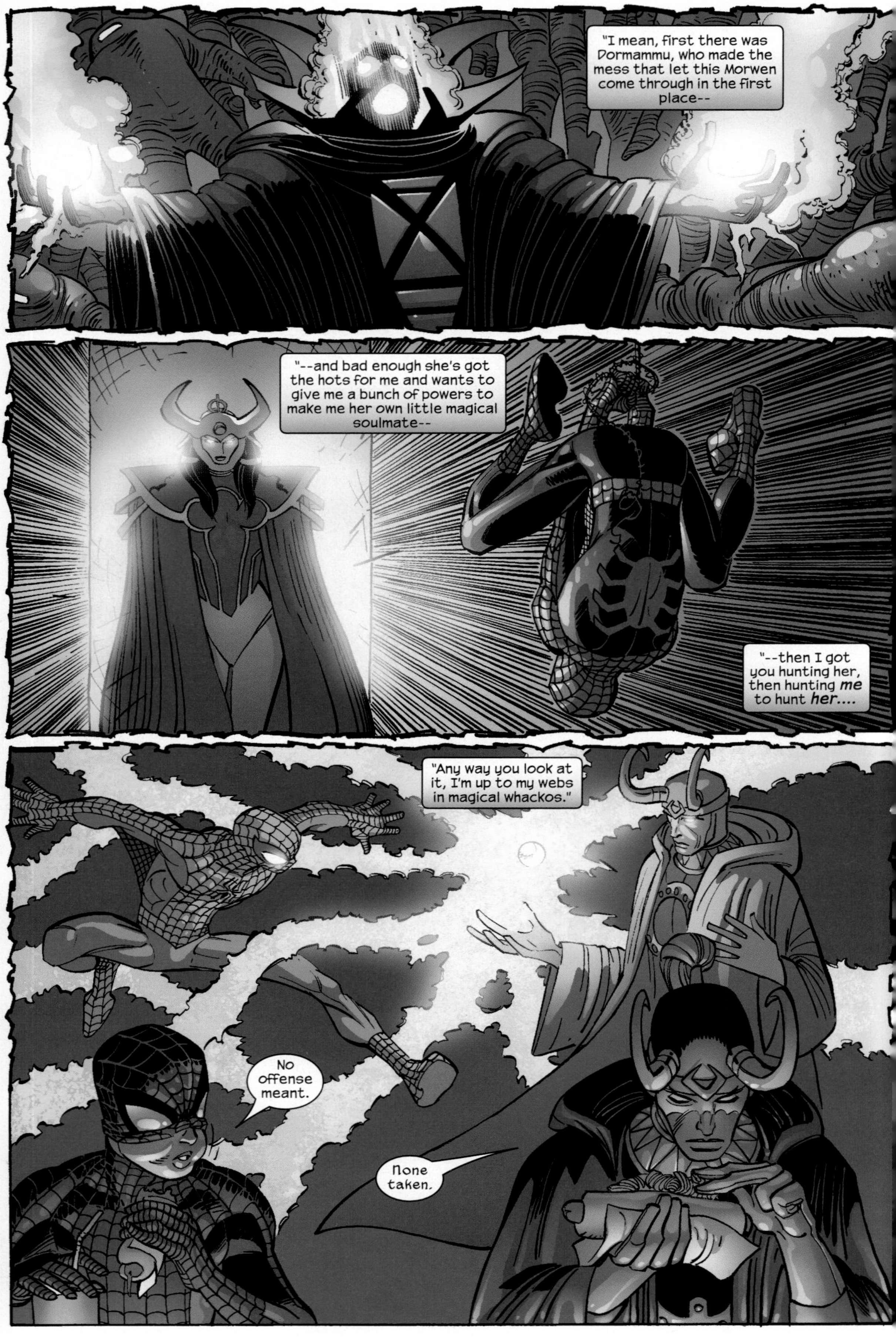
"I mean, first there was Dormammu, who made the mess that let this Morwen come through in the first place--
"--and bad enough she's got the hots for me and wants to give me a bunch of powers to make me her own little magical soulmate--
"--then I got you hunting her, then hunting *me* to hunt *her*....
"Any way you look at it, I'm up to my webs in magical whackos."
No offense meant.
None taken.

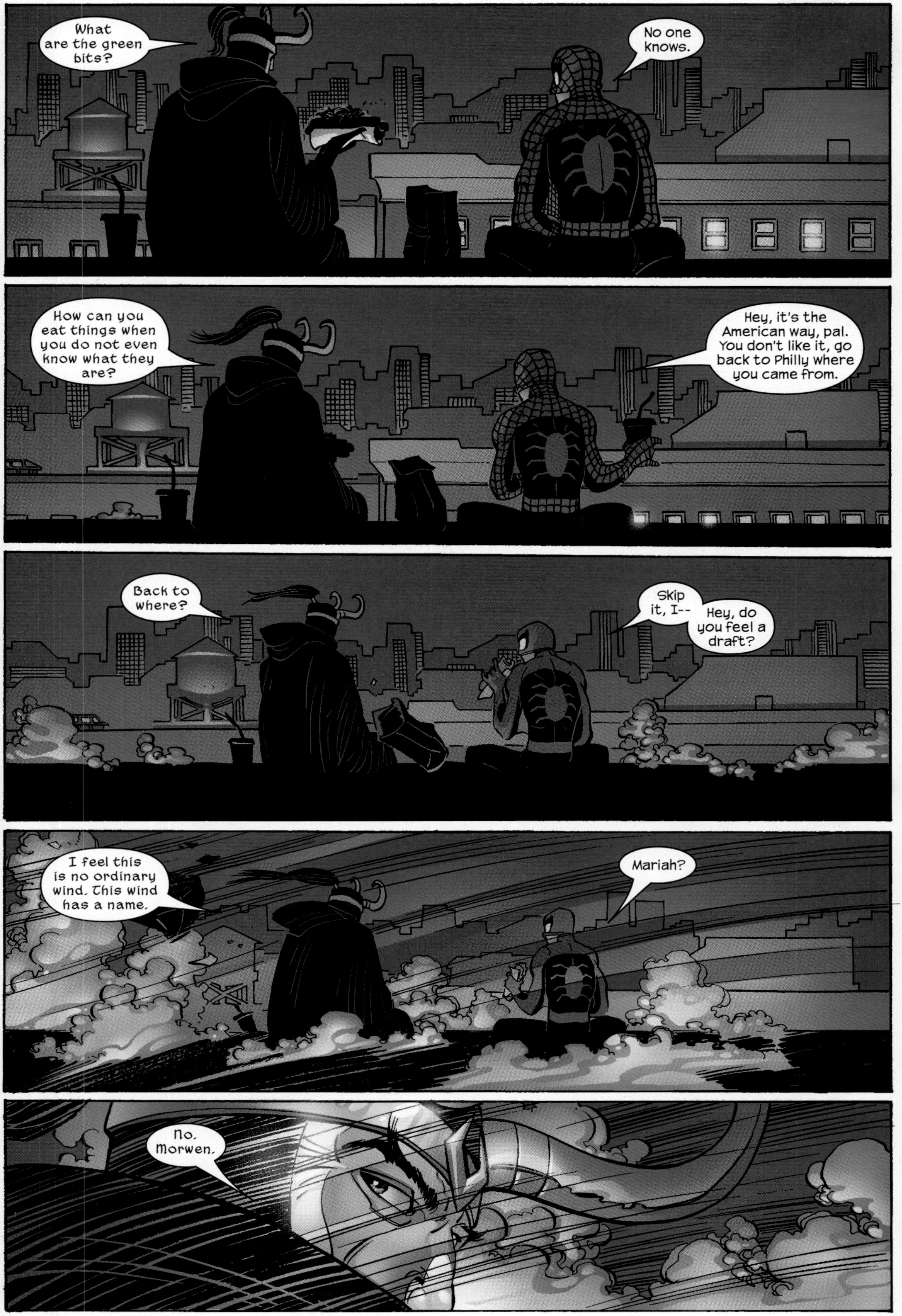
What are the green bits?
No one knows.
How can you eat things when you do not even know what they are?
Hey, it's the American way, pal. You don't like it, go back to Philly where you came from.
Back to where?
Skip it, I--
Hey, do you feel a draft?
I feel this is no ordinary wind. This wind has a name.
Mariah?
No. Morwen.

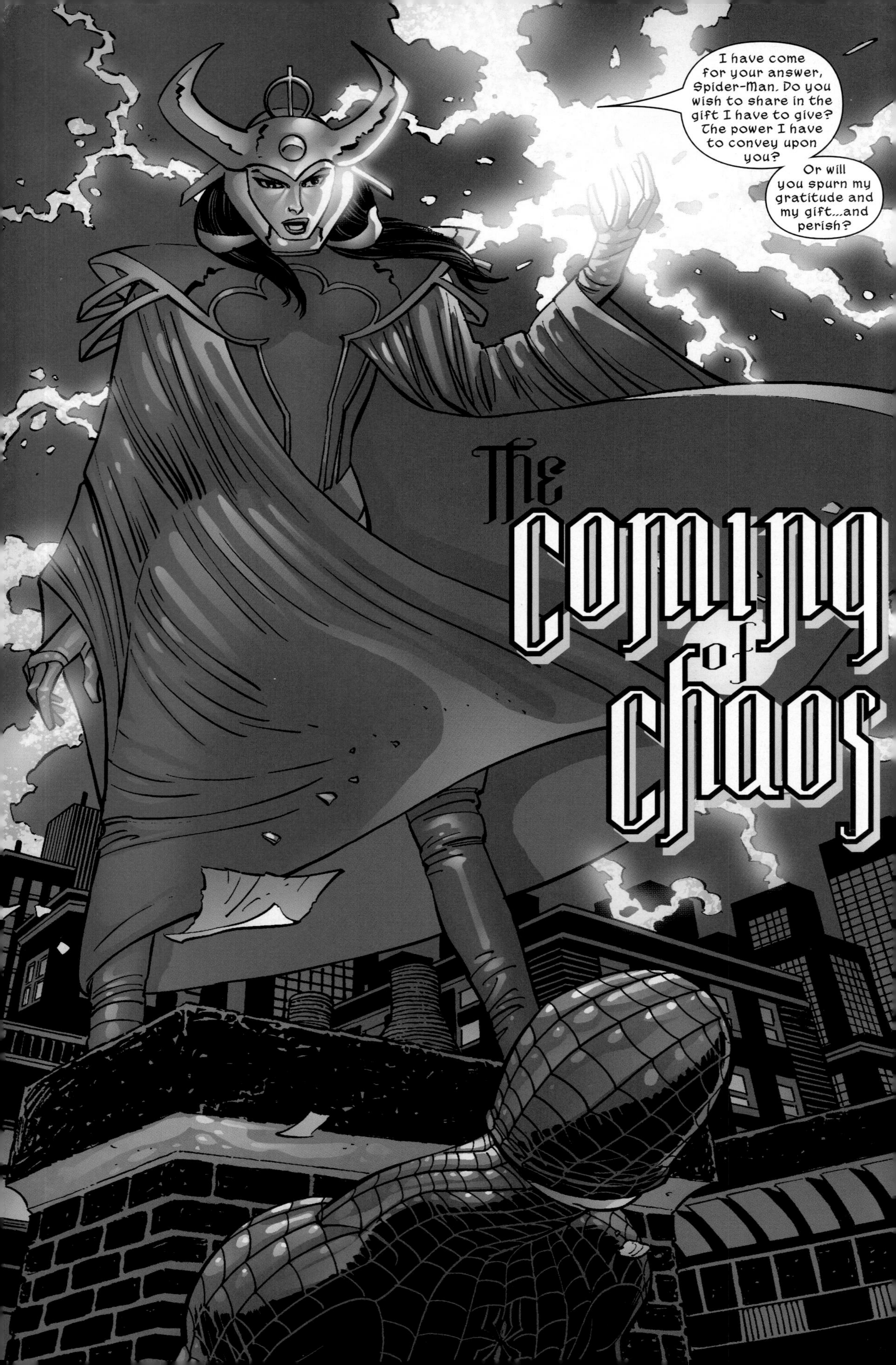
I have come for your answer, Spider-Man. Do you wish to share in the gift I have to give? The power I have to convey upon you?
Or will you spurn my gratitude and my gift...and perish?
The Coming of Chaos

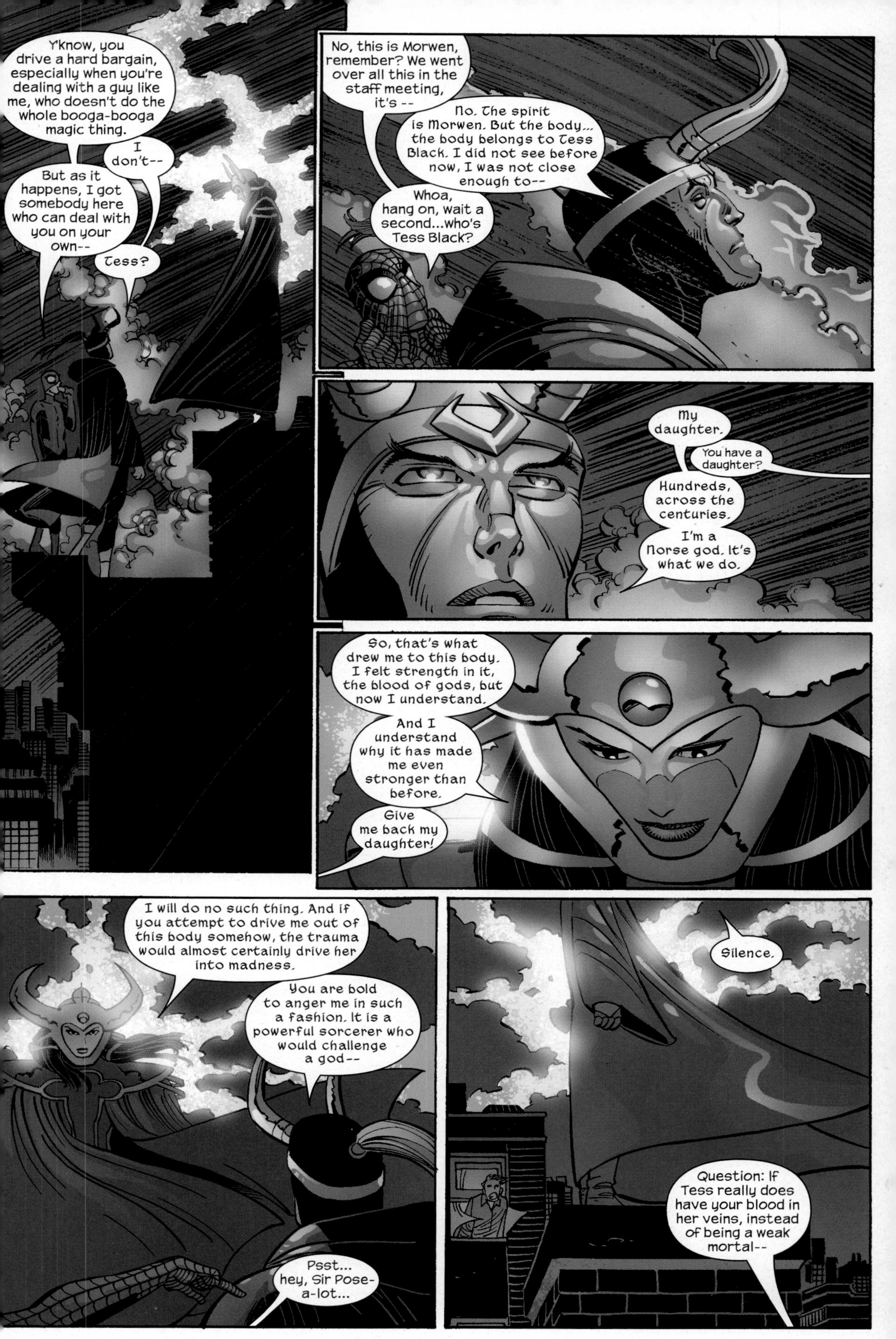
Y'know, you drive a hard bargain, especially when you're dealing with a guy like me, who doesn't do the whole booga-booga magic thing.
I don't--
But as it happens, I got somebody here who can deal with you on your own--
Tess?
No, this is Morwen, remember? We went over all this in the staff meeting, it's --
No. The spirit is Morwen. But the body... the body belongs to Tess Black. I did not see before now, I was not close enough to--
Whoa, hang on, wait a second...who's Tess Black?
My daughter.
You have a daughter?
Hundreds, across the centuries.
I'm a Norse god. It's what we do.
So, that's what drew me to this body. I felt strength in it, the blood of gods, but now I understand.
And I understand why it has made me even stronger than before.
Give me back my daughter!
I will do no such thing. And if you attempt to drive me out of this body somehow, the trauma would almost certainly drive her into madness.
You are bold to anger me in such a fashion. It is a powerful sorcerer who would challenge a god--
Psst... hey, Sir Pose-a-lot...
Silence.
Question: If Tess really does have your blood in her veins, instead of being a weak mortal--

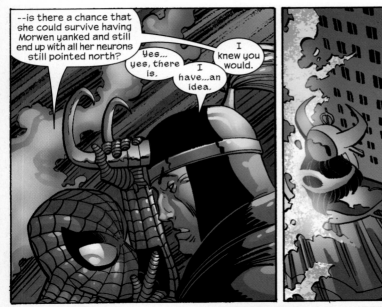

--is there a chance that she could survive having Morwen yanked and still end up with all her neurons still pointed north?

Yes... yes, there is.

I knew you would.

I have...an idea.

How about this? If the Spider-Man doesn't want the power you're offering, I will happily take it and work with you. If it's all about gratitude, surely the assistance of a god is superior to that of a mere mortal.

This by you is an idea?

Being of assistance is not the reason I want this man. My role as sorceress is to serve the forces of chaos. Only through chaos does a race grow stronger.

The Spider-Man is a born agent of Chaos.

Yeah, I get that all the time.

Long have my masters watched him. There is much of the trickster in him, much of chaos...much of the spider.

But I'm the GOD of trickery, how much more chaotic can you get?

At what point, exactly, did this conversation turn into the supernatural version of American Idol? Just asking.

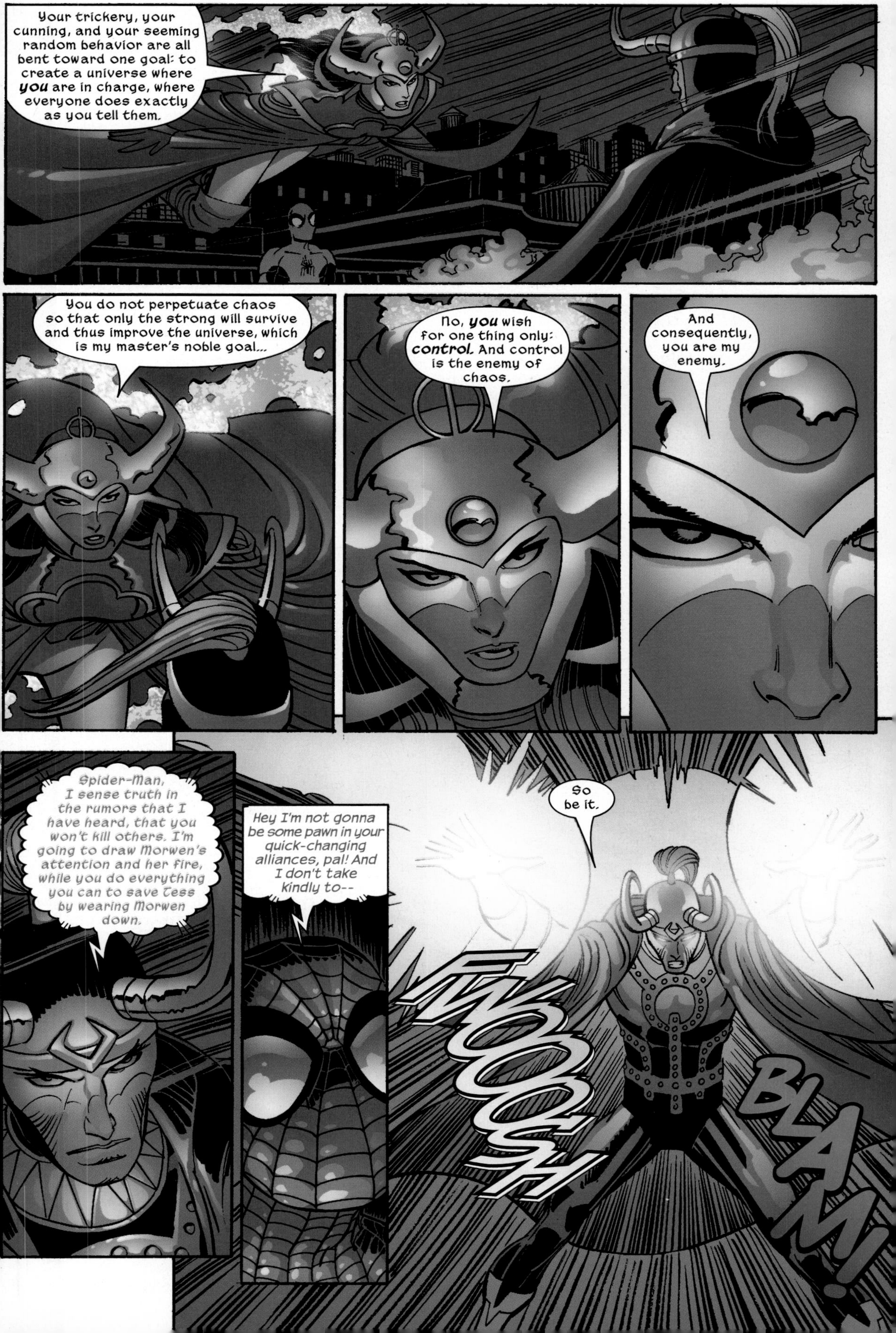
Your trickery, your cunning, and your seeming random behavior are all bent toward one goal: to create a universe where **you** are in charge, where everyone does exactly as you tell them.
You do not perpetuate chaos so that only the strong will survive and thus improve the universe, which is my master's noble goal...
No, **you** wish for one thing only: **control.** And control is the enemy of chaos.
And consequently, you are my enemy.
Spider-Man, I sense truth in the rumors that I have heard, that you won't kill others. I'm going to draw Morwen's attention and her fire, while you do everything you can to save Tess by wearing Morwen down.
Hey I'm not gonna be some pawn in your quick-changing alliances, pal! And I don't take kindly to--
So be it.
FWOOOSH
BLAM!

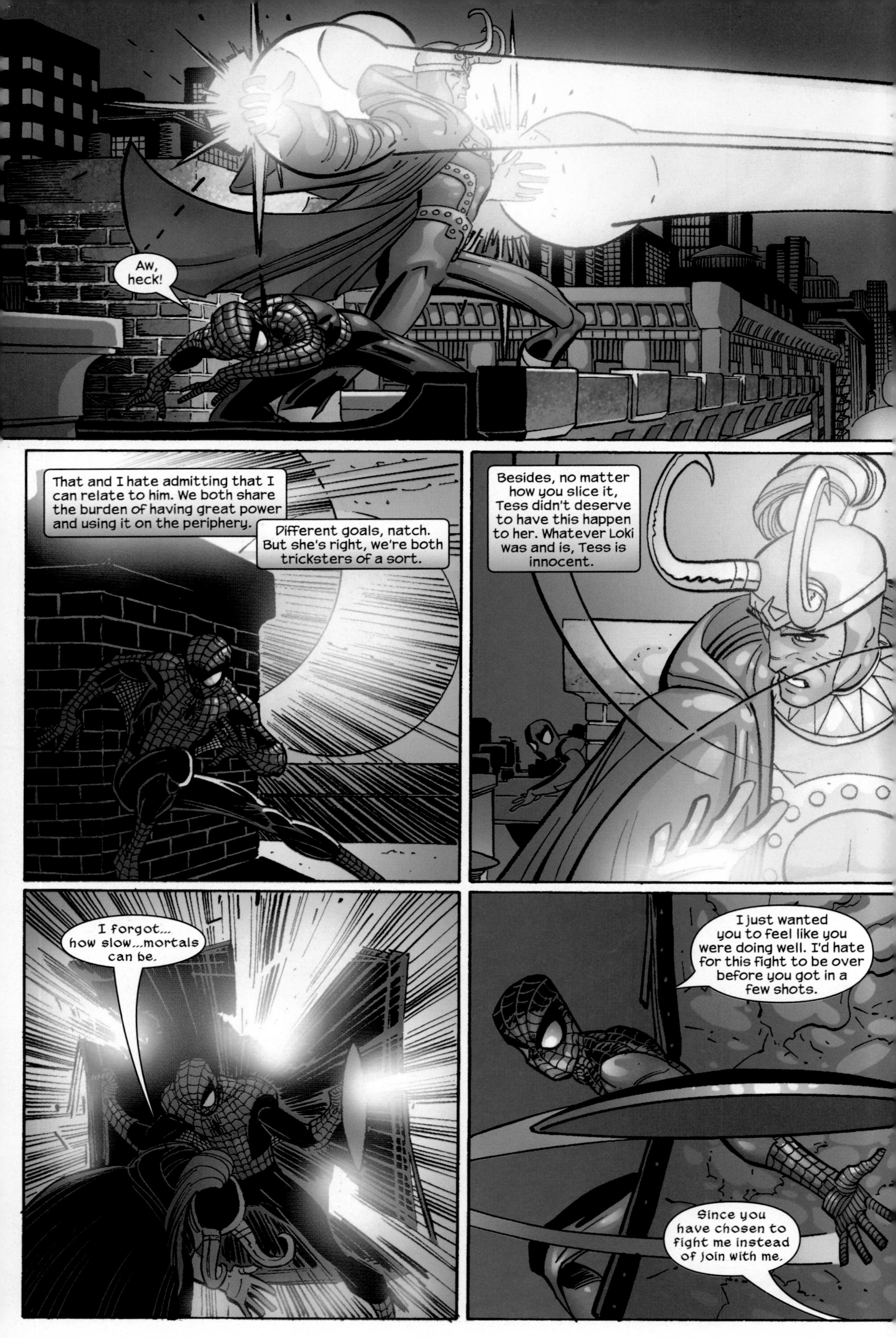

Aw, heck!
That and I hate admitting that I can relate to him. We both share the burden of having great power and using it on the periphery.
Different goals, natch. But she's right, we're both tricksters of a sort.
Besides, no matter how you slice it, Tess didn't deserve to have this happen to her. Whatever Loki was and is, Tess is innocent.
I forgot... how slow...mortals can be.
I just wanted you to feel like you were doing well. I'd hate for this fight to be over before you got in a few shots.
Since you have chosen to fight me instead of join with me.

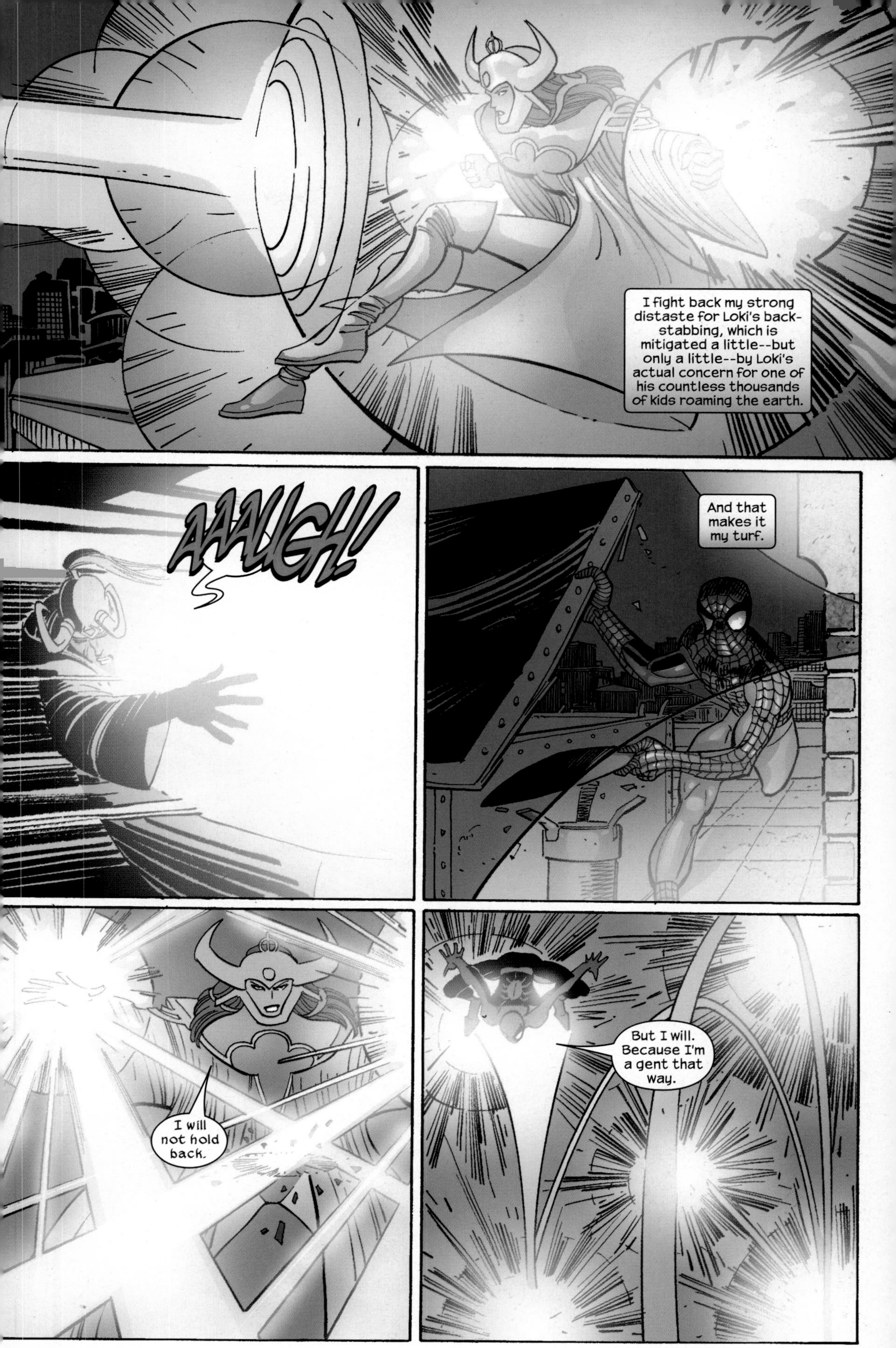
I fight back my strong distaste for Loki's back-stabbing, which is mitigated a little--but only a little--by Loki's actual concern for one of his countless thousands of kids roaming the earth.
AAAUGH!
And that makes it my turf.
I will not hold back.
But I will. Because I'm a gent that way.

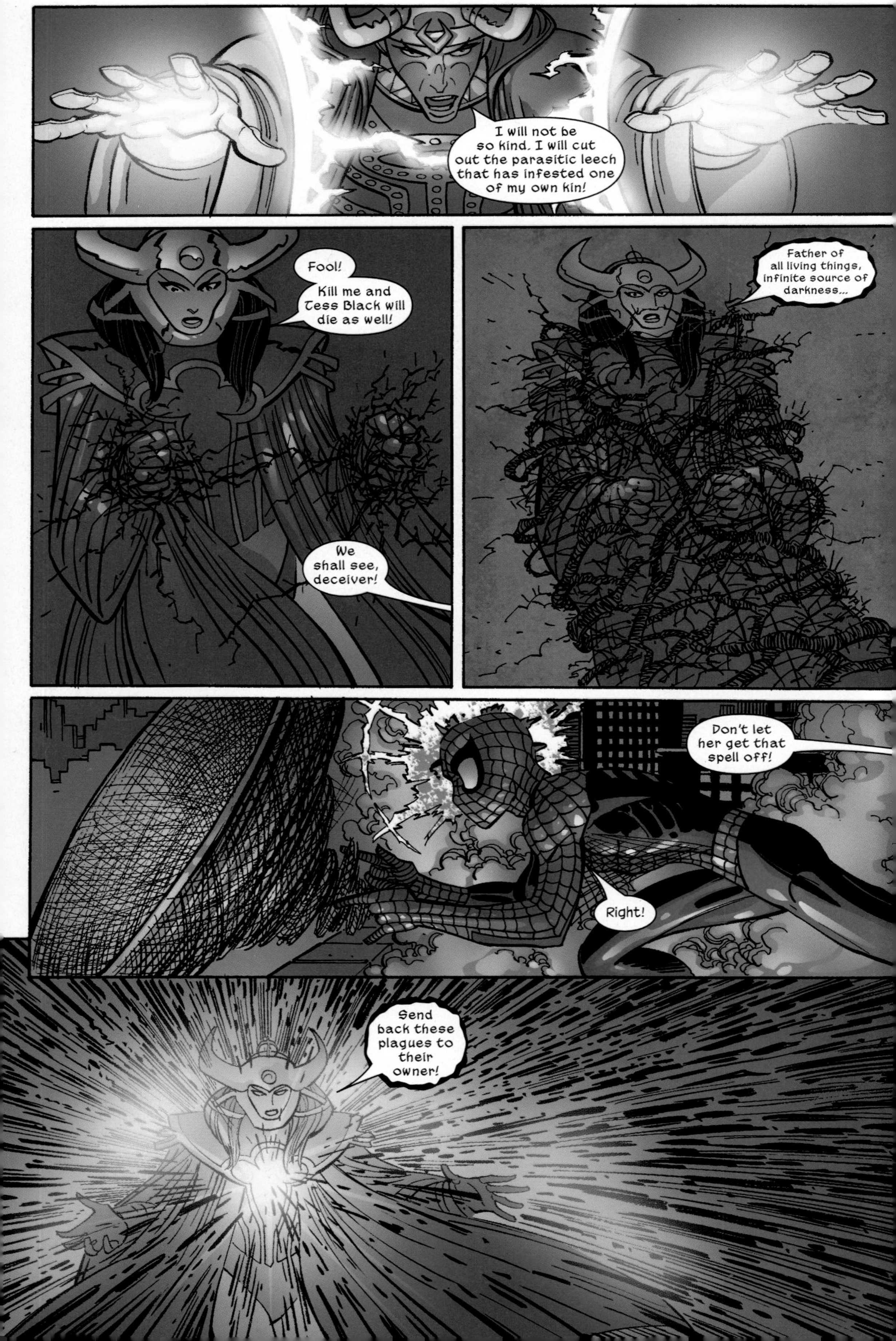
I will not be so kind. I will cut out the parasitic leech that has infested one of my own kin!
Fool!
Kill me and Tess Black will die as well!
We shall see, deceiver!
Father of all living things, infinite source of darkness...
Don't let her get that spell off!
Right!
Send back these plagues to their owner!

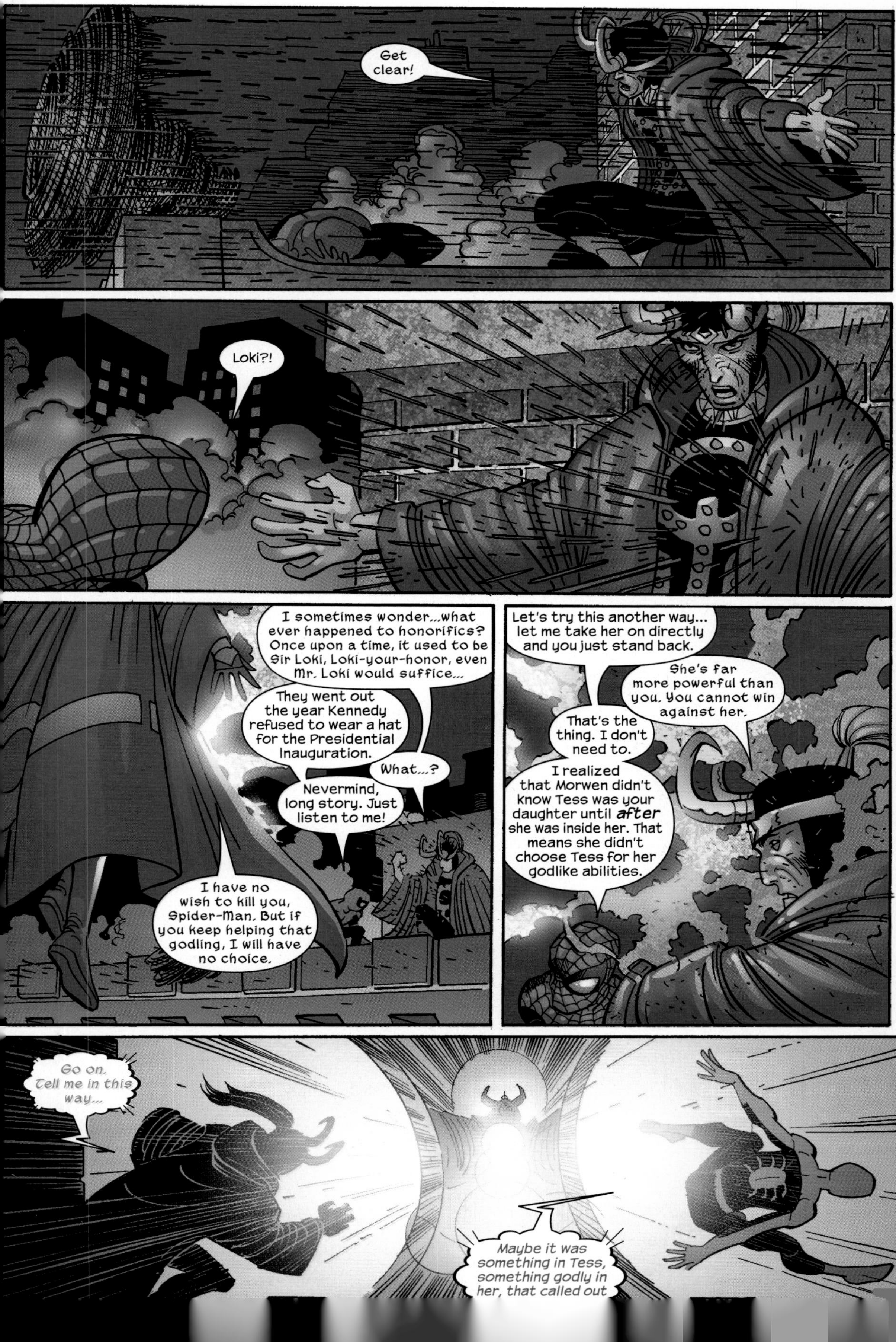
Get clear!
Loki?!
I sometimes wonder...what ever happened to honorifics? Once upon a time, it used to be Sir Loki, Loki-your-honor, even Mr. Loki would suffice...
They went out the year Kennedy refused to wear a hat for the Presidential Inauguration.
What...?
Nevermind, long story. Just listen to me!
I have no wish to kill you, Spider-Man. But if you keep helping that godling, I will have no choice.
Let's try this another way... let me take her on directly and you just stand back.
She's far more powerful than you. You cannot win against her.
That's the thing. I don't need to.
I realized that Morwen didn't know Tess was your daughter until *after* she was inside her. That means she didn't choose Tess for her godlike abilities.
Go on. Tell me in this way...
Maybe it was something in Tess, something godly in her, that called out

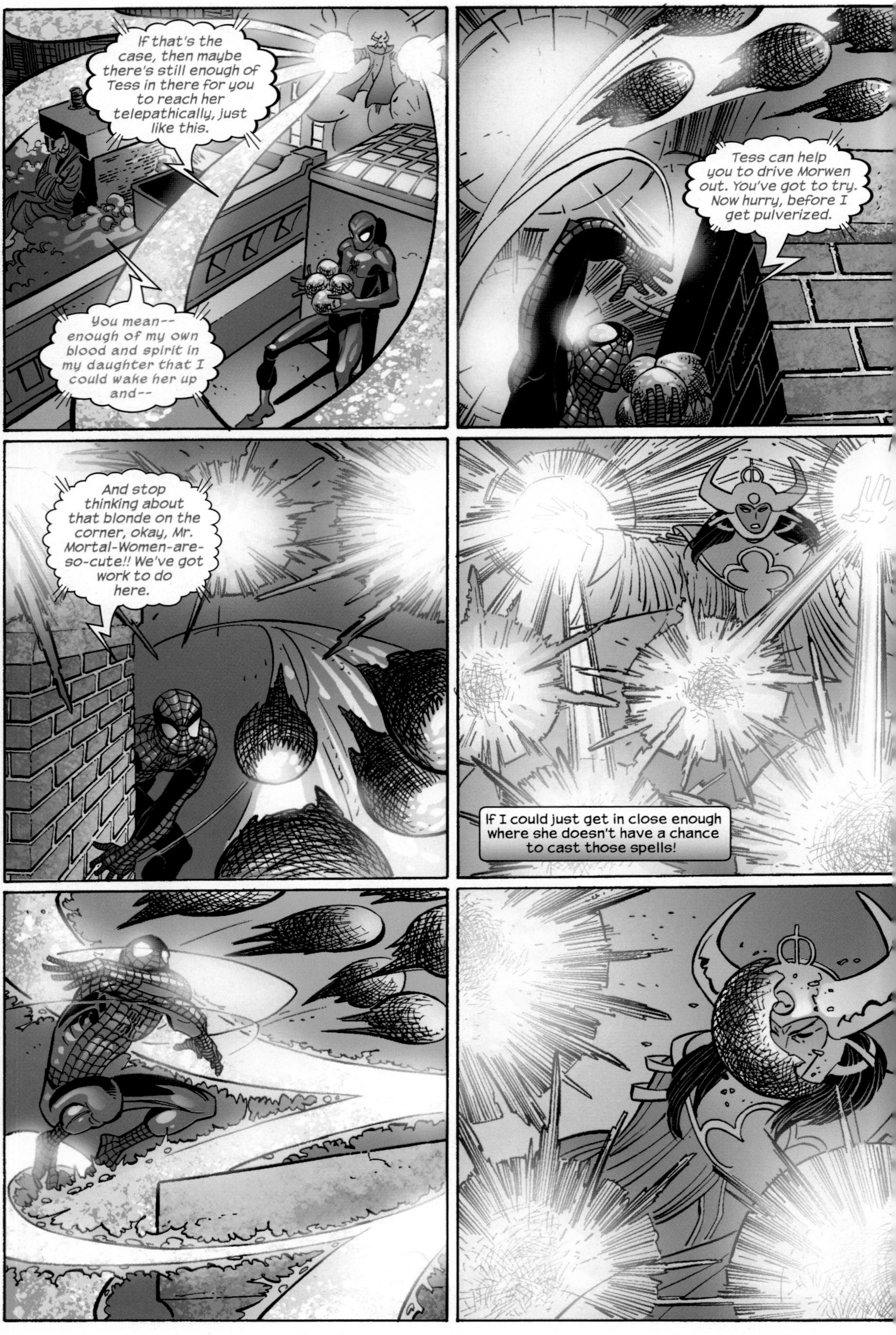

If that's the case, then maybe there's still enough of Tess in there for you to reach her telepathically, just like this.
You mean-- enough of my own blood and spirit in my daughter that I could wake her up and--
Tess can help you to drive Morwen out. You've got to try. Now hurry, before I get pulverized.
And stop thinking about that blonde on the corner, okay, Mr. Mortal-Women-are-so-cute!! We've got work to do here.
If I could just get in close enough where she doesn't have a chance to cast those spells!

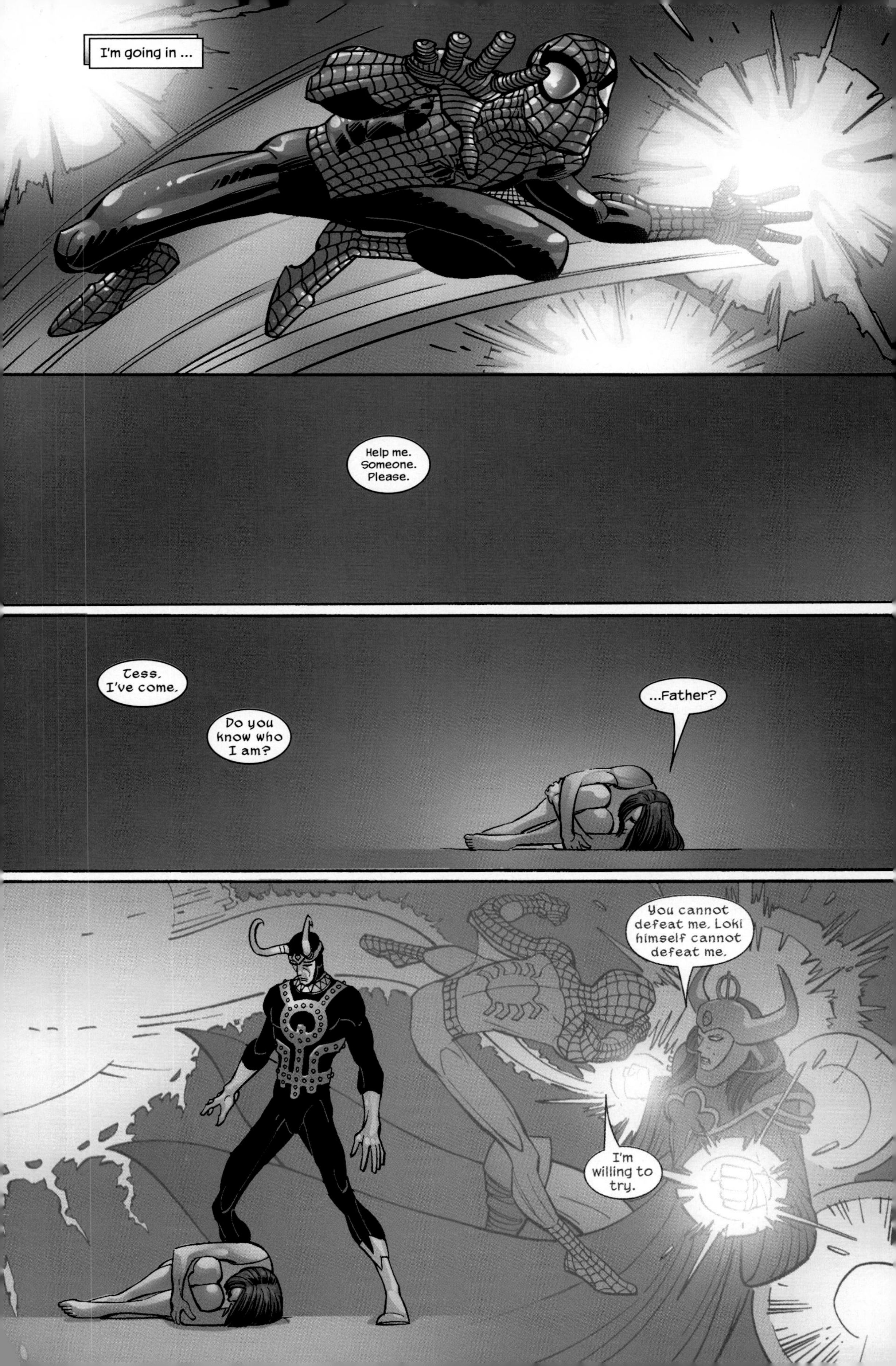
I'm going in ...
Help me. Someone. Please.
Tess. I've come.
Do you know who I am?
...Father?
You cannot defeat me. Loki himself cannot defeat me.
I'm willing to try.

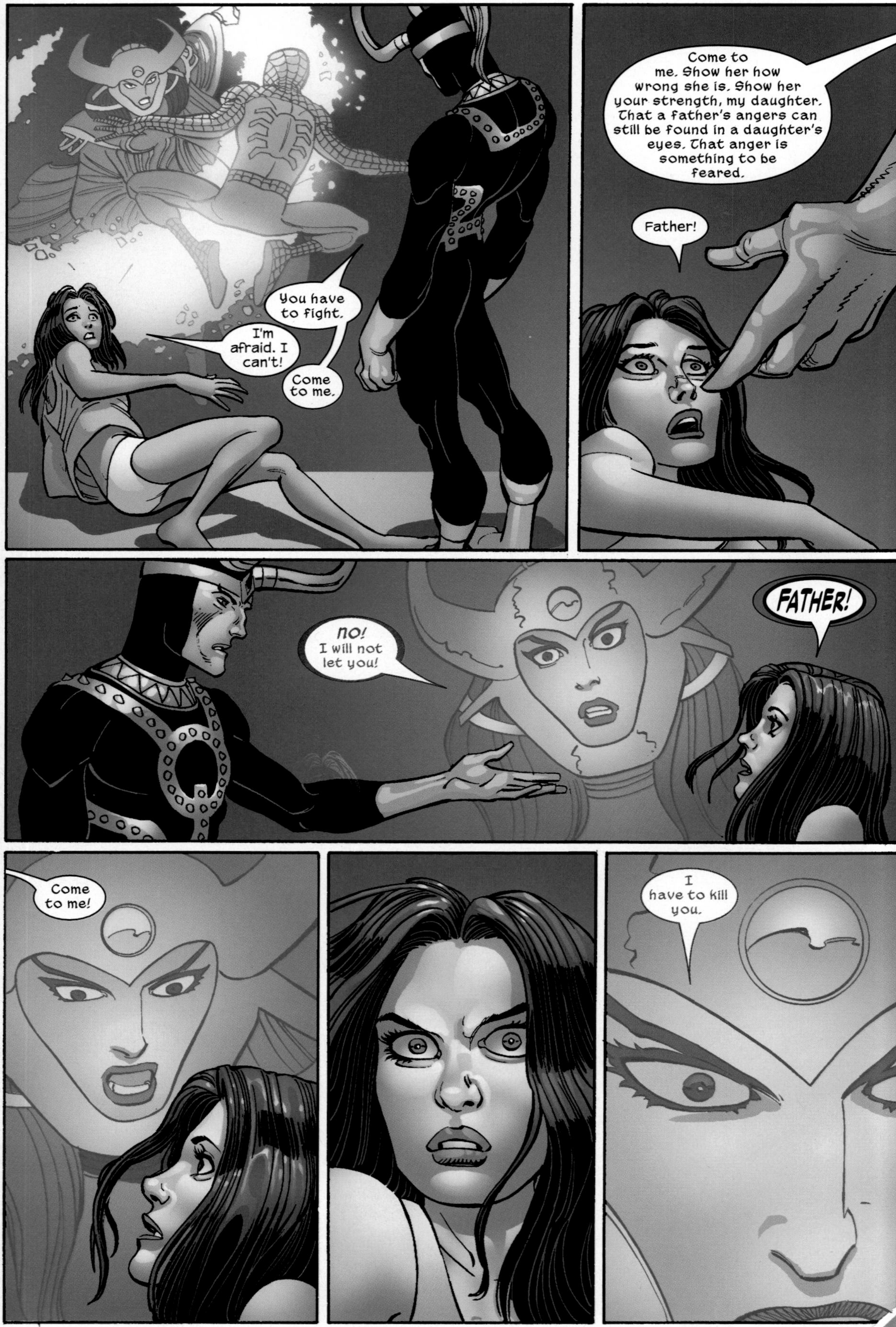
You have to fight.
I'm afraid. I can't!
Come to me.
Come to me. Show her how wrong she is. Show her your strength, my daughter. That a father's angers can still be found in a daughter's eyes. That anger is something to be feared.
Father!
NO! I will not let you!
FATHER!
Come to me!
I have to kill you.

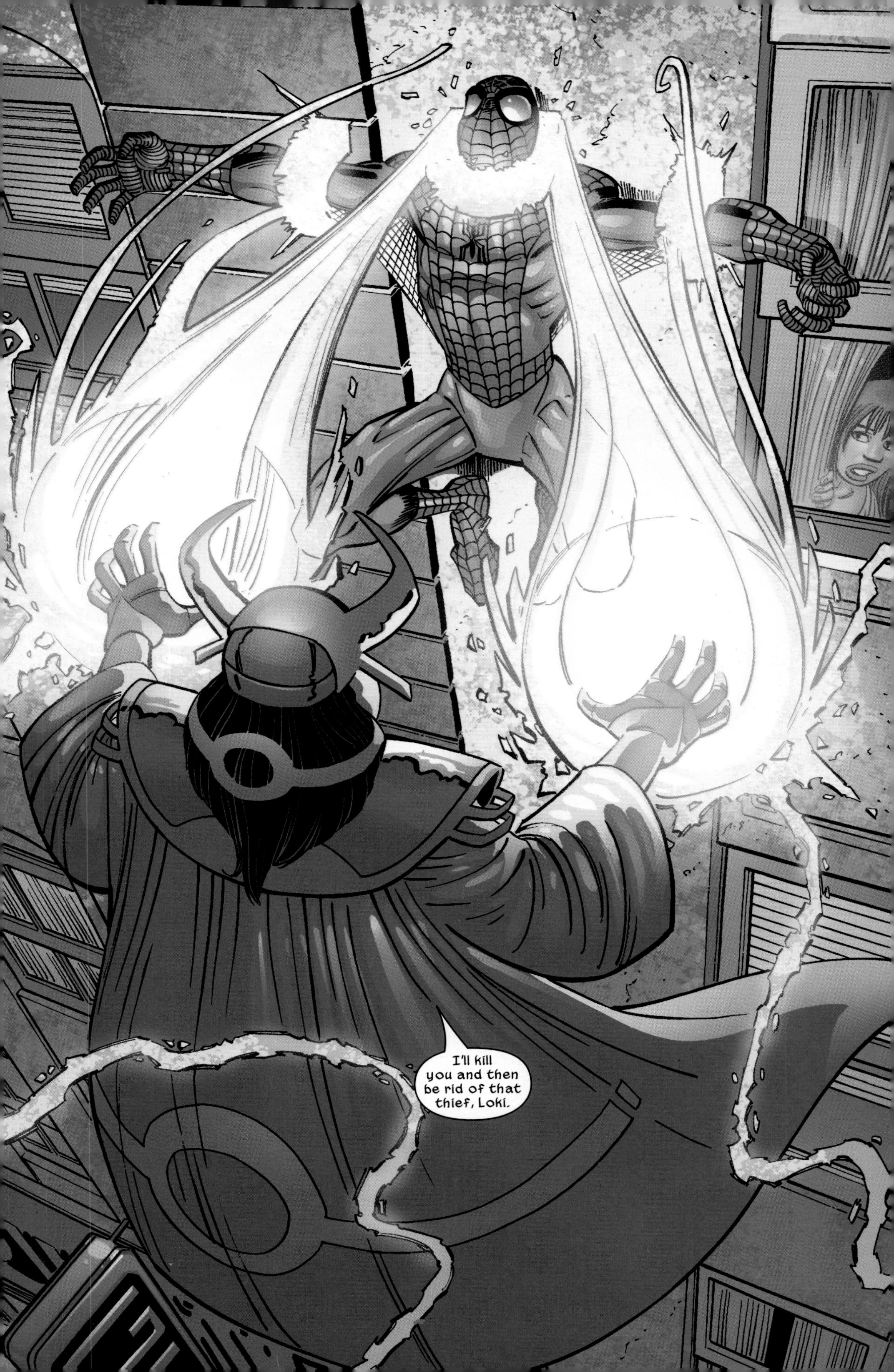
I'll kill you and then be rid of that thief, Loki.

CRACKLE
FTTTz

AUGH!

AAAH! LOKI! HURRY!

It's taking all my power, using it against me. It's not just normal magic.

I could stand a chance against that. But it's like fighting myself-- my own strength--holding me down.

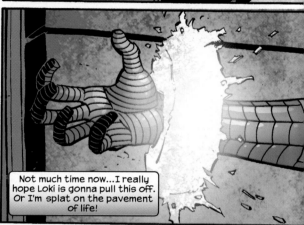

Not much time now...I really hope Loki is gonna pull this off. Or I'm splat on the pavement of life!

I can't linger on you. I have to get to Loki soon or it's all over.

But I will not leave this body.

NOW, DIE!

GUUUURRREEELLE...

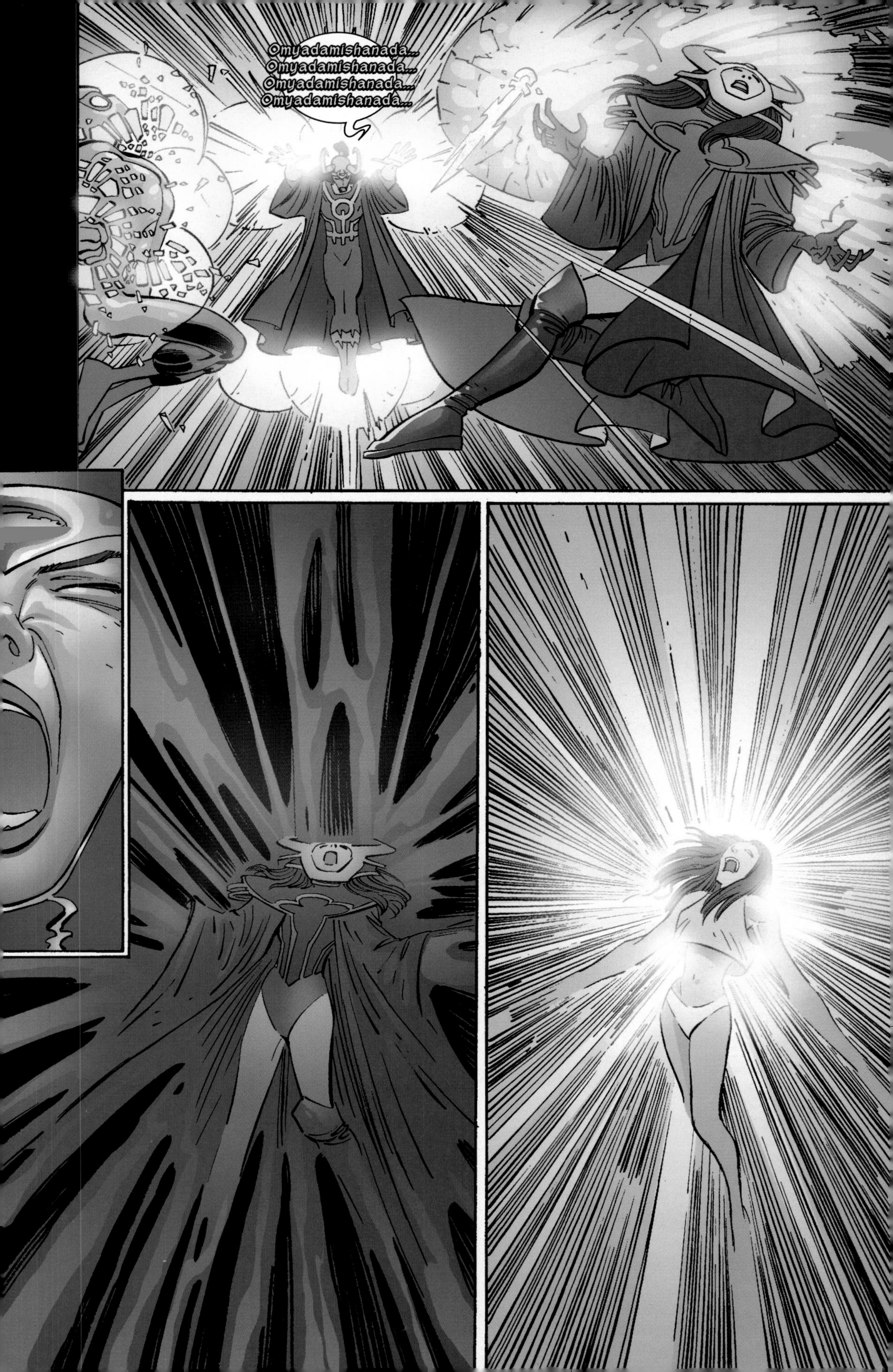
Omyadamishanada... Omyadamishanada... Omyadamishanada... Omyadamishanada...

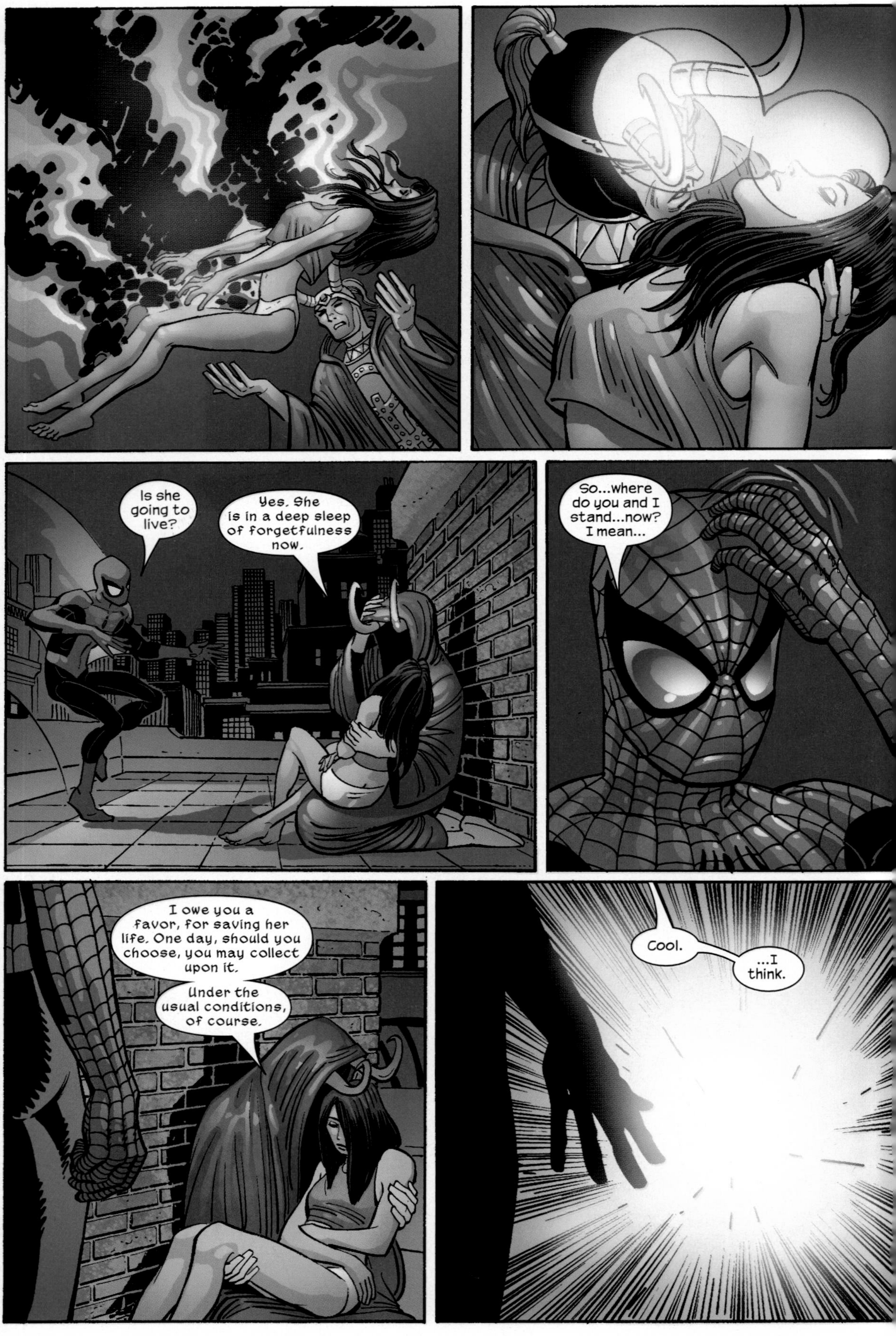
Is she going to live?
Yes. She is in a deep sleep of forgetfulness now.
So...where do you and I stand...now? I mean...
I owe you a favor, for saving her life. One day, should you choose, you may collect upon it.
Under the usual conditions, of course.
Cool.
...I think.

Doc Strange still wasn't in town, so I did a little investigating of my own at the public library.

There was nothing on microfiche or any literature on Morwen, First Sorcerer of Chaos.

I looked her up online too. All I got were X-rated sites. Thankfully the public library has a block on that stuff. Talk about embarrassing!

Shopping   Money   People & Chat

Search   ▷ Morwen + Sorcerer of Chaos

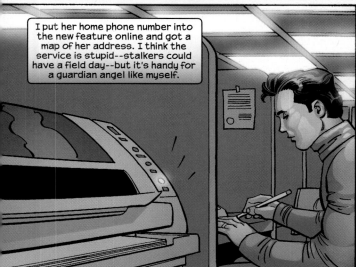

Then I did some checking on Tess Black.

Doesn't seem like Loki's kid. For starters, she's respectable, even made the paper a few times. She's a stock trader and pretty well-off.

I put her home phone number into the new feature online and got a map of her address. I think the service is stupid--stalkers could have a field day--but it's handy for a guardian angel like myself.

Oh, and I made absolutely sure Aunt May's number stayed unlisted. Just 'cuz.

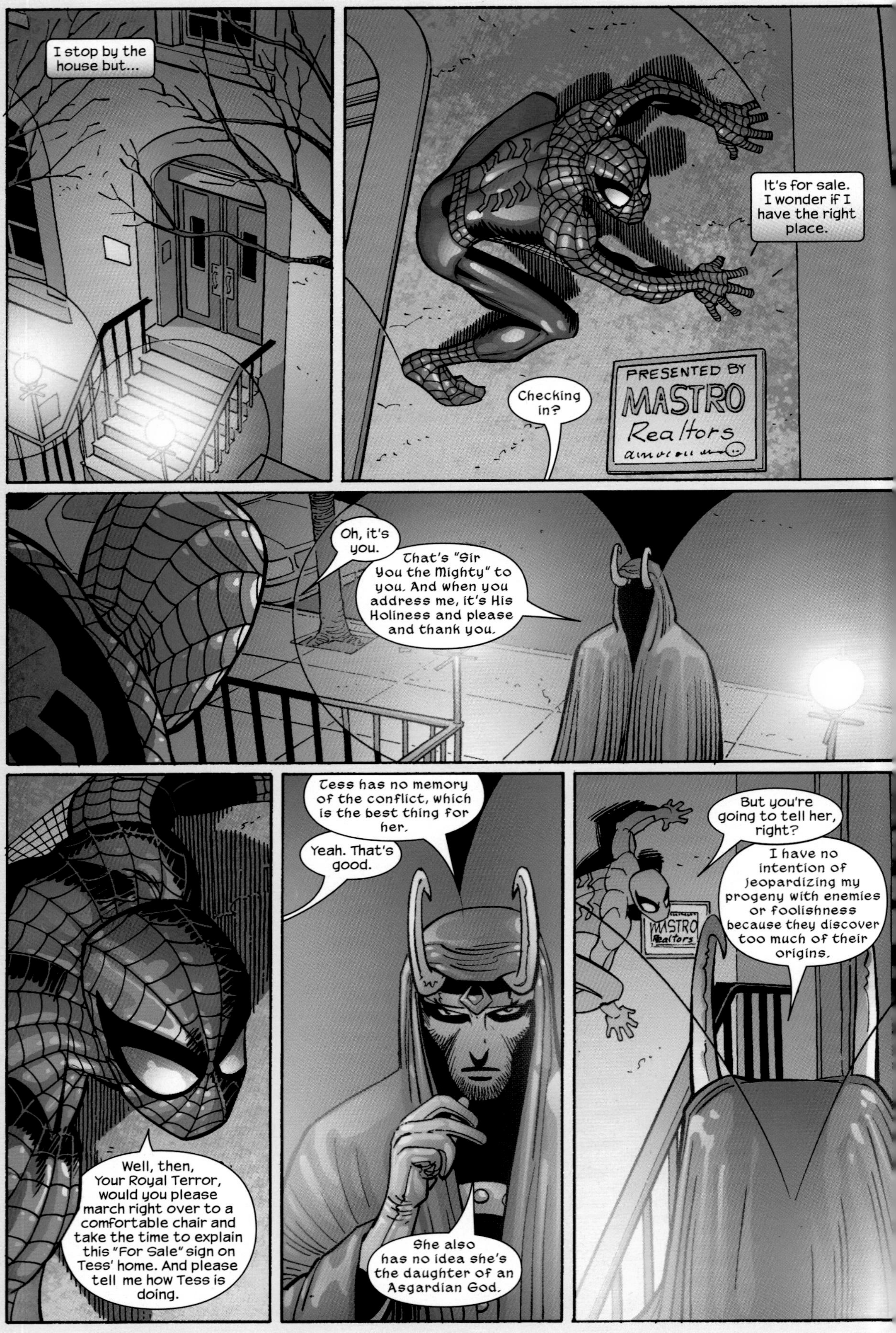
I stop by the house but...
It's for sale. I wonder if I have the right place.
PRESENTED BY MASTRO Realtors
Checking in?
Oh, it's you.
That's "Sir You the Mighty" to you. And when you address me, it's His Holiness and please and thank you.
Well, then, Your Royal Terror, would you please march right over to a comfortable chair and take the time to explain this "For Sale" sign on Tess' home. And please tell me how Tess is doing.
Tess has no memory of the conflict, which is the best thing for her.
Yeah. That's good.
She also has no idea she's the daughter of an Asgardian God.
But you're going to tell her, right?
I have no intention of jeopardizing my progeny with enemies or foolishness because they discover too much of their origins.

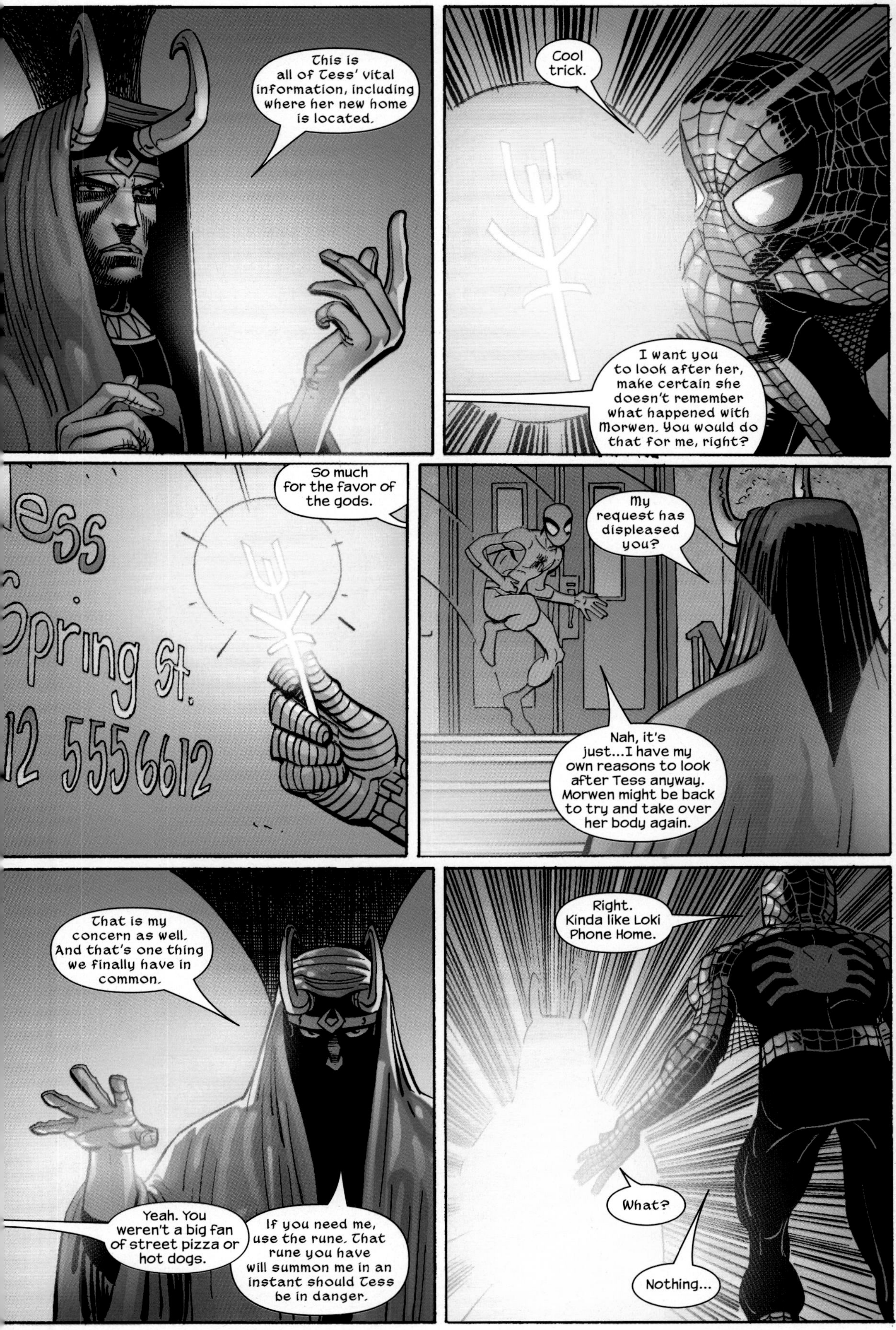
This is all of Tess' vital information, including where her new home is located.
Cool trick.
I want you to look after her, make certain she doesn't remember what happened with Morwen. You would do that for me, right?
So much for the favor of the gods.
Spring St.
12 5556612
My request has displeased you?
Nah, it's just...I have my own reasons to look after Tess anyway. Morwen might be back to try and take over her body again.
That is my concern as well. And that's one thing we finally have in common.
Yeah. You weren't a big fan of street pizza or hot dogs.
If you need me, use the rune. That rune you have will summon me in an instant should Tess be in danger.
Right. Kinda like Loki Phone Home.
What?
Nothing...

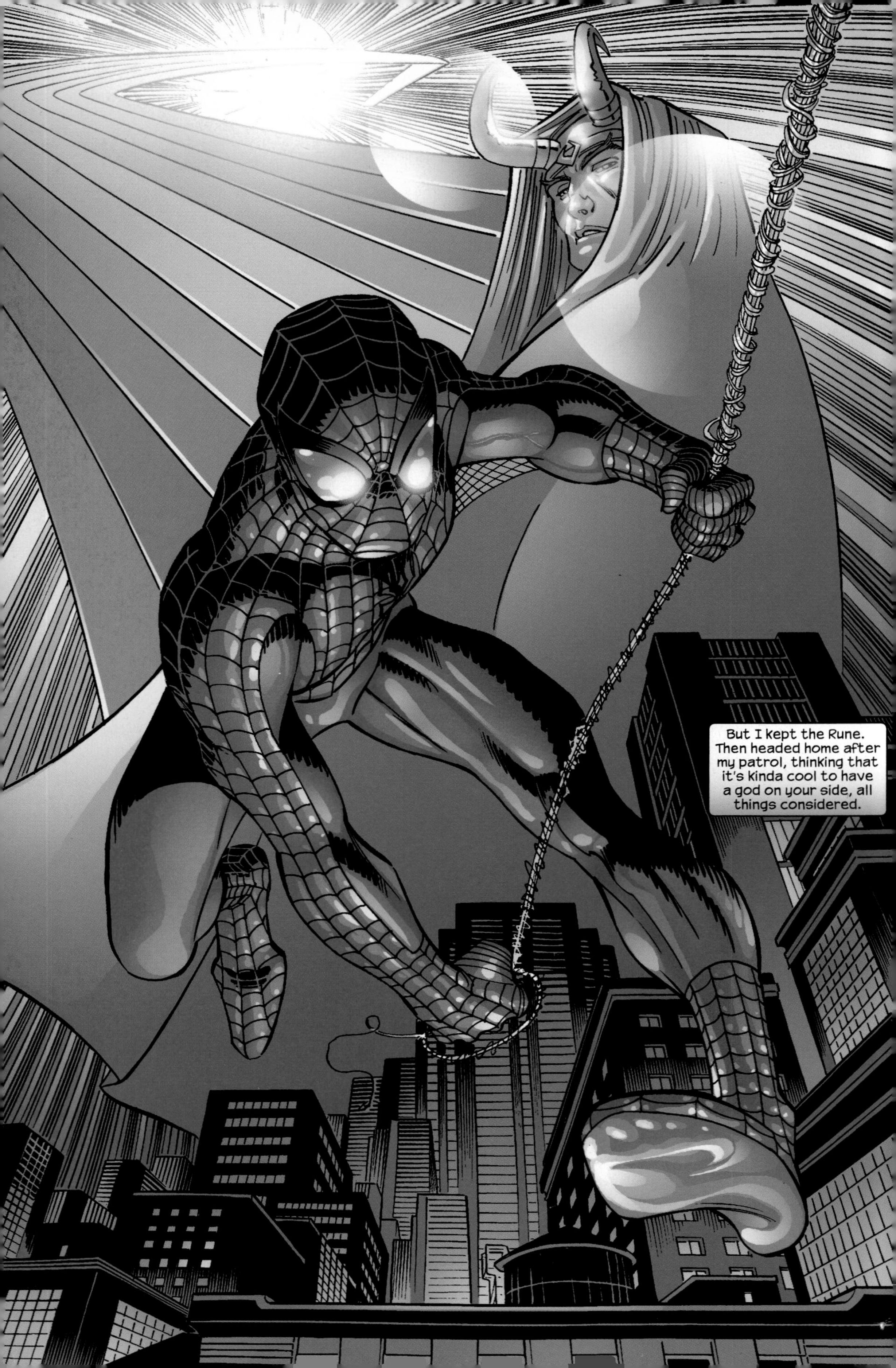
But I kept the Rune. Then headed home after my patrol, thinking that it's kinda cool to have a god on your side, all things considered.

#505

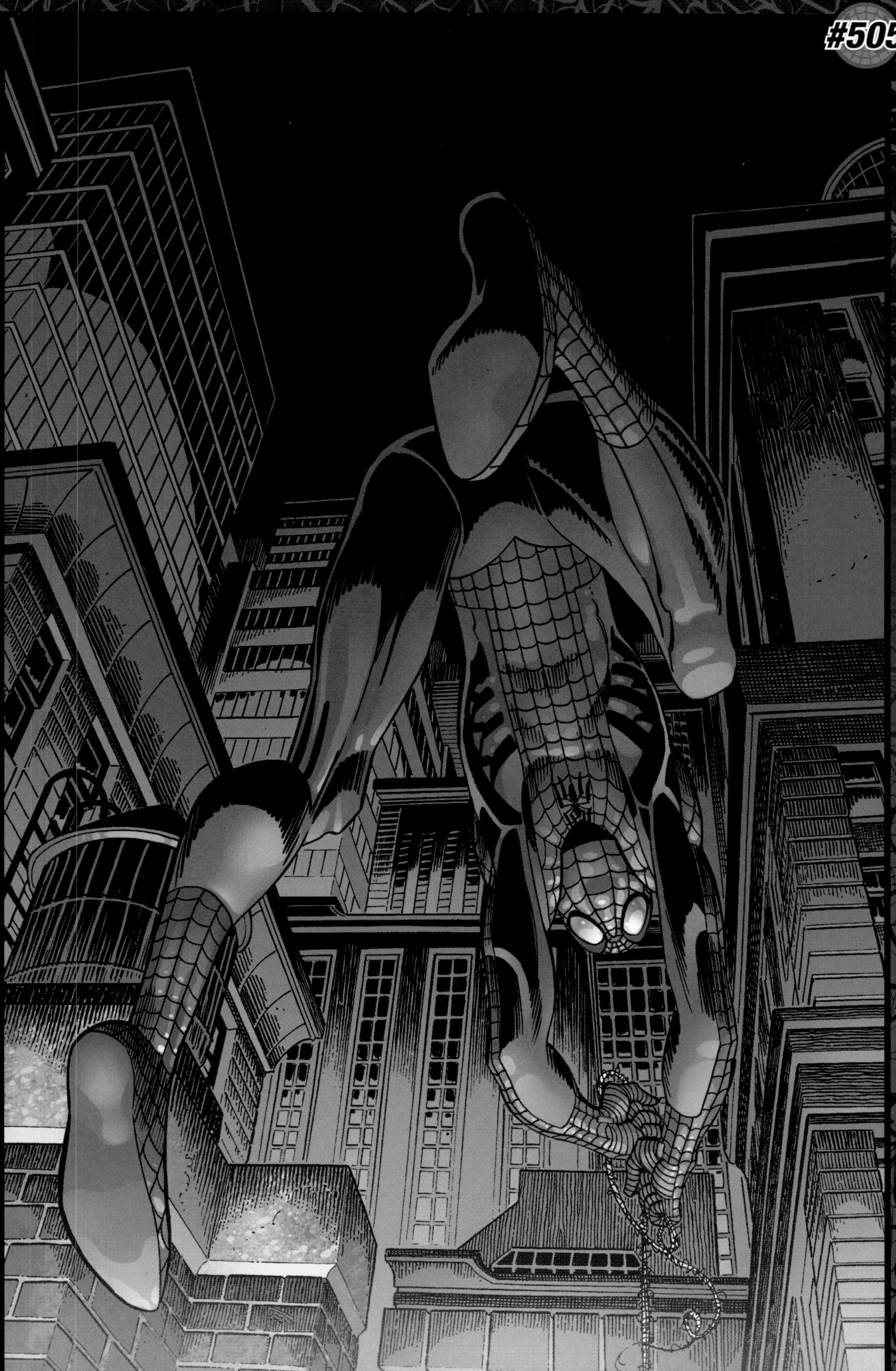

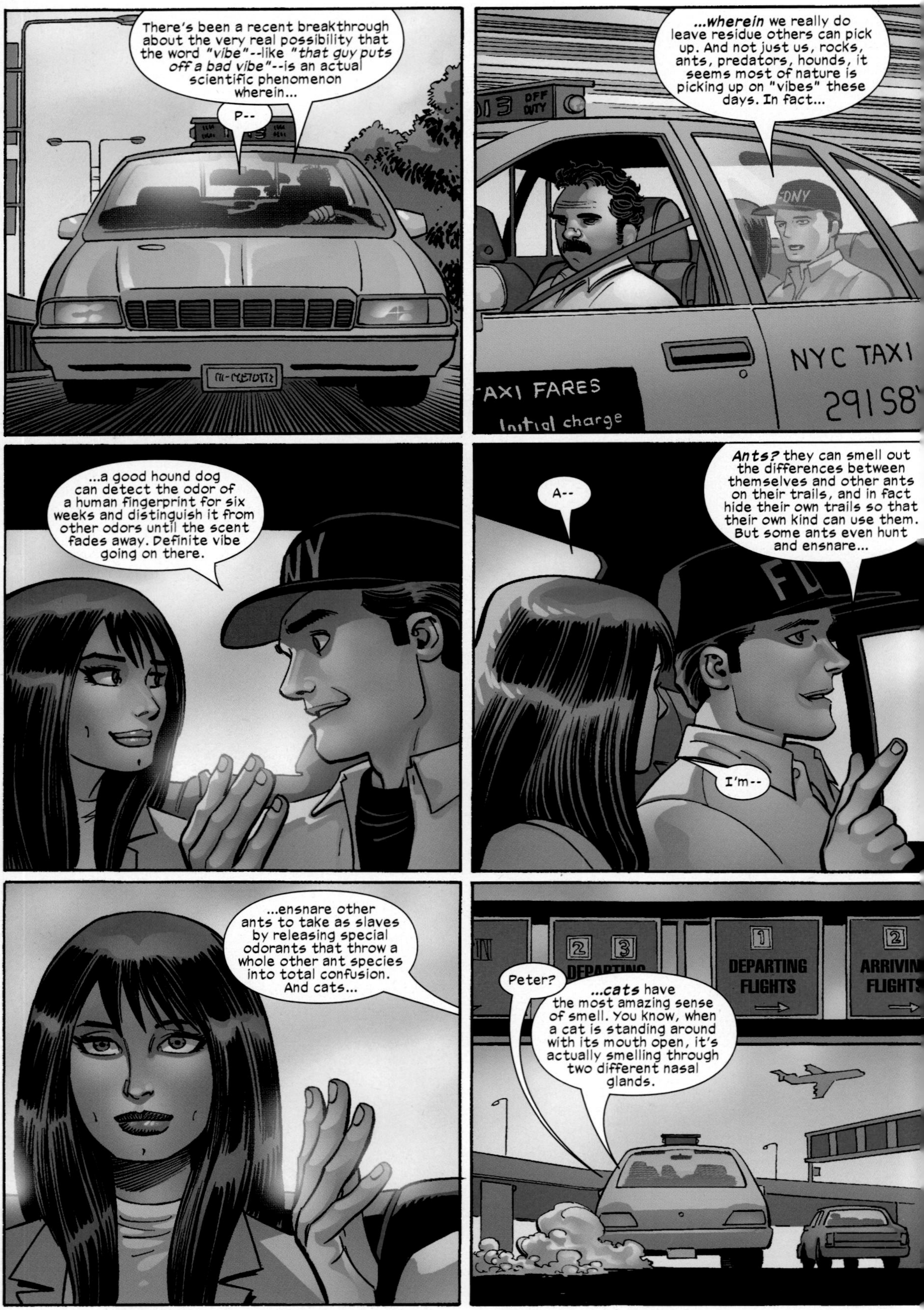
There's been a recent breakthrough about the very real possibility that the word *"vibe"*--like *"that guy puts off a bad vibe"*--is an actual scientific phenomenon wherein...
P--
...wherein we really do leave residue others can pick up. And not just us, rocks, ants, predators, hounds, it seems most of nature is picking up on "vibes" these days. In fact...
OFF DUTY
FDNY
NYC TAXI
TAXI FARES
Initial charge
...a good hound dog can detect the odor of a human fingerprint for six weeks and distinguish it from other odors until the scent fades away. Definite vibe going on there.
A--
Ants? they can smell out the differences between themselves and other ants on their trails, and in fact hide their own trails so that their own kind can use them. But some ants even hunt and ensnare...
I'm--
...ensnare other ants to take as slaves by releasing special odorants that throw a whole other ant species into total confusion. And cats...
DEPARTING FLIGHTS
Peter?
...cats have the most amazing sense of smell. You know, when a cat is standing around with its mouth open, it's actually smelling through two different nasal glands.

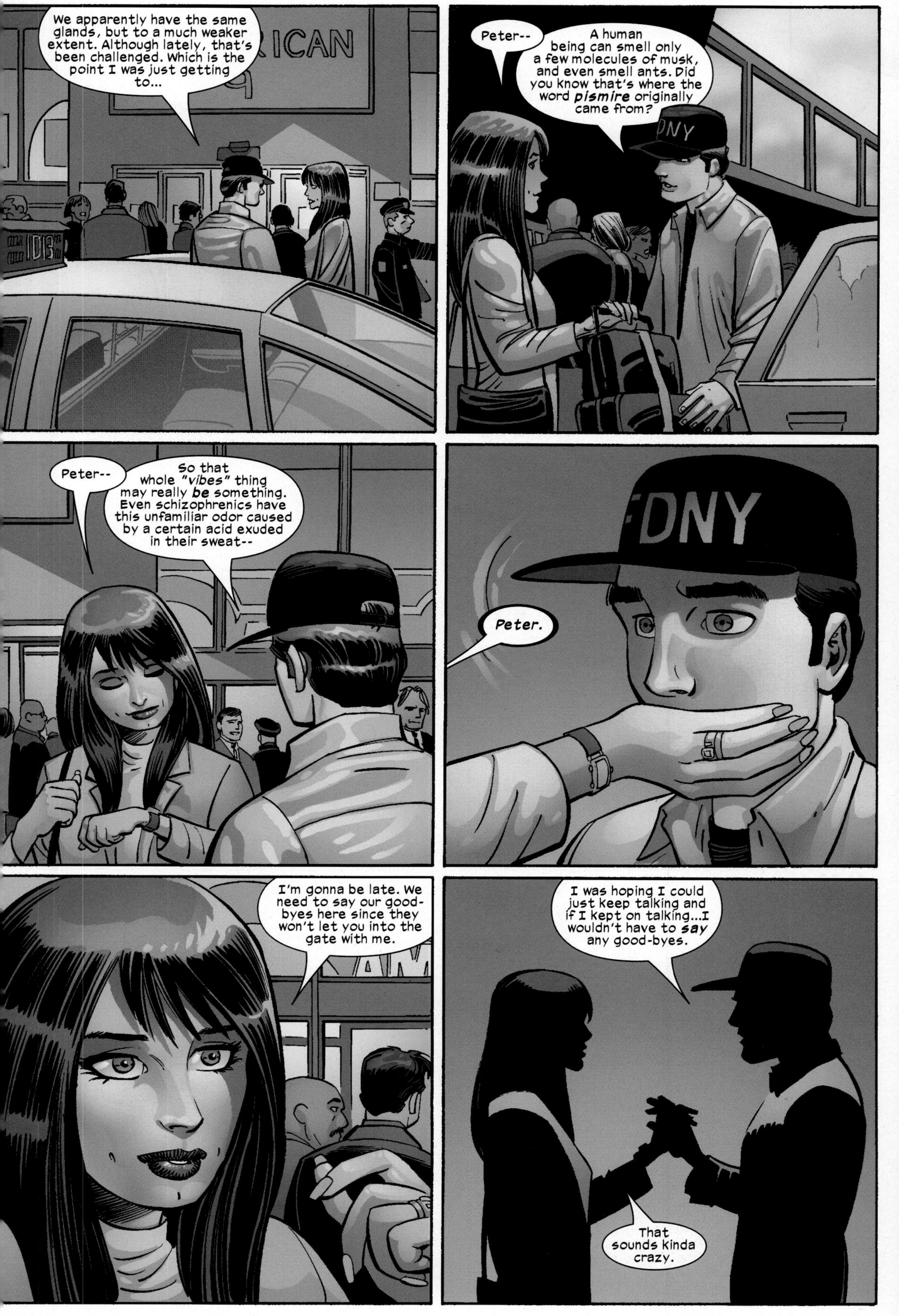

We apparently have the same glands, but to a much weaker extent. Although lately, that's been challenged. Which is the point I was just getting to...
ICAN
Peter--
A human being can smell only a few molecules of musk, and even smell ants. Did you know that's where the word *pismire* originally came from?
DNY
Peter--
So that whole *"vibes"* thing may really *be* something. Even schizophrenics have this unfamiliar odor caused by a certain acid exuded in their sweat--
FDNY
Peter.
I'm gonna be late. We need to say our good-byes here since they won't let you into the gate with me.
I was hoping I could just keep talking and if I kept on talking...I wouldn't have to *say* any good-byes.
That sounds kinda crazy.

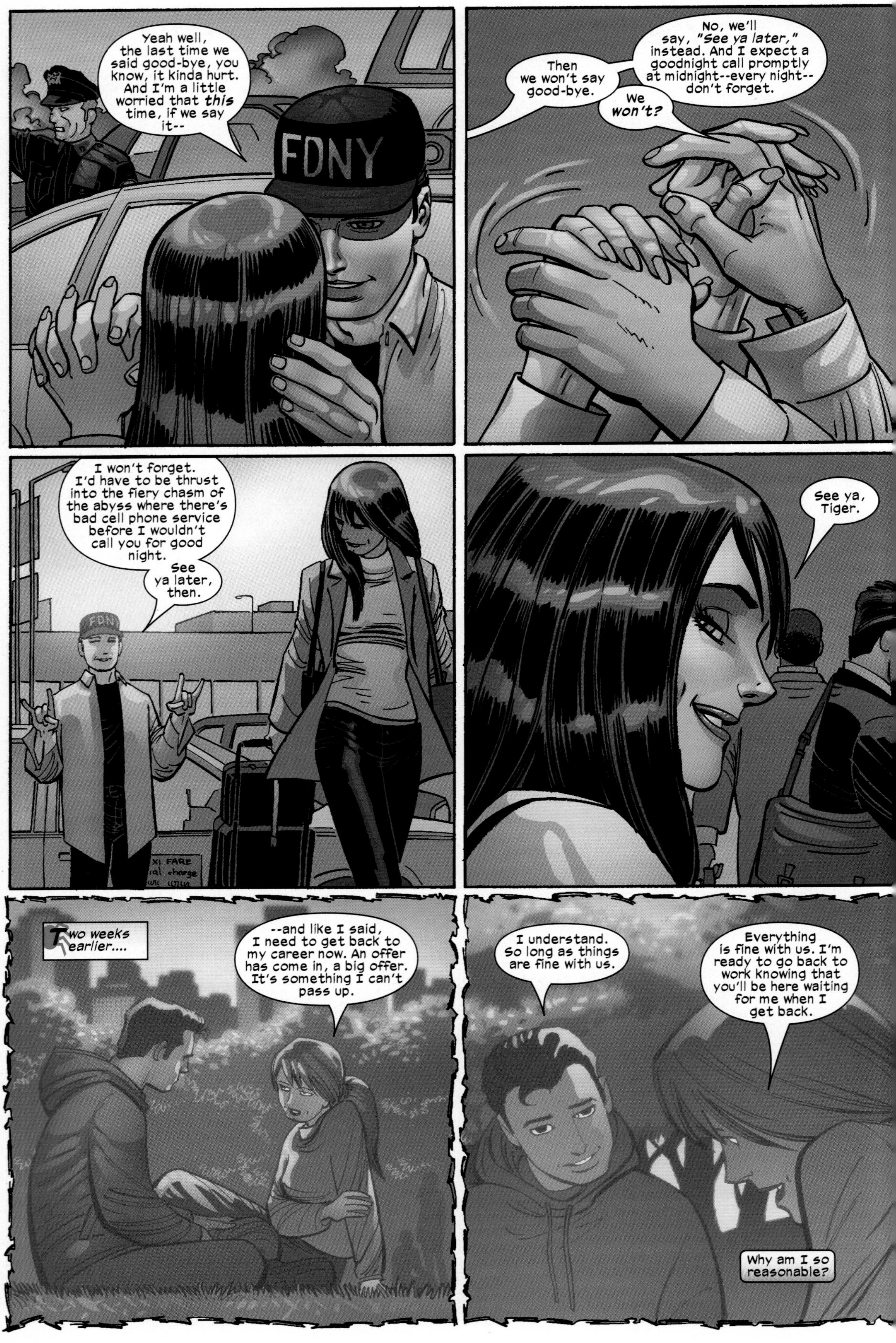
Yeah well, the last time we said good-bye, you know, it kinda hurt. And I'm a little worried that *this* time, if we say it--
FDNY
Then we won't say good-bye.
We *won't?*
No, we'll say, *"See ya later,"* instead. And I expect a goodnight call promptly at midnight--every night--don't forget.
I won't forget. I'd have to be thrust into the fiery chasm of the abyss where there's bad cell phone service before I wouldn't call you for good night.
See ya later, then.
FDNY
See ya, Tiger.
Two weeks earlier....
--and like I said, I need to get back to my career now. An offer has come in, a big offer. It's something I can't pass up.
I understand. So long as things are fine with us.
Everything is fine with us. I'm ready to go back to work knowing that you'll be here waiting for me when I get back.
Why am I so reasonable?

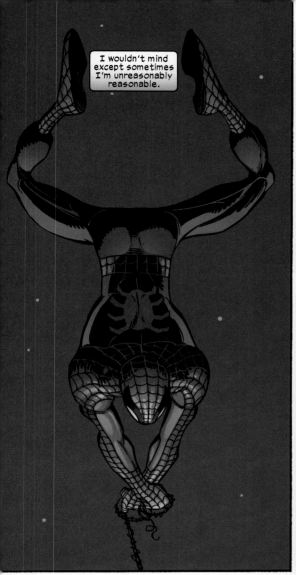

I wouldn't mind except sometimes I'm unreasonably reasonable.

So I decided to bury myself in the work, knowing that if I just sat around, I would miss MJ. I would worry. In other words, I'd be stupid.

But it's a happy-skippy night. Seems like everyone's behaving just when I need some rowdiness.

I wonder how MJ is doing.

BEVERLY HILLS, CALIFORNIA.

It's three hours earlier in L.A., but I bet she's feeling New York time nonetheless.

Baramont Pictures

This is the biggest break in her entire career. I feel weird not being there.

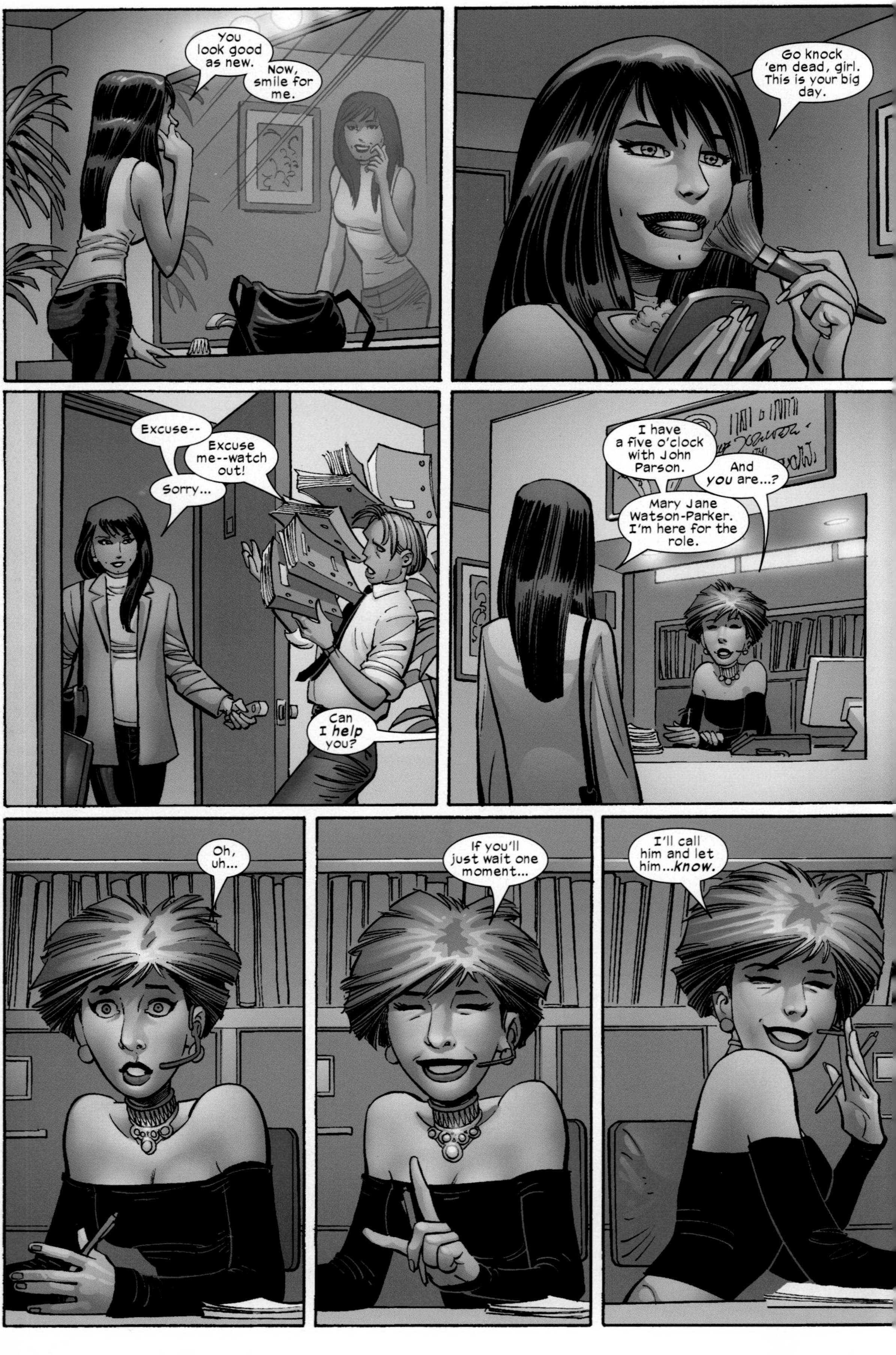
You look good as new.
Now, smile for me.
Go knock 'em dead, girl. This is your big day.
Excuse--
Excuse me--watch out!
Sorry...
Can I *help* you?
I have a five o'clock with John Parson.
And *you* are...?
Mary Jane Watson-Parker. I'm here for the role.
Oh, uh...
If you'll just wait one moment...
I'll call him and let him...*know.*

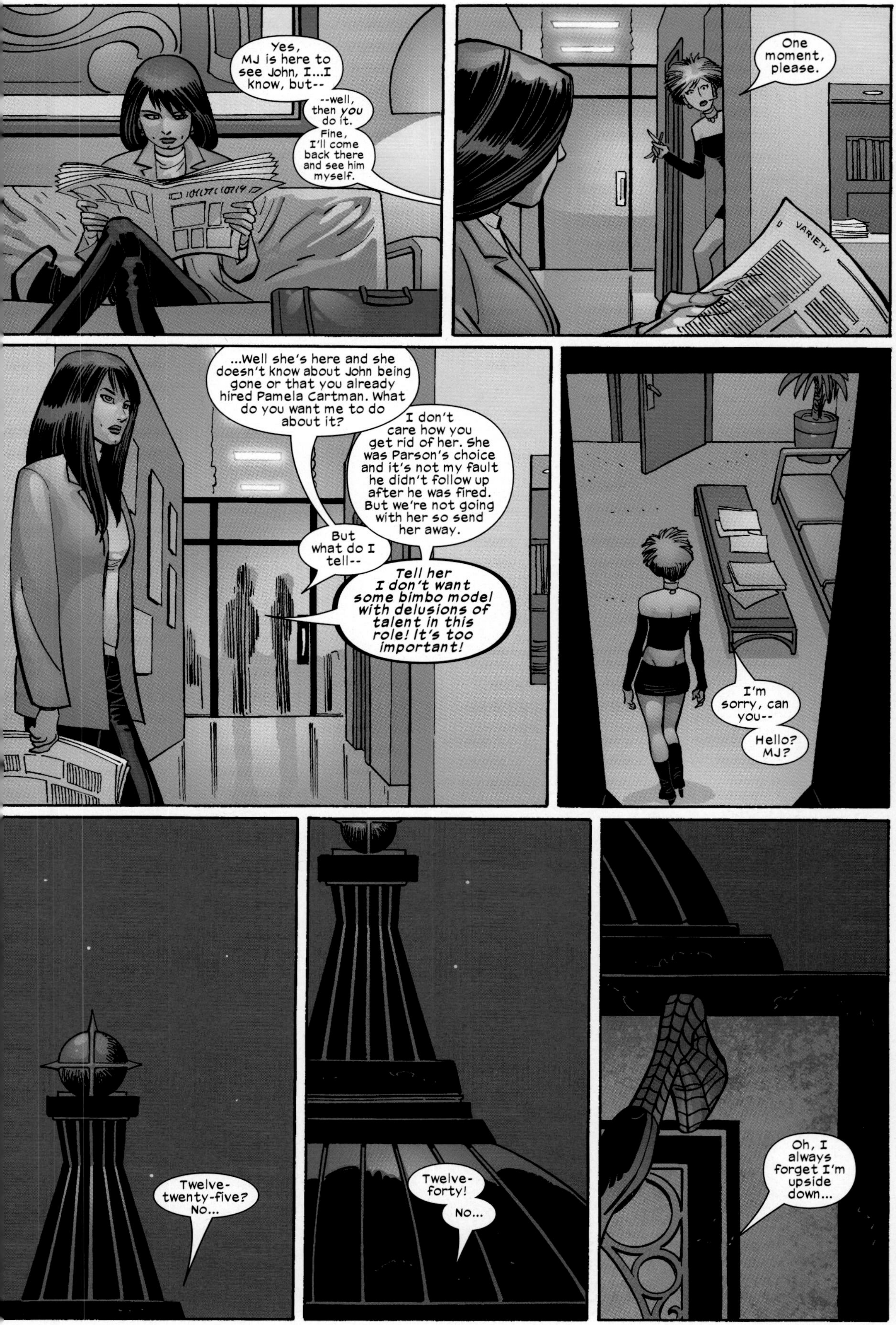
Yes, MJ is here to see John, I...I know, but--
--well, then you do it. Fine, I'll come back there and see him myself.
One moment, please.
VARIETY
...Well she's here and she doesn't know about John being gone or that you already hired Pamela Cartman. What do you want me to do about it?
I don't care how you get rid of her. She was Parson's choice and it's not my fault he didn't follow up after he was fired. But we're not going with her so send her away.
But what do I tell--
Tell her I don't want some bimbo model with delusions of talent in this role! It's too important!
I'm sorry, can you--
Hello? MJ?
Twelve-twenty-five? No...
Twelve-forty!
No...
Oh, I always forget I'm upside down...

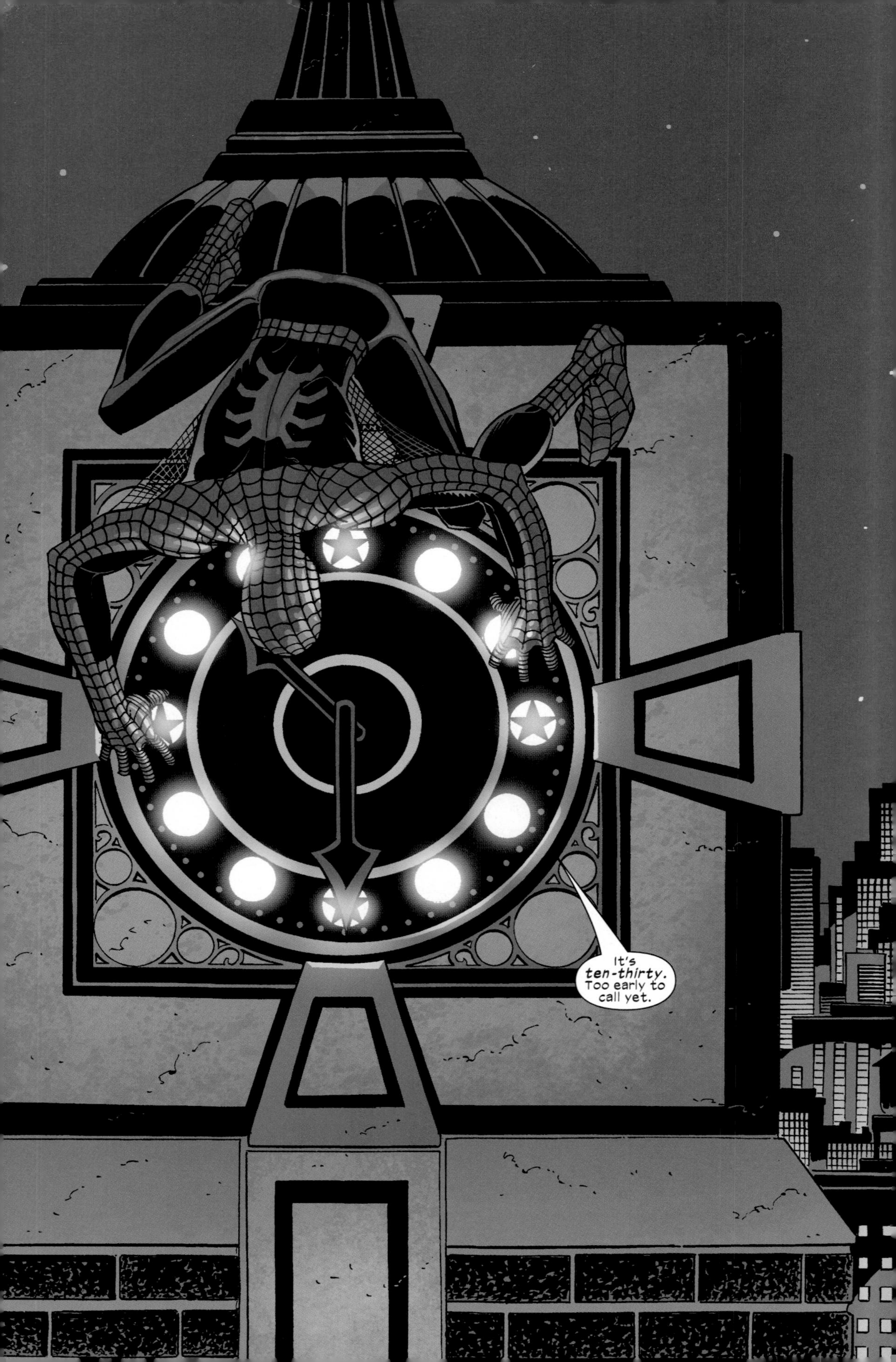
It's ten-thirty. Too early to call yet.

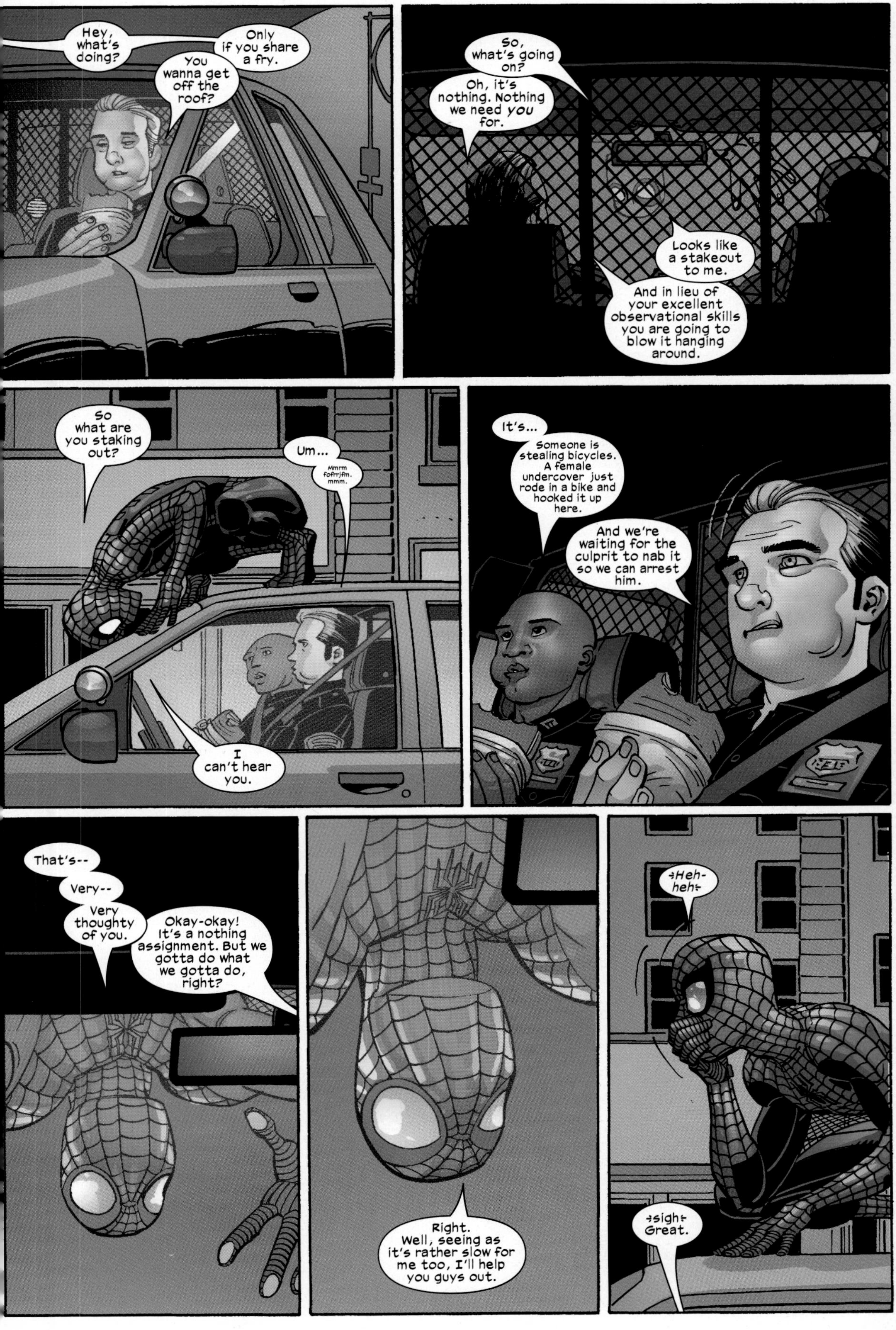
Hey, what's doing?
Only if you share a fry.
You wanna get off the roof?
So, what's going on?
Oh, it's nothing. Nothing we need *you* for.
Looks like a stakeout to me.
And in lieu of your excellent observational skills you are going to blow it hanging around.
So what are you staking out?
Um...
Mmrm fofrrjfm. mmm.
I can't hear you.
It's...
Someone is stealing bicycles. A female undercover just rode in a bike and hooked it up here.
And we're waiting for the culprit to nab it so we can arrest him.
That's--
Very--
Very thoughty of you.
Okay-okay! It's a nothing assignment. But we gotta do what we gotta do, right?
Right. Well, seeing as it's rather slow for me too, I'll help you guys out.
-Heh-heh-
-sigh- Great.

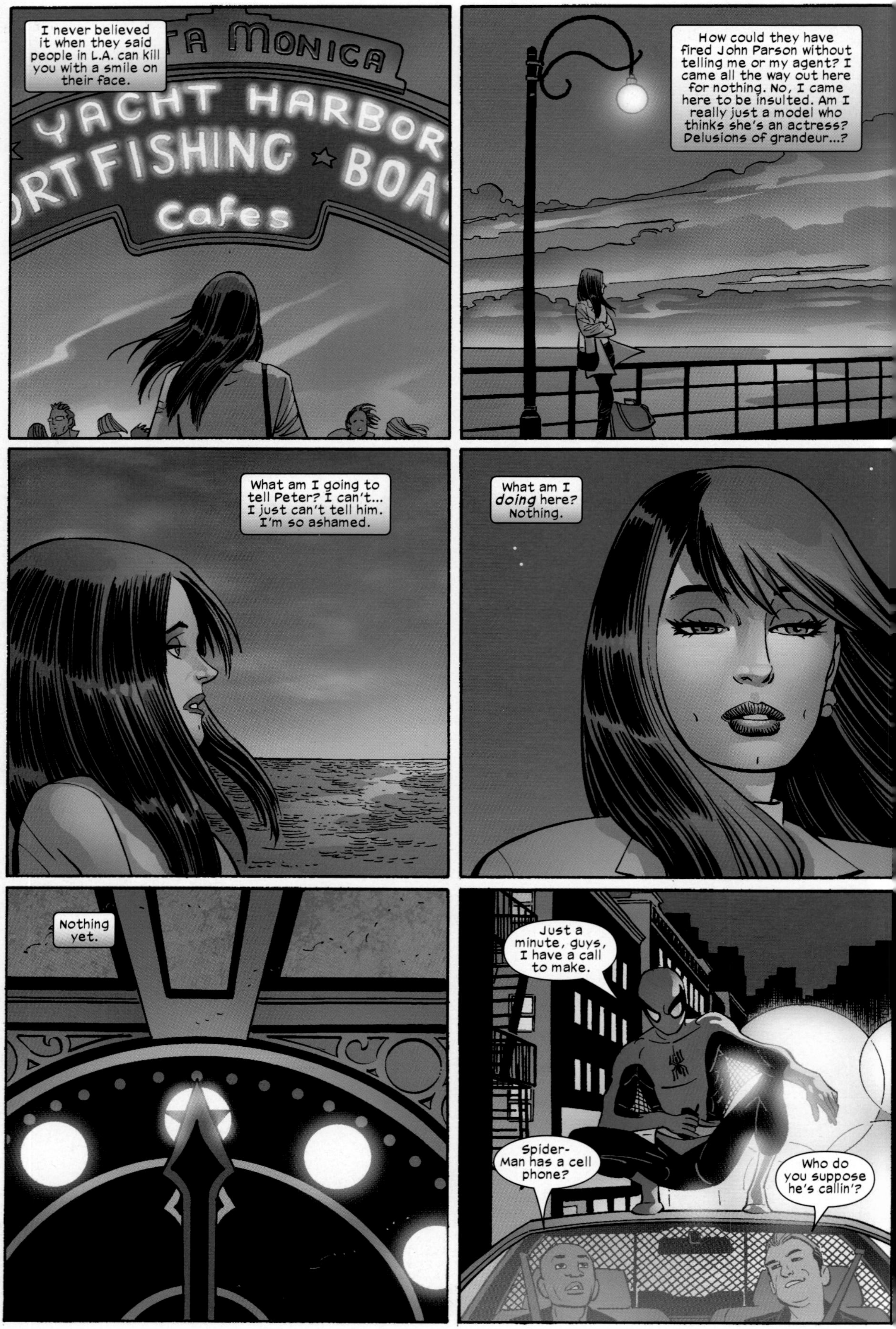
I never believed it when they said people in L.A. can kill you with a smile on their face.
TA MONICA
YACHT HARBOR
ORT FISHING BOA
Cafes
How could they have fired John Parson without telling me or my agent? I came all the way out here for nothing. No, I came here to be insulted. Am I really just a model who thinks she's an actress? Delusions of grandeur...?
What am I going to tell Peter? I can't... I just can't tell him. I'm so ashamed.
What am I *doing* here? Nothing.
Nothing yet.
Just a minute, guys, I have a call to make.
Spider-Man has a cell phone?
Who do you suppose he's callin'?

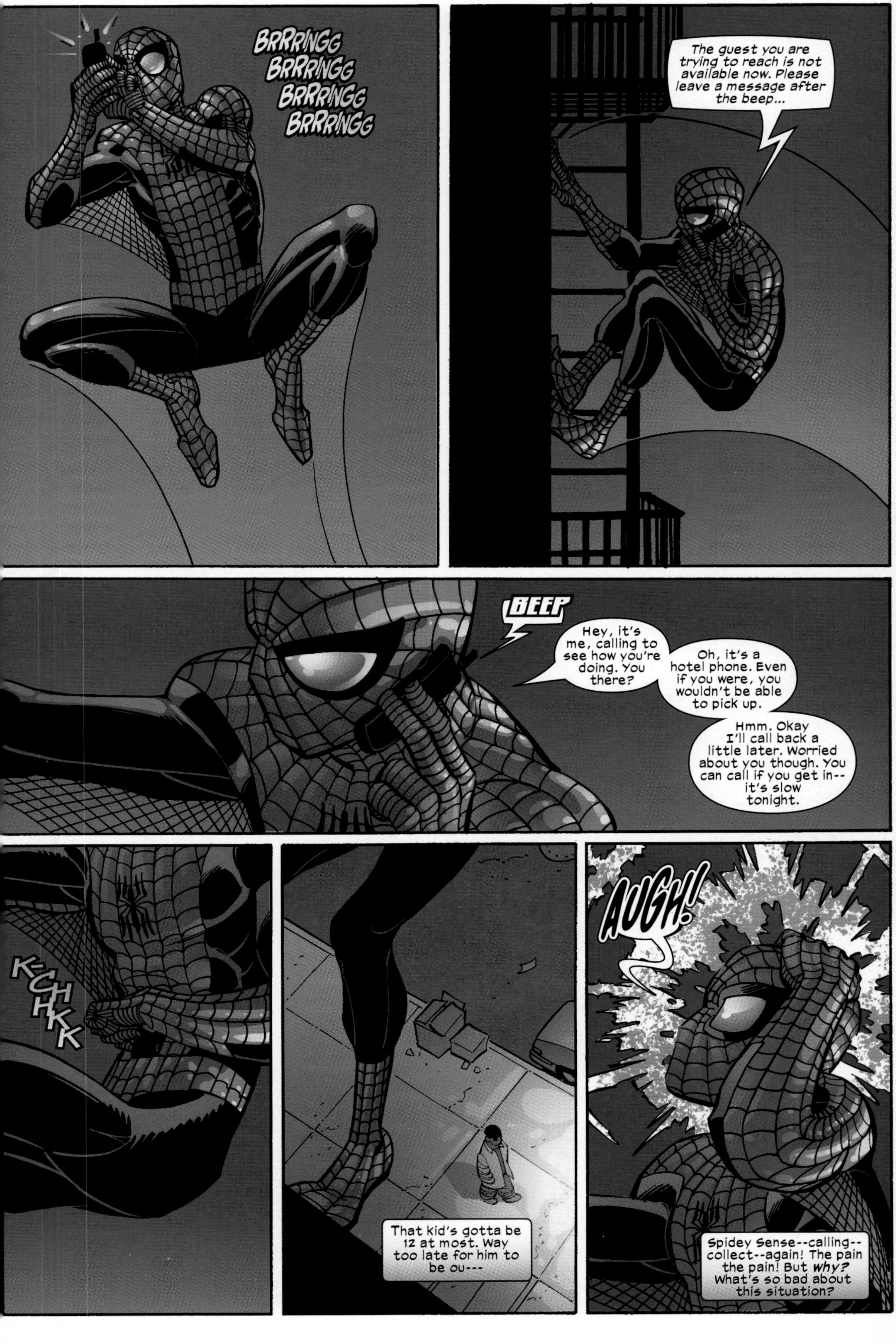
BRRRINGG BRRRINGG BRRRINGG BRRRINGG
The guest you are trying to reach is not available now. Please leave a message after the beep...
BEEP
Hey, it's me, calling to see how you're doing. You there?
Oh, it's a hotel phone. Even if you were, you wouldn't be able to pick up.
Hmm. Okay I'll call back a little later. Worried about you though. You can call if you get in-- it's slow tonight.
K-CHKK
That kid's gotta be 12 at most. Way too late for him to be ou---
AUGH!
Spidey Sense--calling--collect--again! The pain the pain! But *why?* What's so bad about this situation?

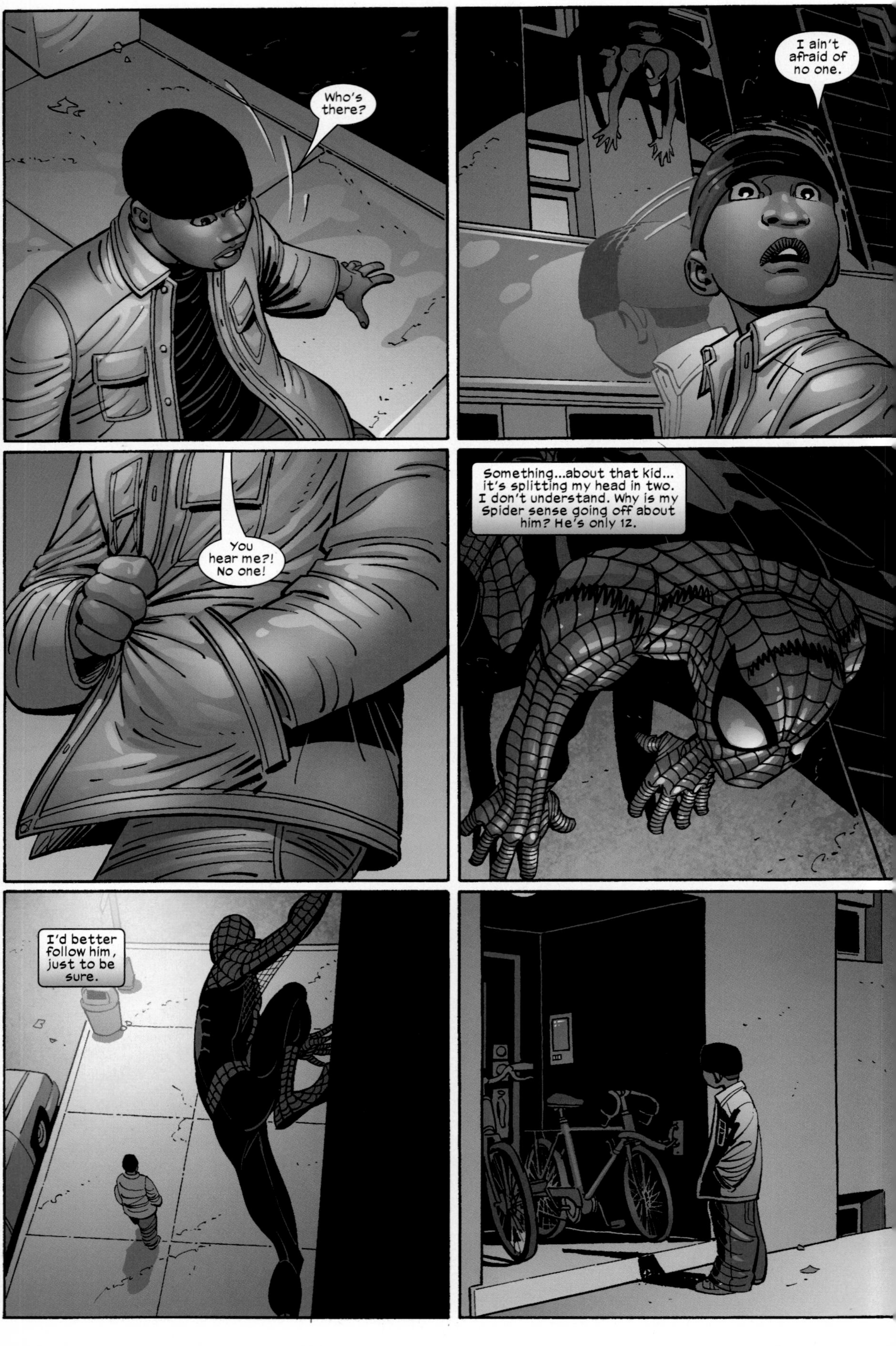
Who's there?
I ain't afraid of no one.
You hear me?! No one!
Something...about that kid... it's splitting my head in two. I don't understand. Why is my Spider sense going off about him? He's only 12.
I'd better follow him, just to be sure.

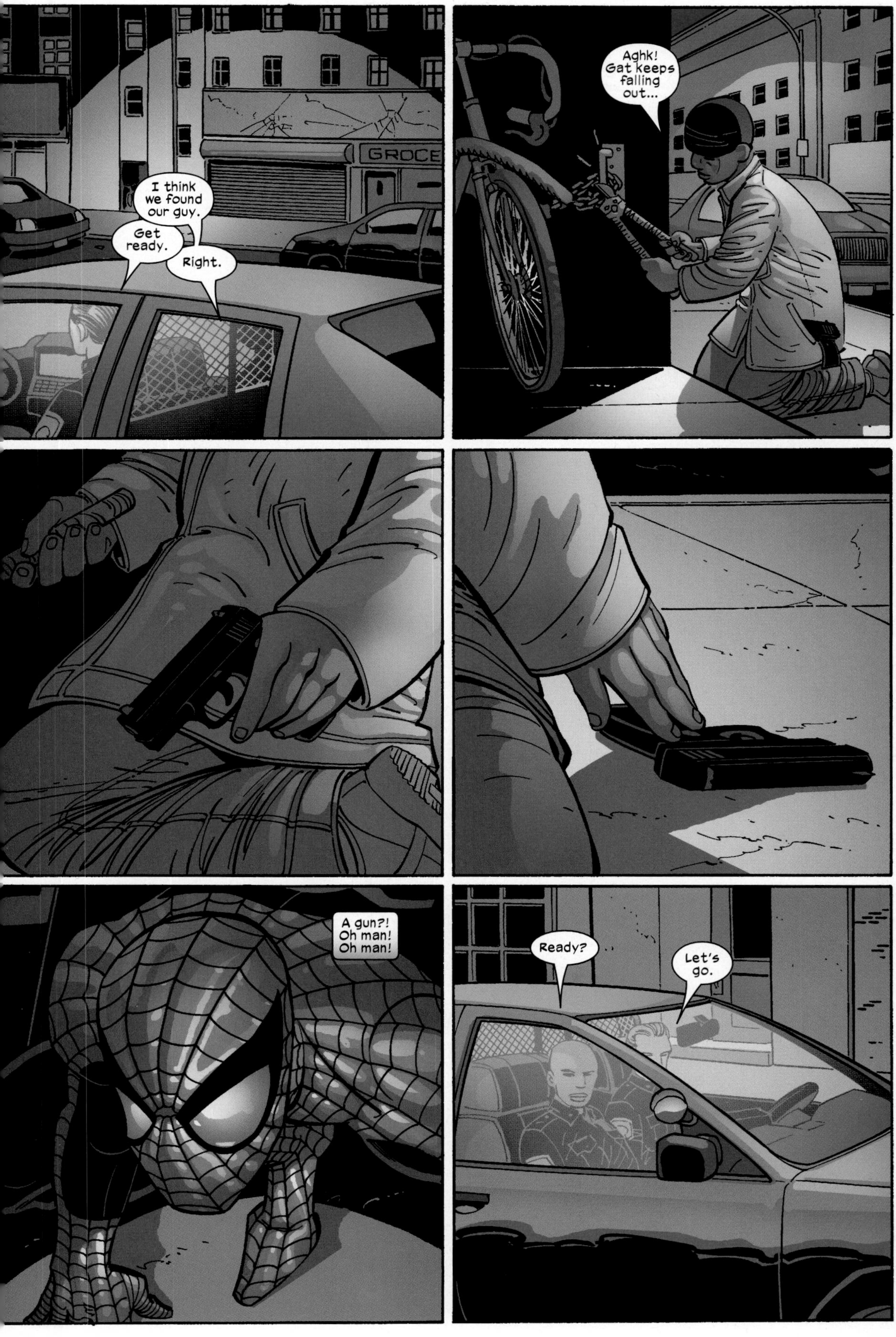
I think we found our guy.
Get ready.
Right.
Aghk! Gat keeps falling out...
A gun?! Oh man! Oh man!
Ready?
Let's go.

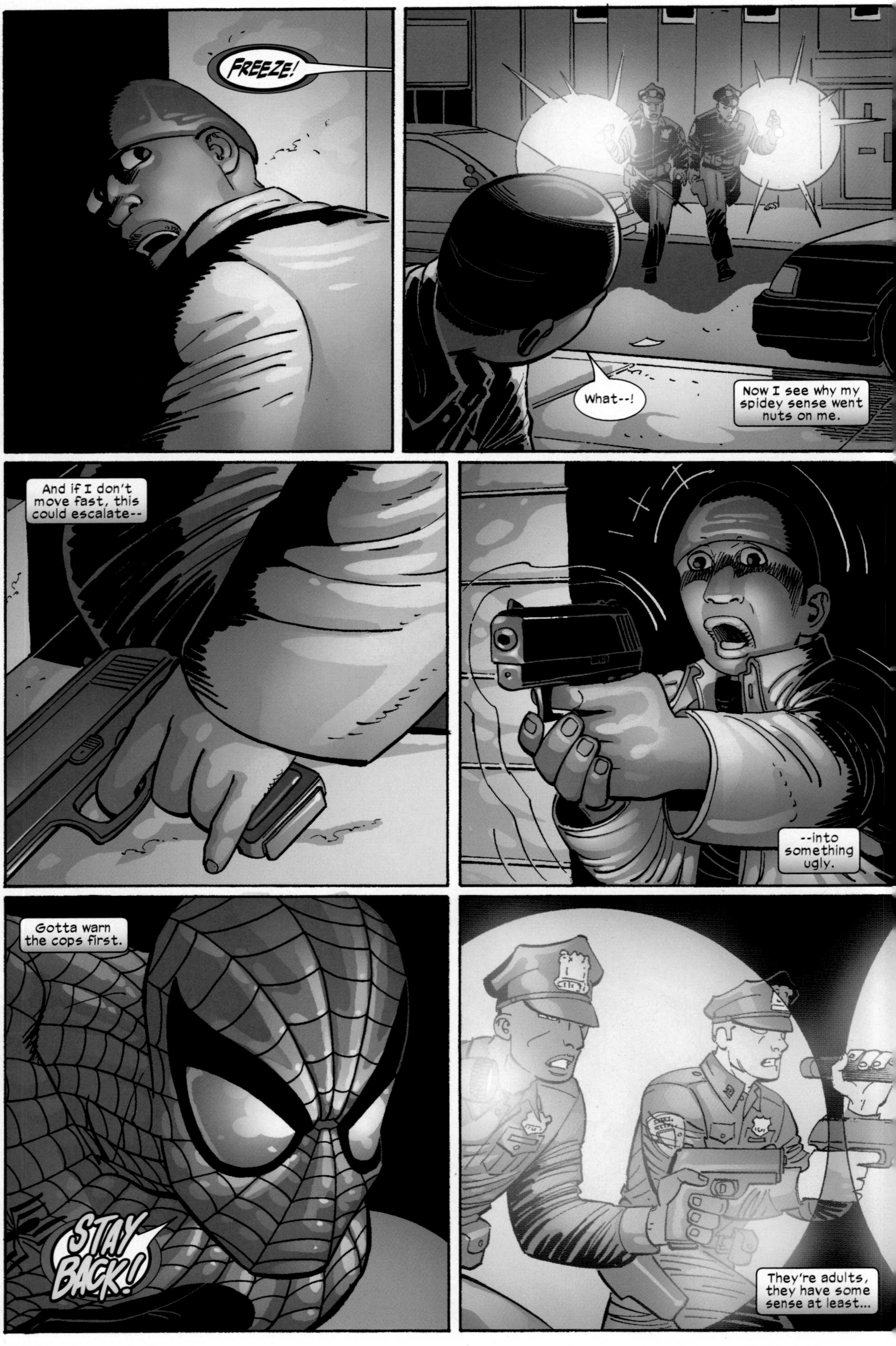
FREEZE!
What--!
Now I see why my spidey sense went nuts on me.
And if I don't move fast, this could escalate--
--into something ugly.
Gotta warn the cops first.
STAY BACK!
They're adults, they have some sense at least...

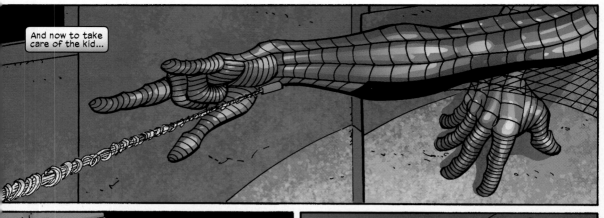

And now to take care of the kid...

Without anyone getting hurt by the gun...

What the--

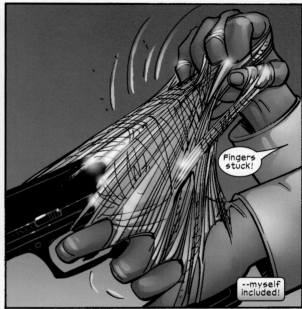

Fingers stuck!

--myself included!

Gotta be careful, knock him down without hurting him--

Oof!

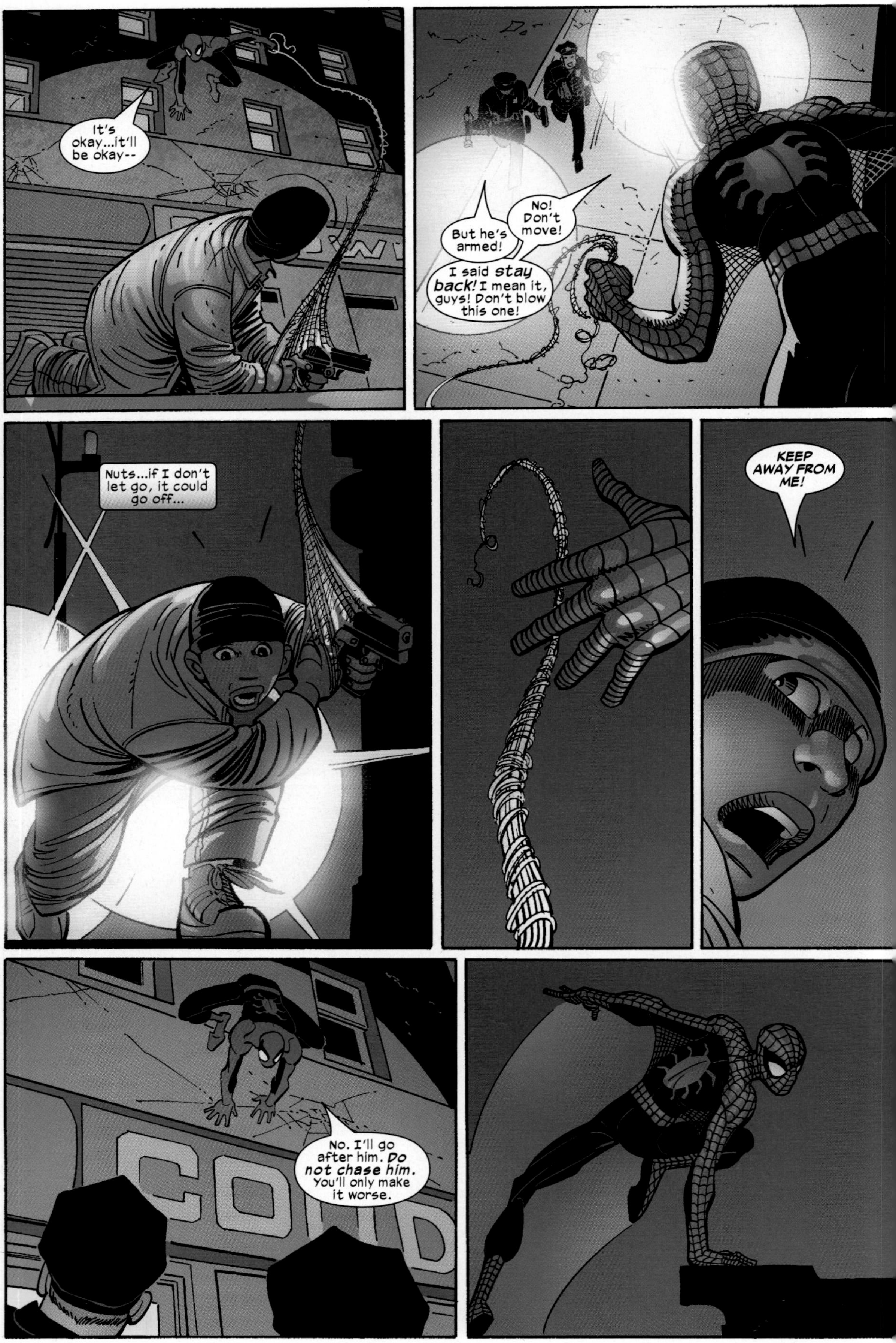

It's okay...it'll be okay--
No! Don't move!
But he's armed!
I said *stay back!* I mean it, guys! Don't blow this one!
Nuts...if I don't let go, it could go off...
KEEP AWAY FROM ME!
No. I'll go after him. *Do not chase him.* You'll only make it worse.

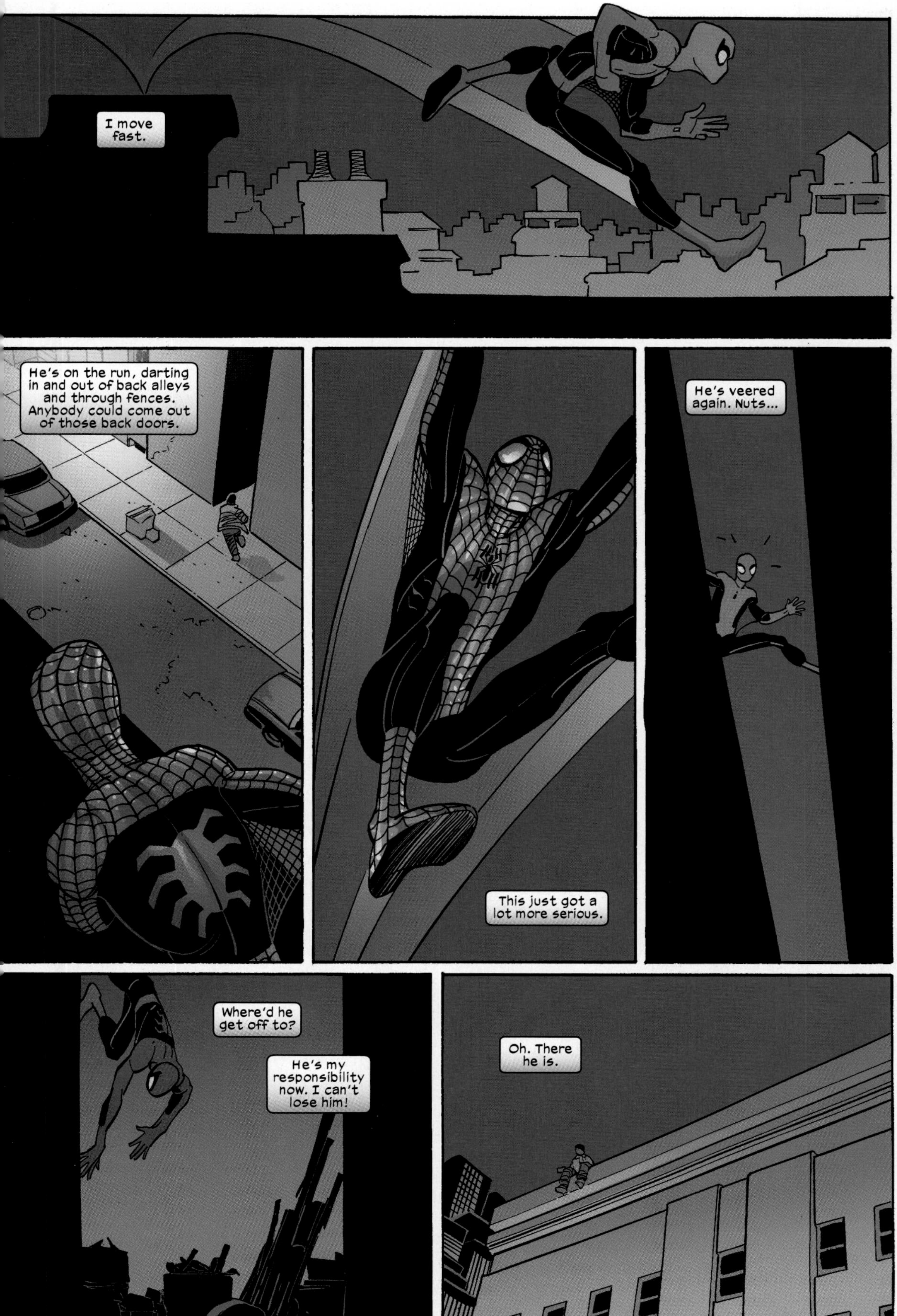
I move fast.
He's on the run, darting in and out of back alleys and through fences. Anybody could come out of those back doors.
This just got a lot more serious.
He's veered again. Nuts...
Where'd he get off to?
He's my responsibility now. I can't lose him!
Oh. There he is.

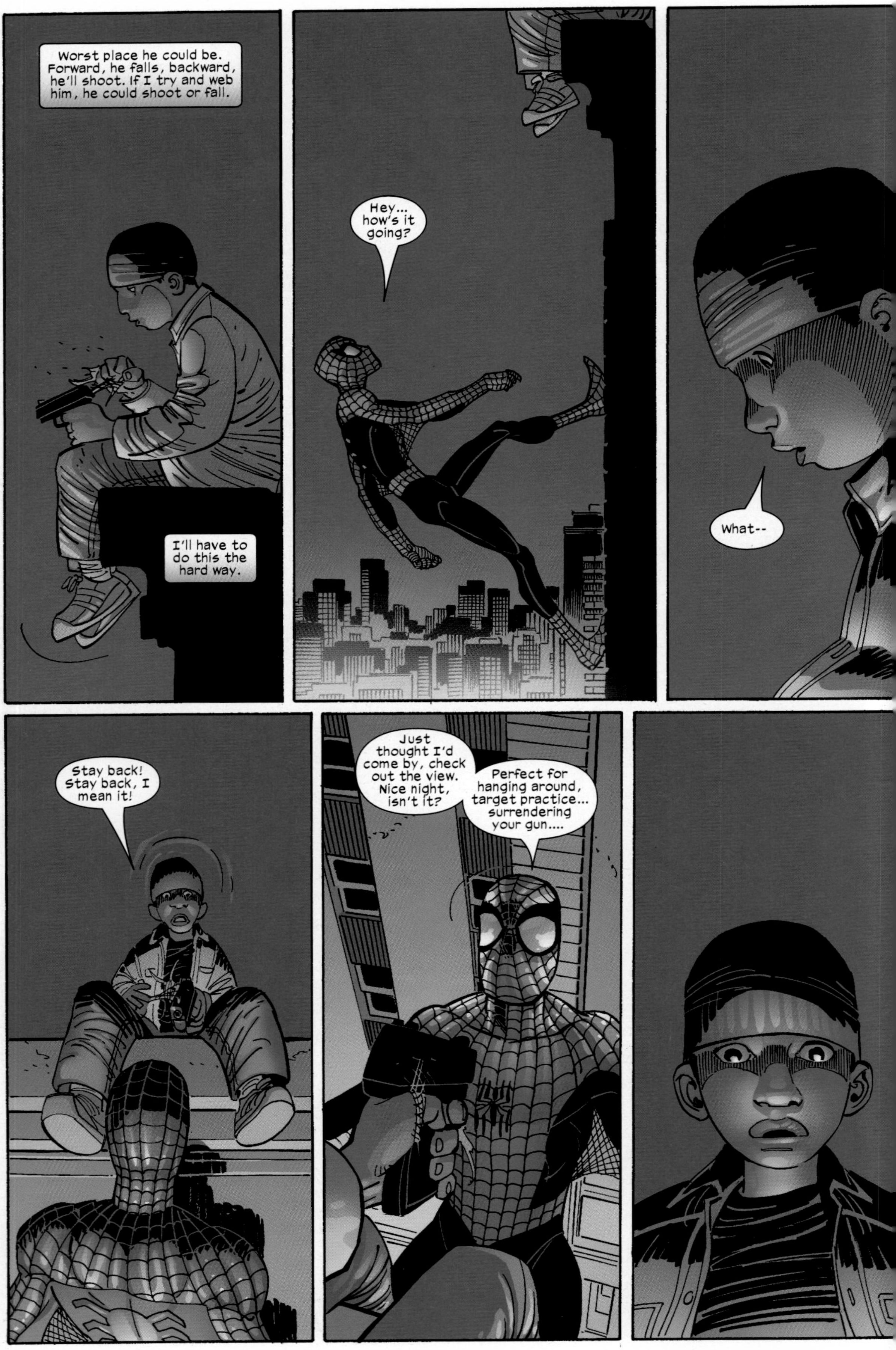
Worst place he could be. Forward, he falls, backward, he'll shoot. If I try and web him, he could shoot or fall.
I'll have to do this the hard way.
Hey... how's it going?
What--
Stay back! Stay back, I mean it!
Just thought I'd come by, check out the view. Nice night, isn't it?
Perfect for hanging around, target practice... surrendering your gun....

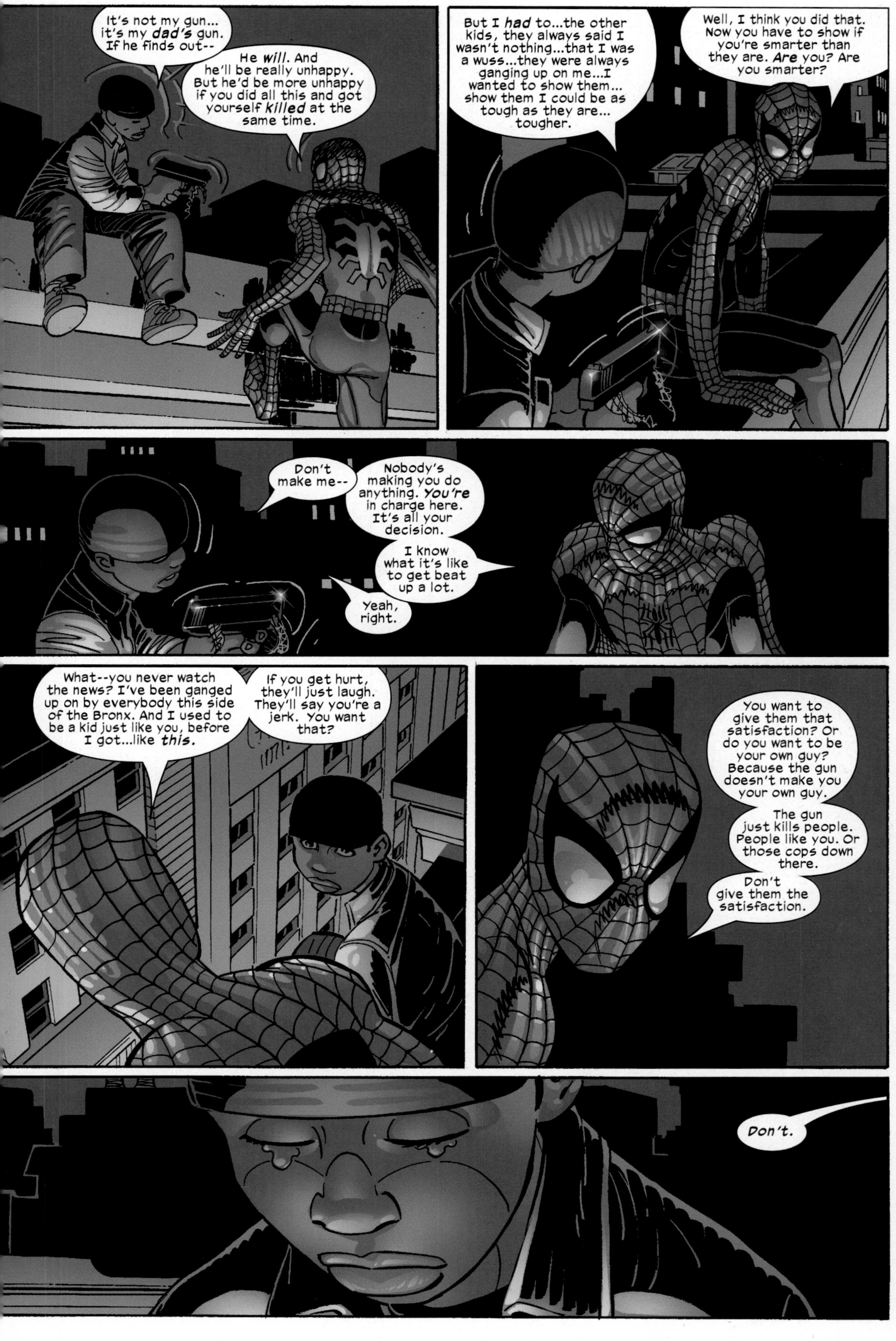

It's not my gun... it's my *dad's* gun. If he finds out--
He *will*. And he'll be really unhappy. But he'd be more unhappy if you did all this and got yourself *killed* at the same time.
But I *had* to...the other kids, they always said I wasn't nothing...that I was a wuss...they were always ganging up on me...I wanted to show them... show them I could be as tough as they are... tougher.
Well, I think you did that. Now you have to show if you're smarter than they are. *Are* you? Are you smarter?
Don't make me--
Nobody's making you do anything. *You're* in charge here. It's all your decision.
I know what it's like to get beat up a lot.
Yeah, right.
What--you never watch the news? I've been ganged up on by everybody this side of the Bronx. And I used to be a kid just like you, before I got...like *this.*
If you get hurt, they'll just laugh. They'll say you're a jerk. You want that?
You want to give them that satisfaction? Or do you want to be your own guy? Because the gun doesn't make you your own guy.
The gun just kills people. People like you. Or those cops down there.
Don't give them the satisfaction.
Don't.

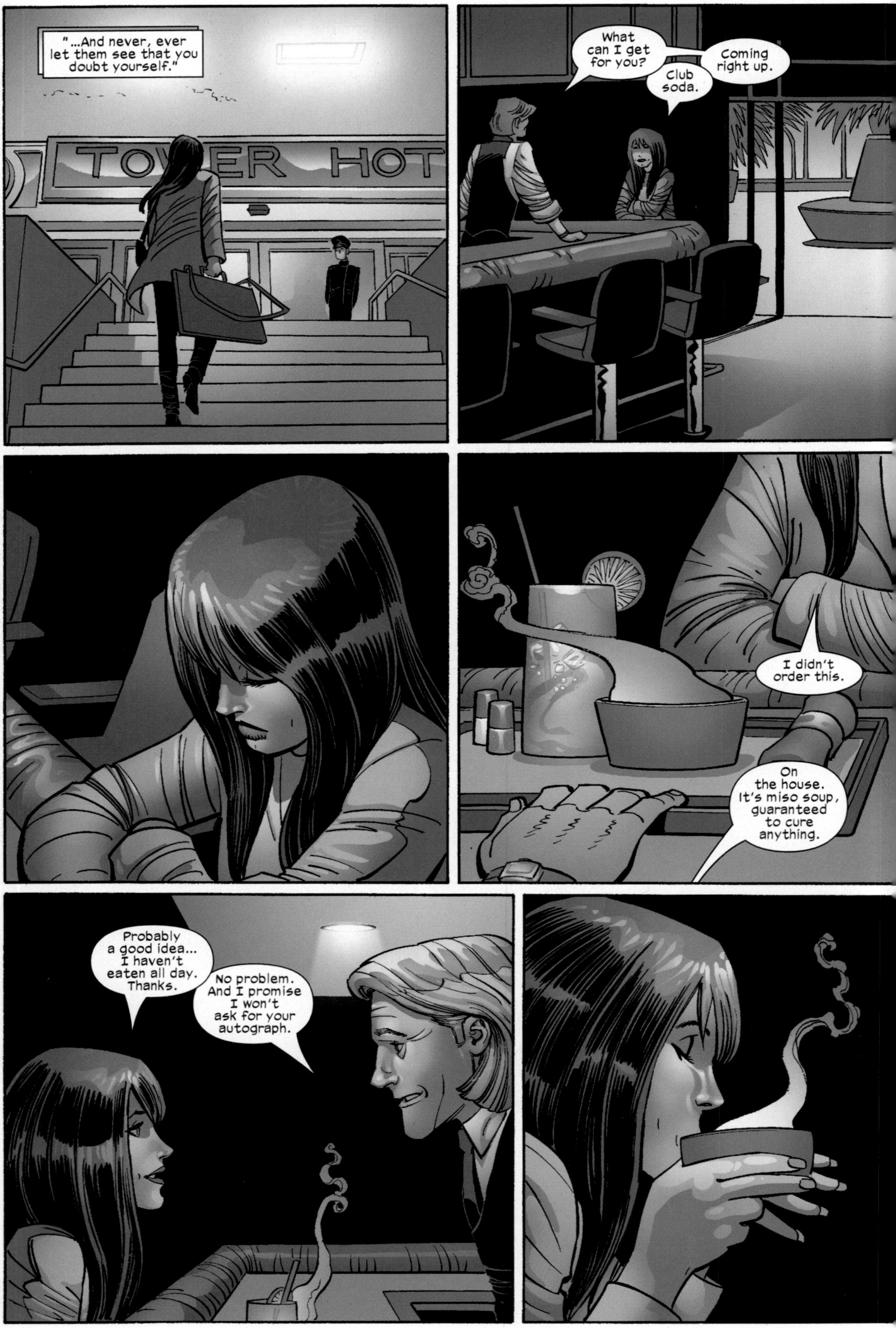
"...And never, ever let them see that you doubt yourself."
TOWER HOT
What can I get for you?
Club soda.
Coming right up.
I didn't order this.
On the house. It's miso soup, guaranteed to cure anything.
Probably a good idea... I haven't eaten all day. Thanks.
No problem. And I promise I won't ask for your autograph.

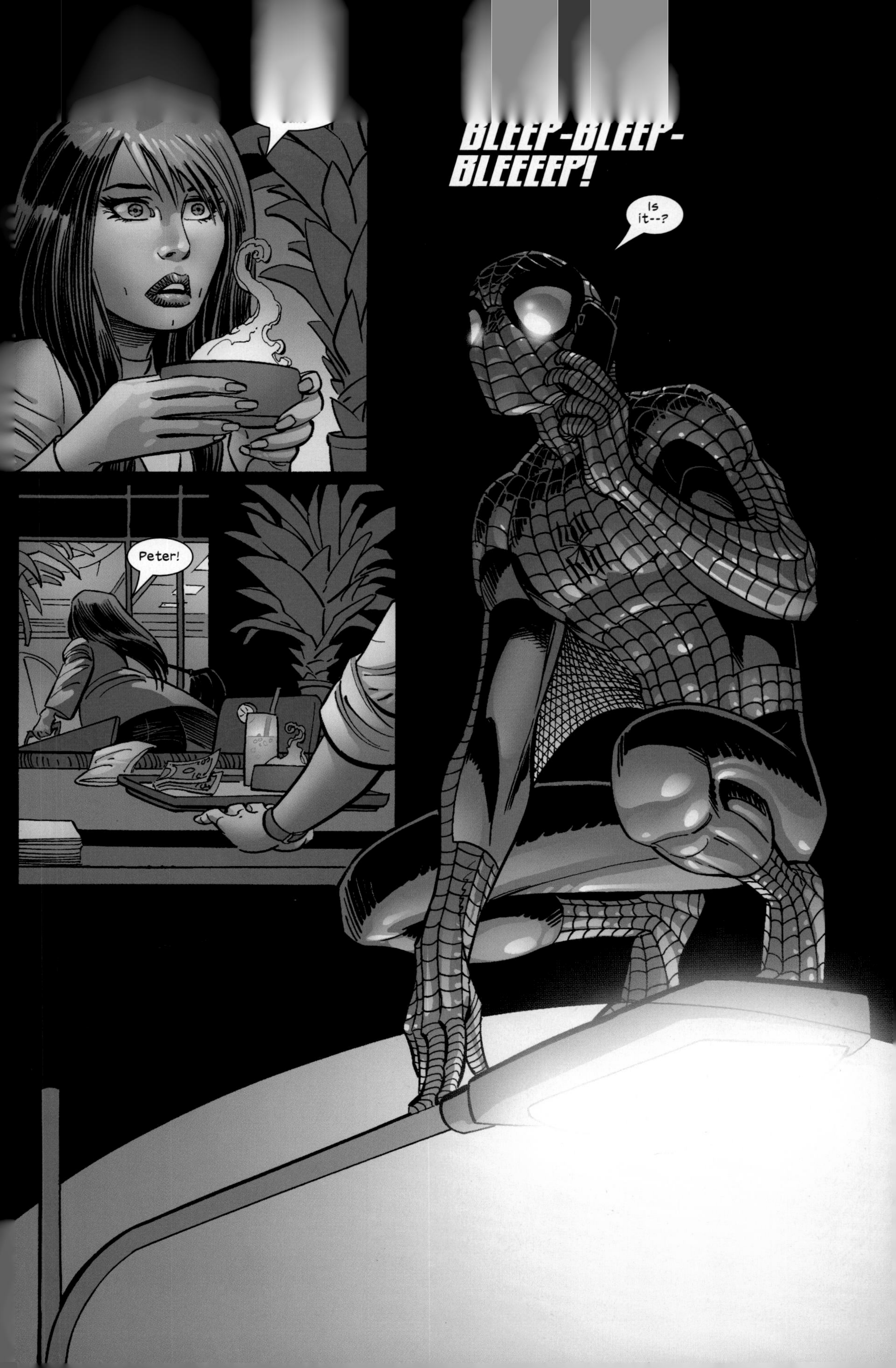

BLEEP-BLEEP-BLEEEEP!
Is it--?
Peter!

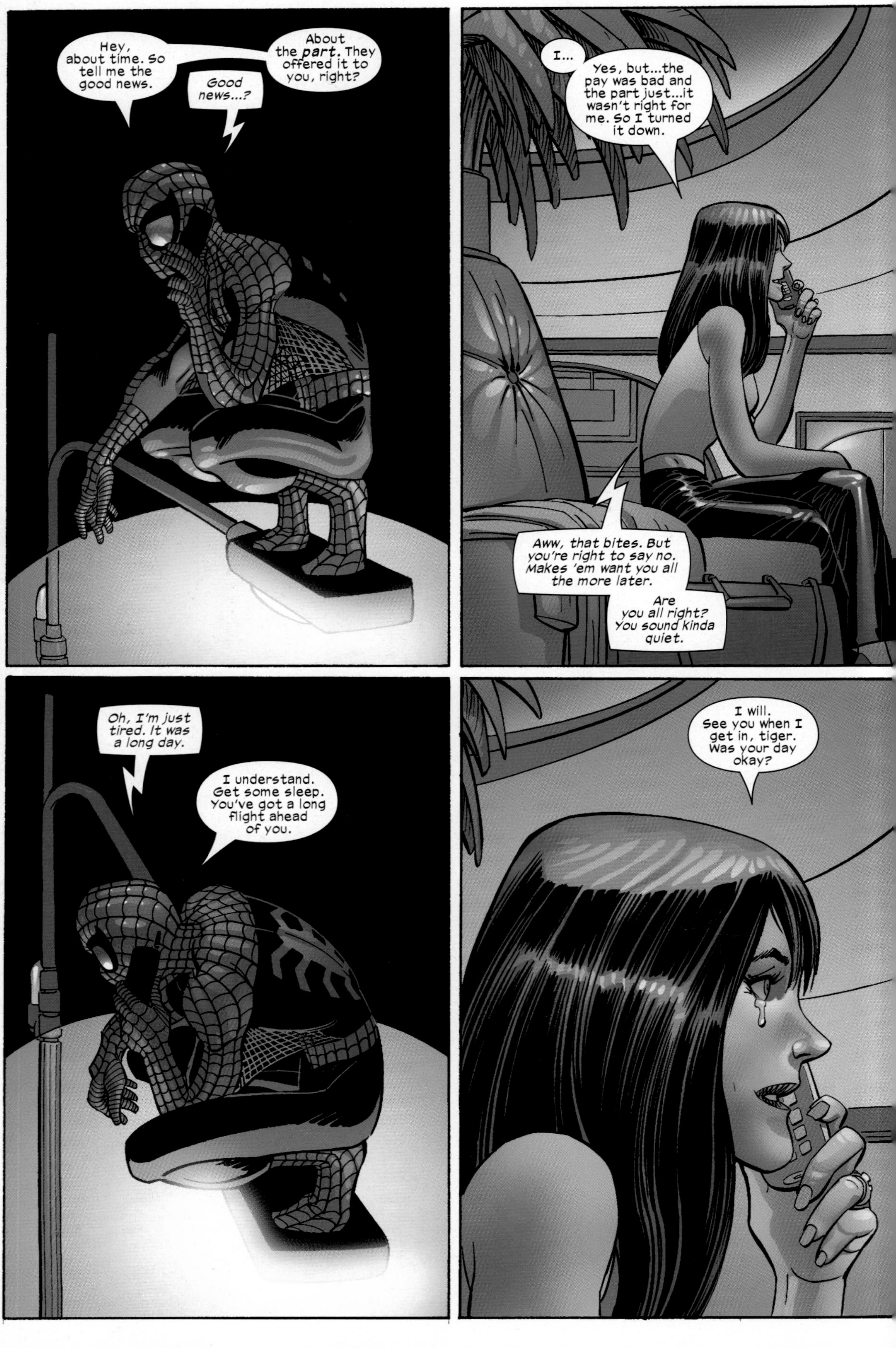

Hey, about time. So tell me the good news.
Good news...?
About the *part.* They offered it to you, right?
I...
Yes, but...the pay was bad and the part just...it wasn't right for me. So I turned it down.
Aww, that bites. But you're right to say no. Makes 'em want you all the more later.
Are you all right? You sound kinda quiet.
Oh, I'm just tired. It was a long day.
I understand. Get some sleep. You've got a long flight ahead of you.
I will. See you when I get in, tiger. Was your day okay?

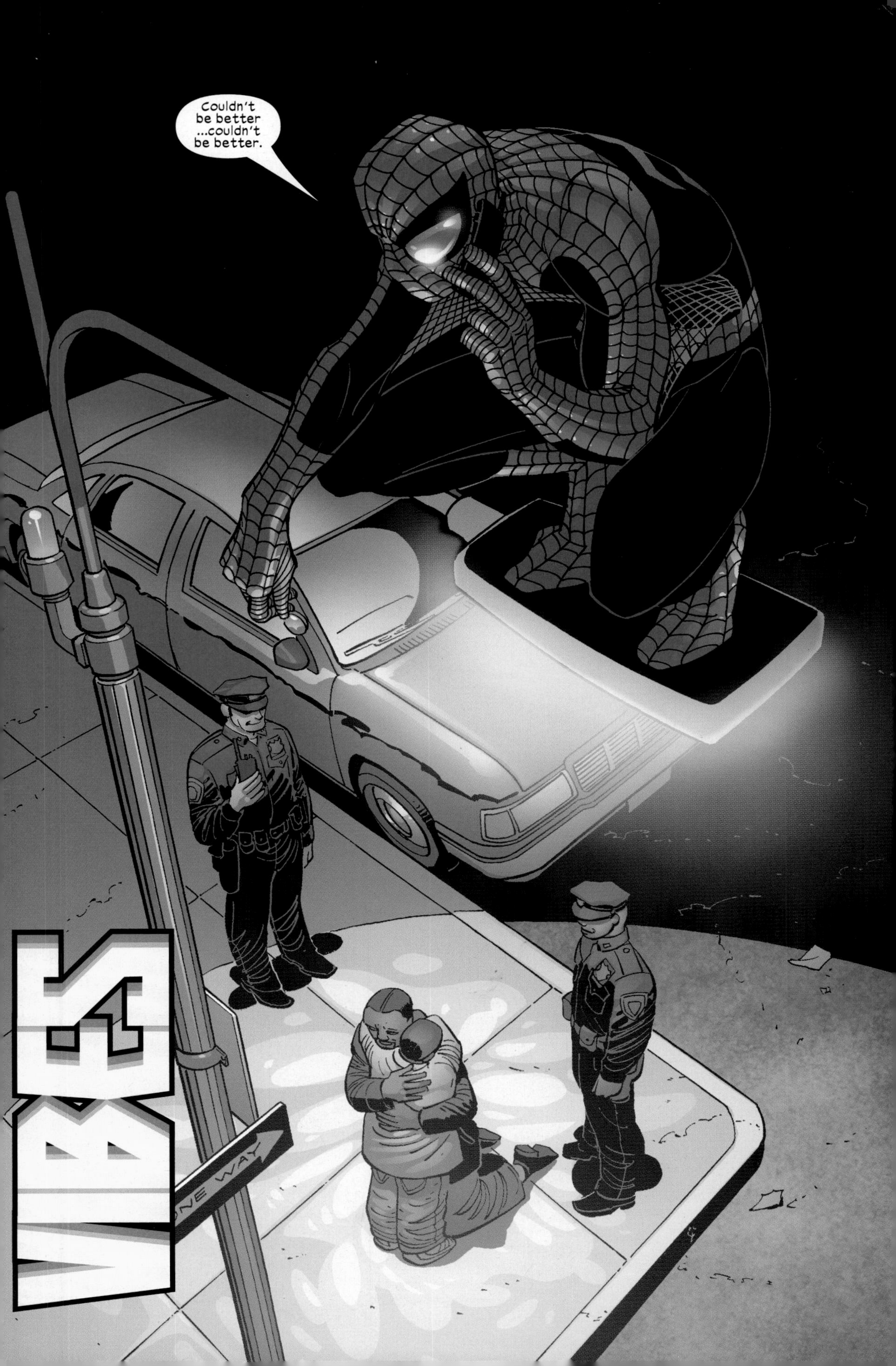
Couldn't be better ...couldn't be better.
VIBES

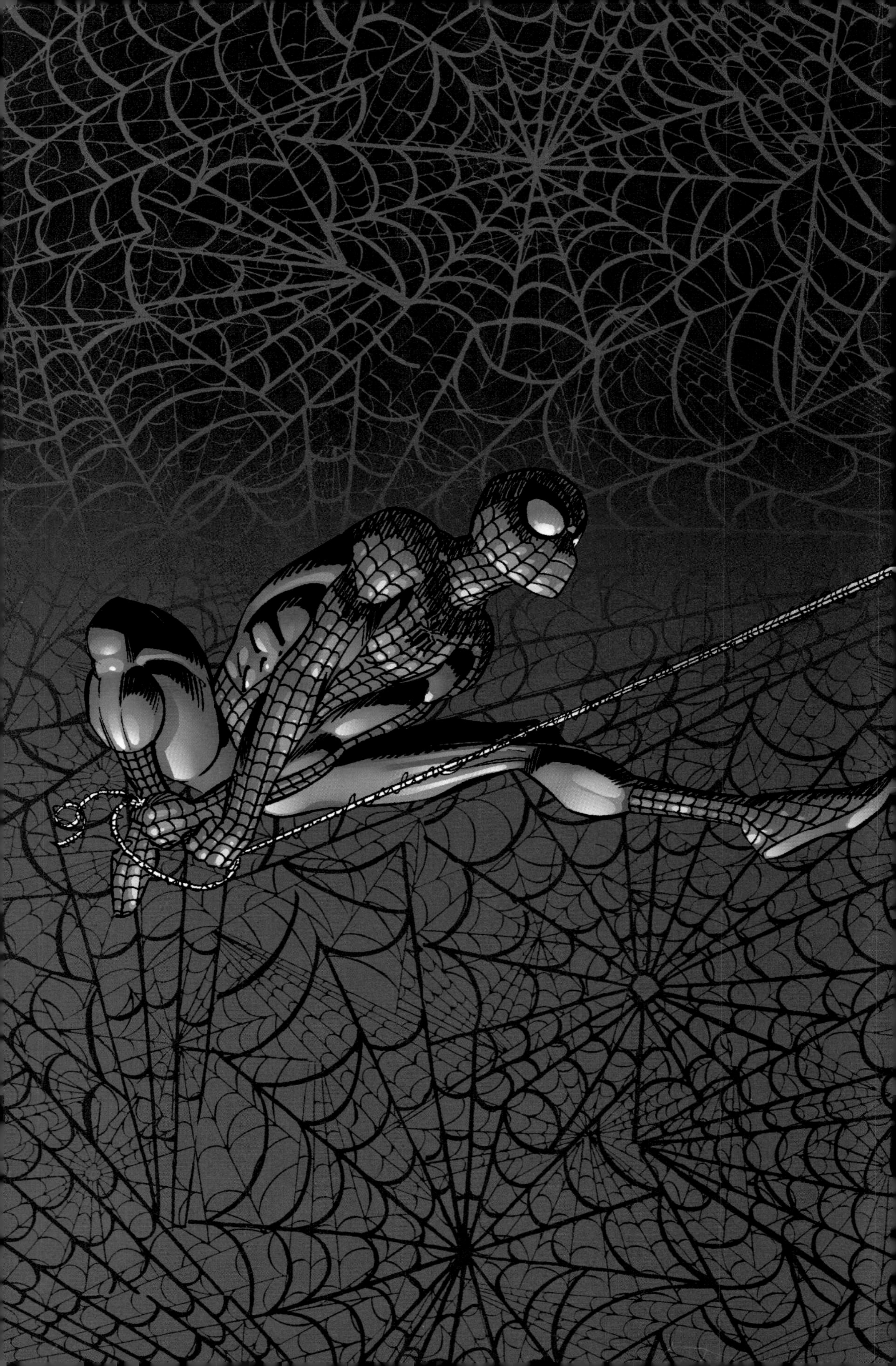

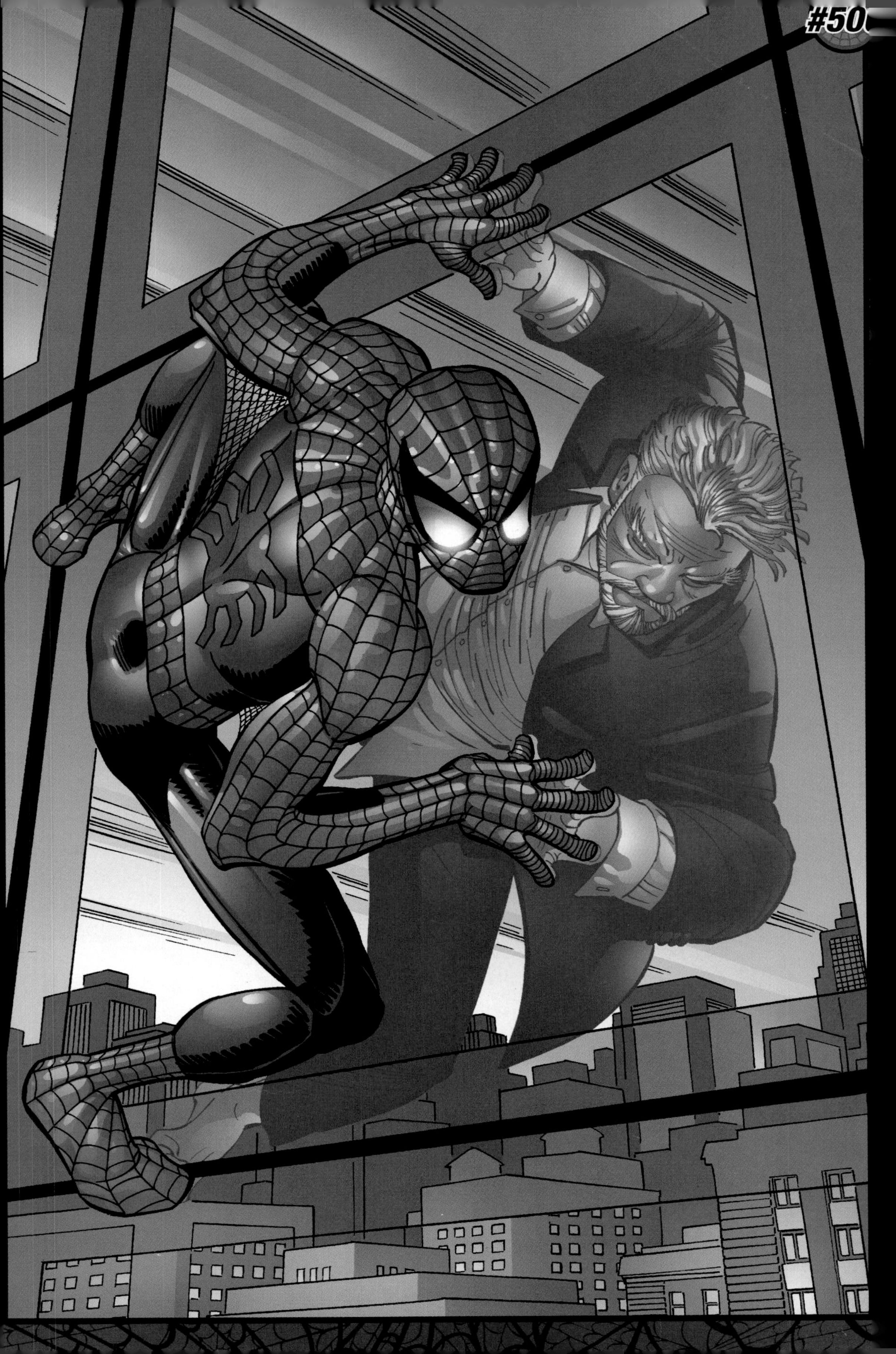
#50

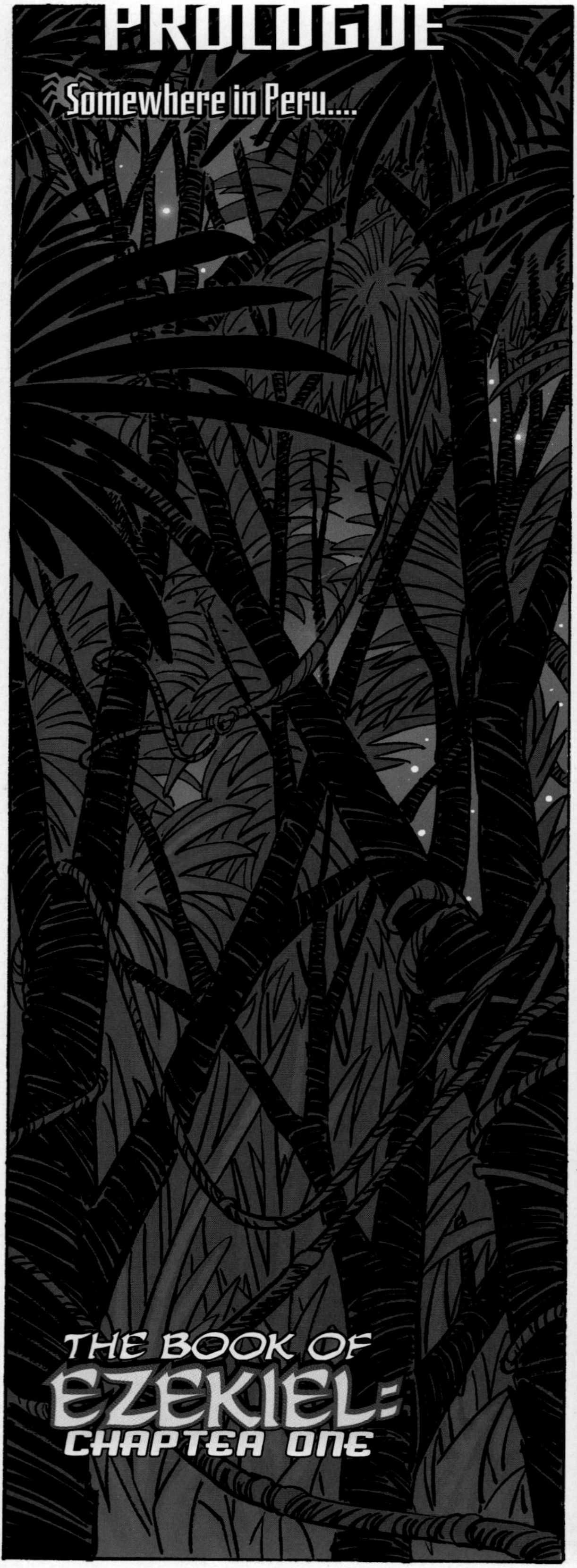
PROLOGUE
Somewhere in Peru....
THE BOOK OF
EZEKIEL:
CHAPTER ONE

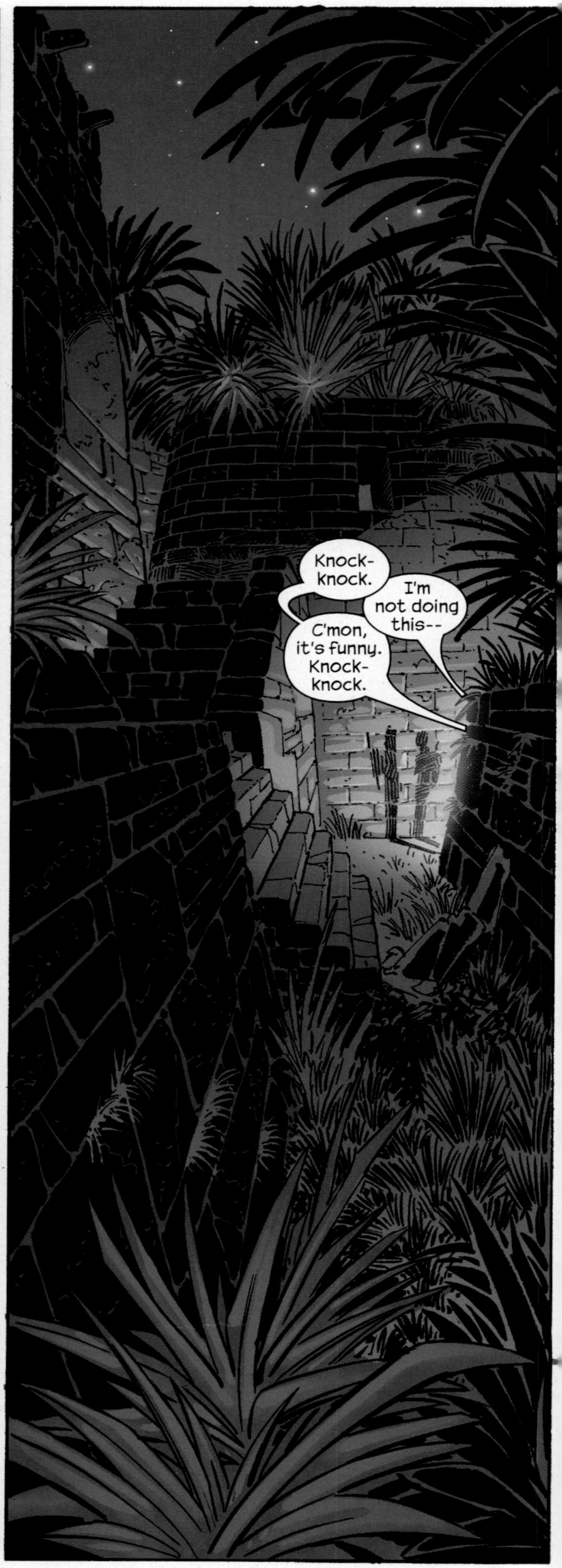
Knock-knock.
I'm not doing this--
C'mon, it's funny. Knock-knock.

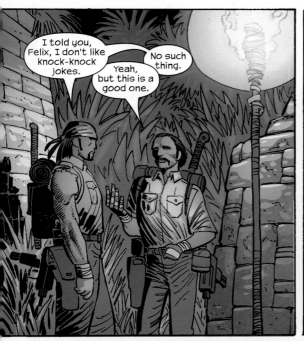

I told you, Felix, I don't like knock-knock jokes.

No such thing.

Yeah, but this is a good one.

C'mon, Ramon, just once. Trust me.

Sigh.... All right. Go on.

Knock-knock.

Who's there?

Michael Jackson.

This better be freaking good, Felix. You're talking to somebody who's got *Thriller* on tape, LP, CD and MP3.

It is. Come on.

Knock-knock.

Who's there?

Michael Jackson.

Michael Jackson who?

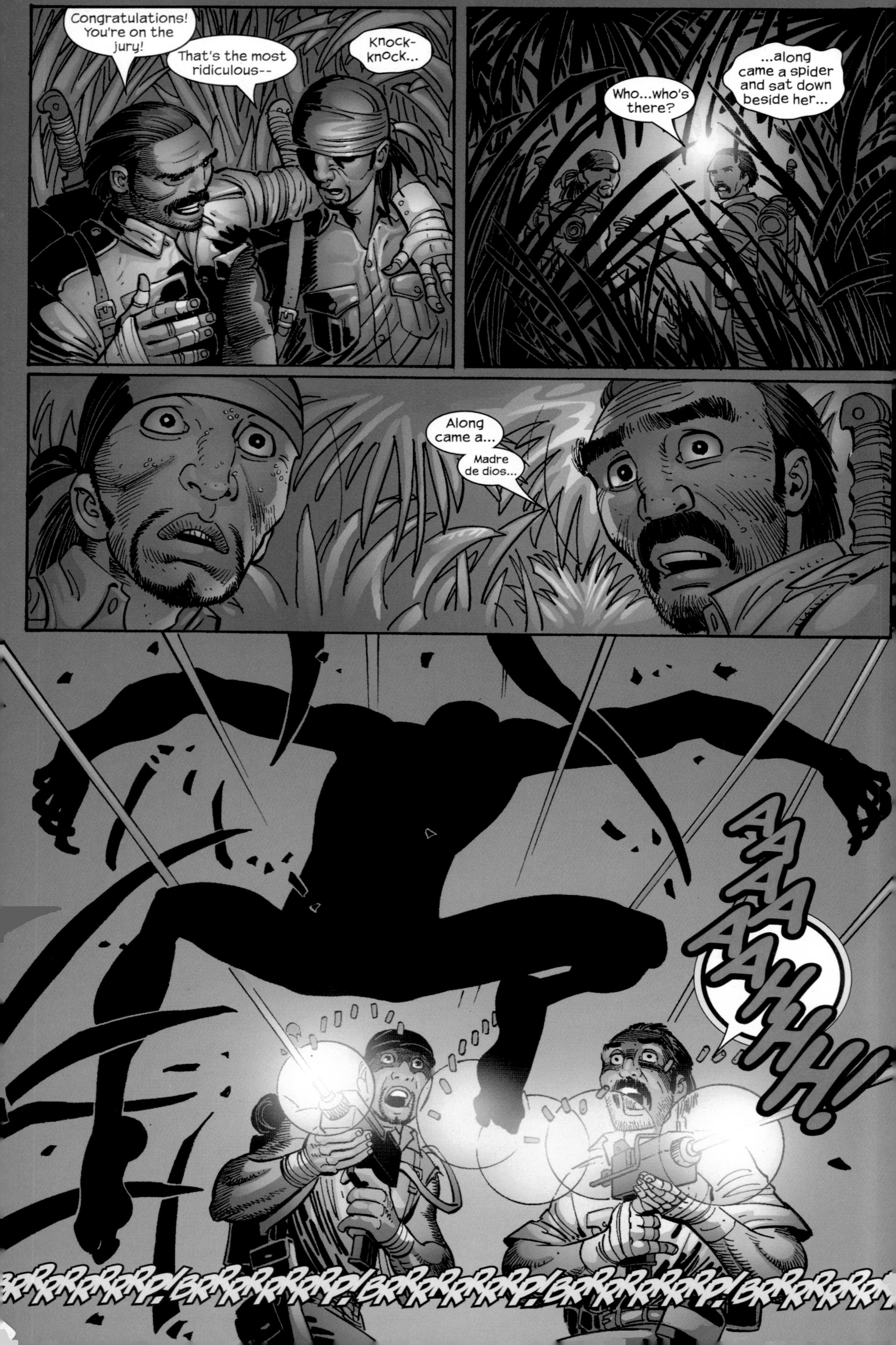
Congratulations! You're on the jury!
That's the most ridiculous--
Knock-knock...
...along came a spider and sat down beside her...
Who...who's there?
Along came a...
Madre de dios...
AAAAAAHHH!
BRRRRRRRP! BRRRRRRRP! BRRRRRRRP! BRRRRRRRP! BRRRRRRRP!

BRRRRRRRP!

BRRRRRRRP!

BRRRRRRRRP!

BRRRRR-

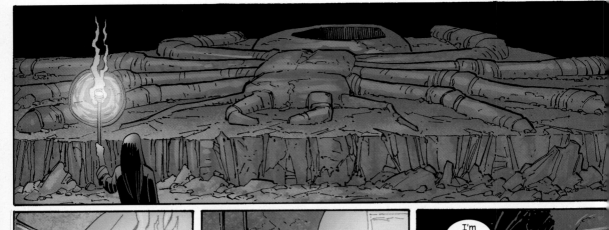

I knew you would come tonight. They wanted to protect me, but I said it would do no good. That you would come regardless.

Did you--

They'll live.

Good. Then there is still hope for you--

--Ezekiel.

For a little while, at least.

I'm burning up.

I know.

You have to help me.

Inca blood flows in my veins. The blood of kings. Of Pachacuti and Inca Roca. When all this was known as Tiwantinsuya, a place of secrets. A place of power.

I am a descendant of kings. I do not *have* to do anything.

I will help you because I *choose* to help you. For what you have done to help my people.

And in sadness for what will happen to you.

Don't write me off yet, Miguel.

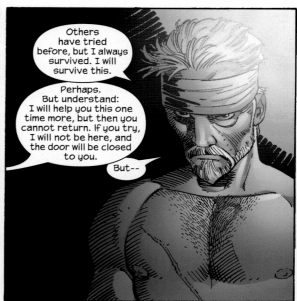

Others have tried before, but I always survived. I will survive this.

Perhaps. But understand: I will help you this one time more, but then you cannot return. If you try, I will not be here, and the door will be closed to you.

But--

I must do this, because if you return again, you will not be as you are now. And either you will die... or I will die.

This is the last.

I'm sorry.

Just...do it. The bleeding. Bleed it out of me, out of my system, enough to buy me the time I need.

And then?

And then... I'll do what I have to.

He'll help me. I've worked hard to make sure of it. He'll help.

You mean he will die, do you not?

Just do it, all right? Just... do it.

You cut the man...you bleed the spider. You cut the spider, you bleed the man.

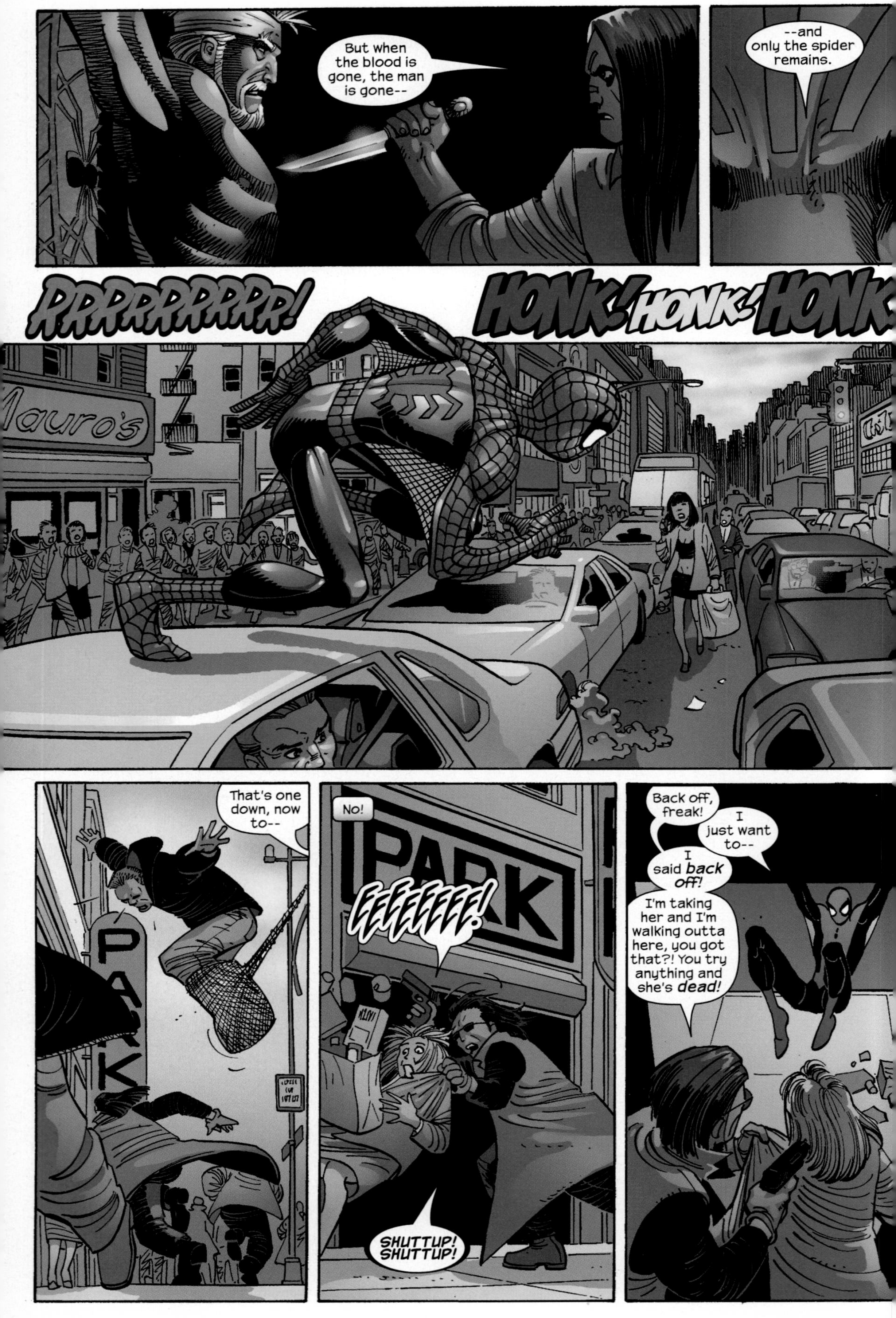

But when the blood is gone, the man is gone--
--and only the spider remains.
RRRRRRRRRR!
HONK! HONK! HONK!
Mauro's
That's one down, now to--
PARK
No!
PARK
EEEEEEEE!
SHUTTUP! SHUTTUP!
Back off, freak!
I just want to--
I said *back off*!
I'm taking her and I'm walking outta here, you got that?! You try anything and she's *dead*!

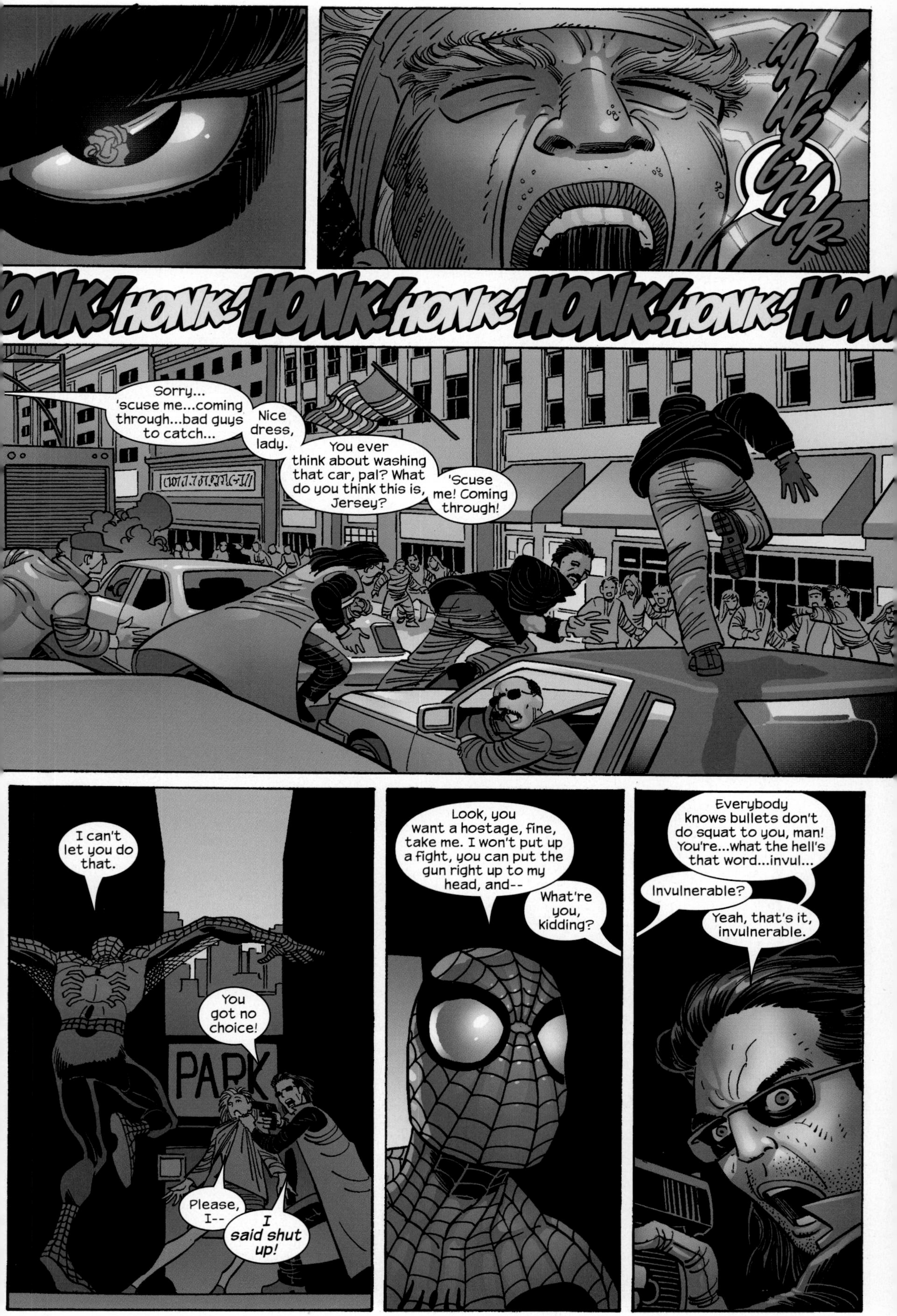
AAAGGHHR!
HONK! HONK! HONK! HONK! HONK! HONK! HONK
Sorry... 'scuse me...coming through...bad guys to catch...
Nice dress, lady.
You ever think about washing that car, pal? What do you think this is, Jersey?
'Scuse me! Coming through!
I can't let you do that.
You got no choice!
PARK
Please, I--
I said shut up!
Look, you want a hostage, fine, take me. I won't put up a fight, you can put the gun right up to my head, and--
What're you, kidding?
Everybody knows bullets don't do squat to you, man! You're...what the hell's that word...invul...
Invulnerable?
Yeah, that's it, invulnerable.

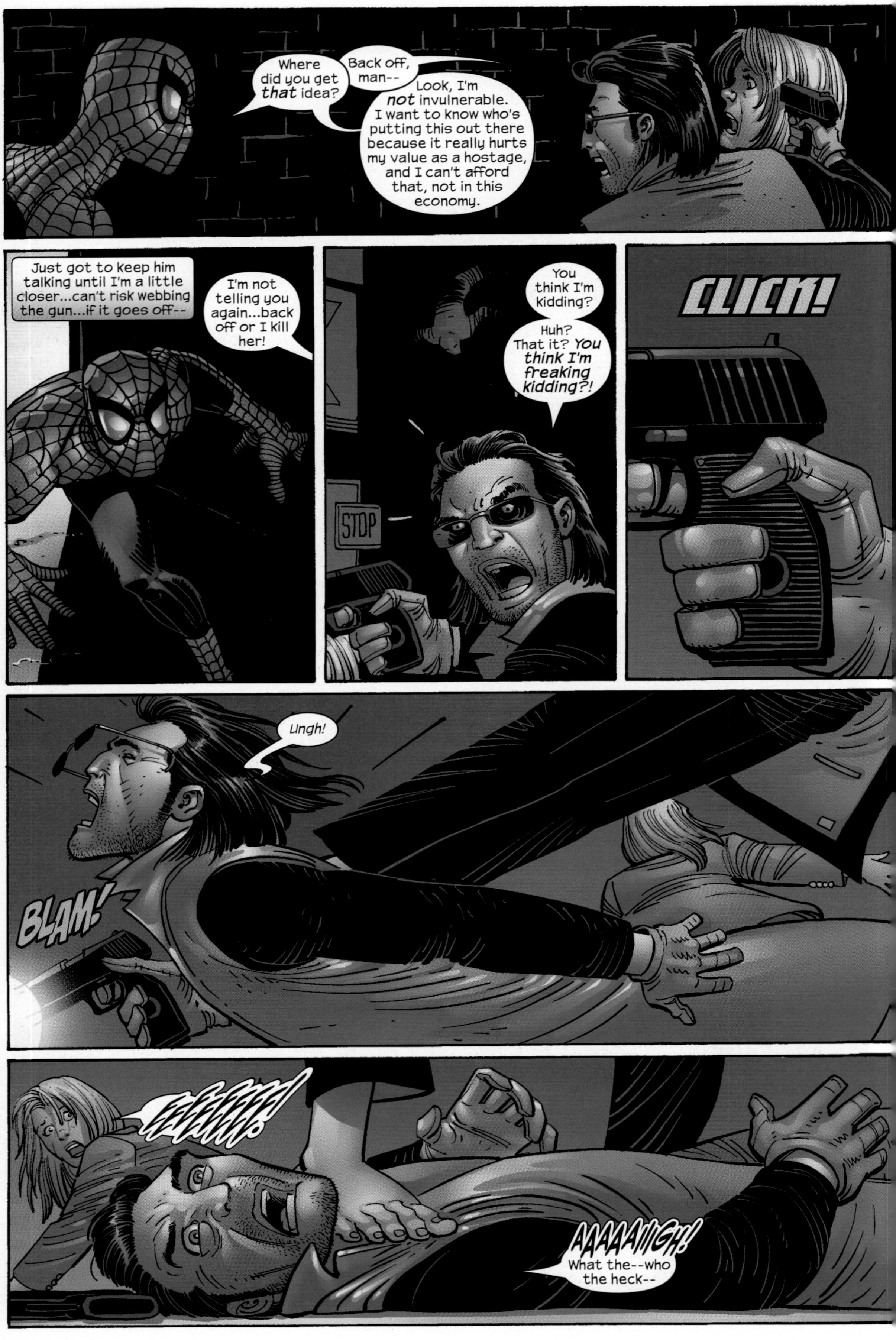

Where did you get that idea?
Back off, man--
Look, I'm not invulnerable. I want to know who's putting this out there because it really hurts my value as a hostage, and I can't afford that, not in this economy.
Just got to keep him talking until I'm a little closer...can't risk webbing the gun...if it goes off--
I'm not telling you again...back off or I kill her!
You think I'm kidding?
Huh? That it? You think I'm freaking kidding?!
CLICK!
Ungh!
BLAM!
AAAAAIIGH!
What the--who the heck--

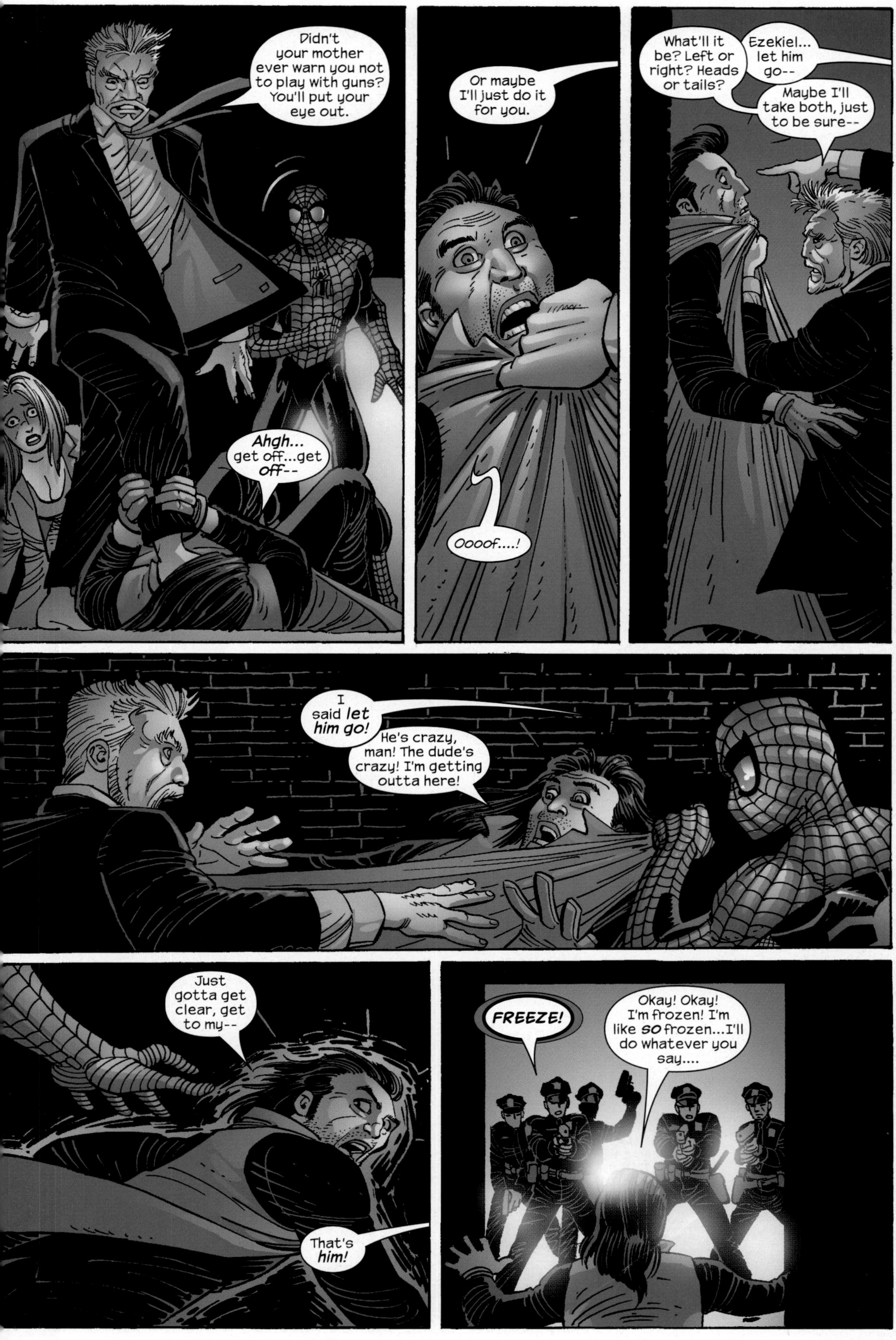

Didn't your mother ever warn you not to play with guns? You'll put your eye out.
Ahgh... get off...get off--
Or maybe I'll just do it for you.
Oooof....!
What'll it be? Left or right? Heads or tails?
Ezekiel... let him go--
Maybe I'll take both, just to be sure--
I said let him go!
He's crazy, man! The dude's crazy! I'm getting outta here!
Just gotta get clear, get to my--
That's him!
FREEZE!
Okay! Okay! I'm frozen! I'm like SO frozen...I'll do whatever you say....

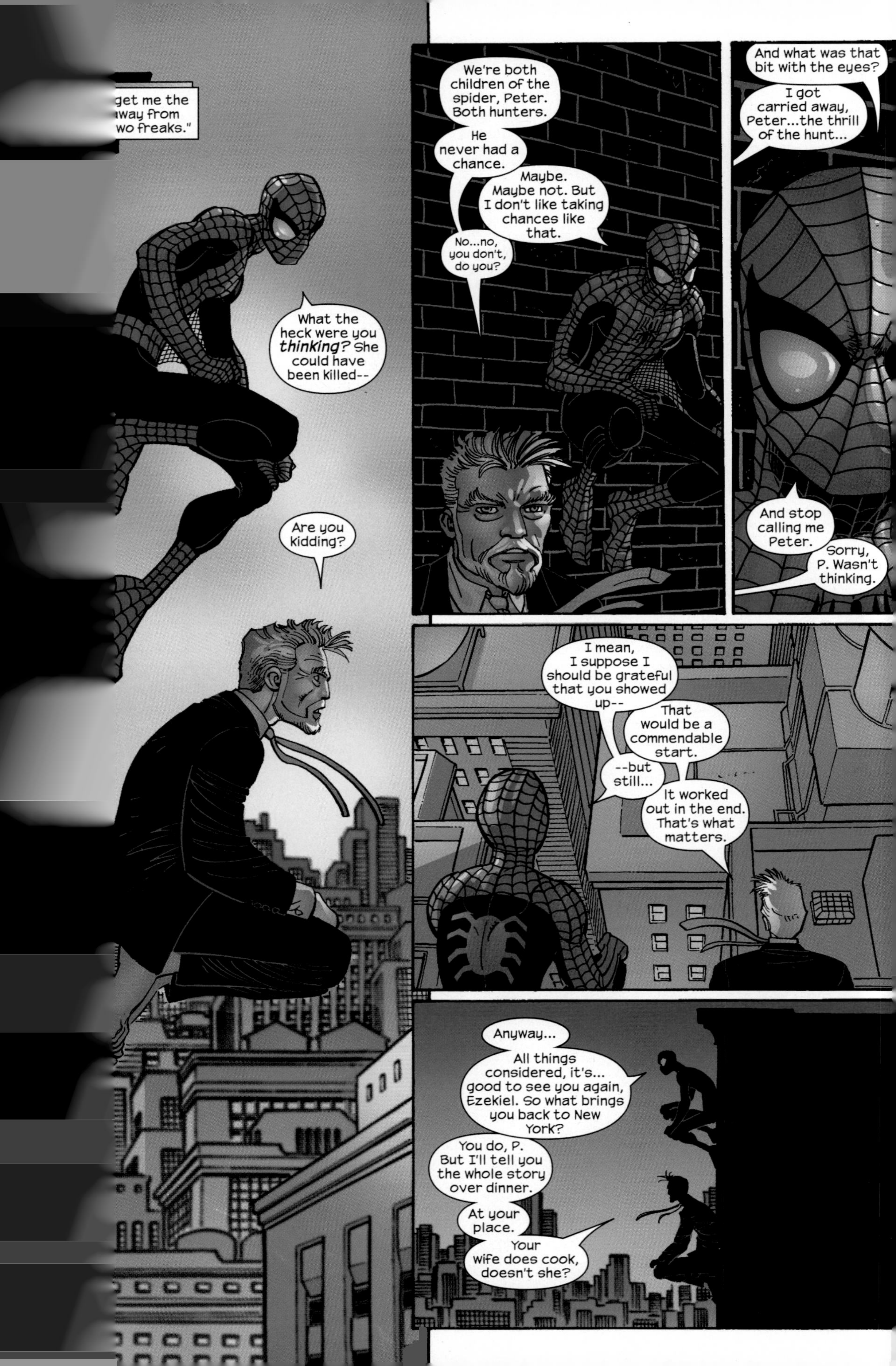
get me the
away from
wo freaks."
What the heck were you *thinking?* She could have been killed--
Are you kidding?
We're both children of the spider, Peter. Both hunters.
He never had a chance.
Maybe. Maybe not. But I don't like taking chances like that.
No...no, you don't, do you?
And what was that bit with the eyes?
I got carried away, Peter...the thrill of the hunt...
And stop calling me Peter.
Sorry, P. Wasn't thinking.
I mean, I suppose I should be grateful that you showed up--
That would be a commendable start.
--but still...
It worked out in the end. That's what matters.
Anyway...
All things considered, it's... good to see you again, Ezekiel. So what brings you back to New York?
You do, P. But I'll tell you the whole story over dinner.
At your place.
Your wife does cook, doesn't she?

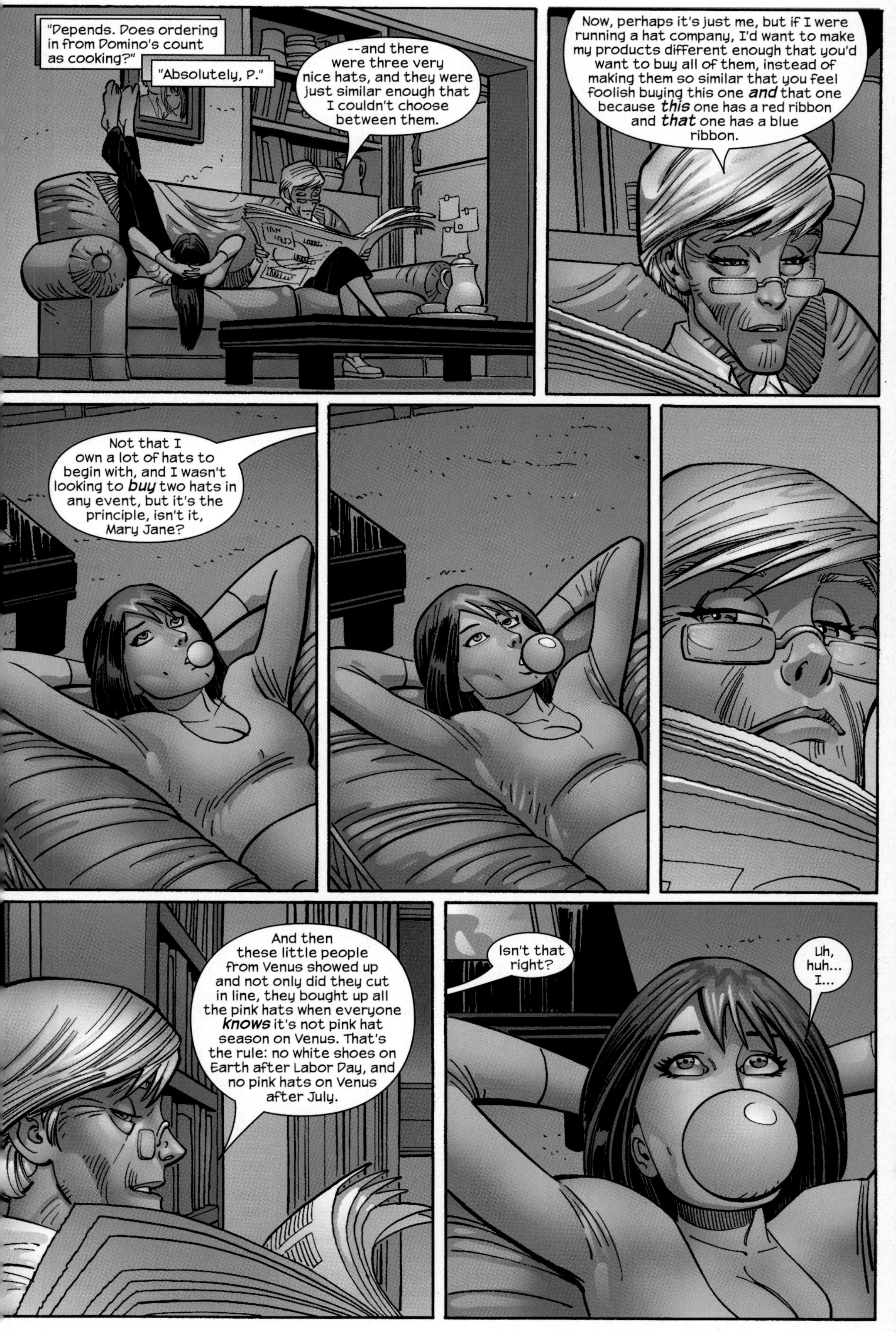
"Depends. Does ordering in from Domino's count as cooking?"
"Absolutely, P."
--and there were three very nice hats, and they were just similar enough that I couldn't choose between them.
Now, perhaps it's just me, but if I were running a hat company, I'd want to make my products different enough that you'd want to buy all of them, instead of making them so similar that you feel foolish buying this one *and* that one because *this* one has a red ribbon and *that* one has a blue ribbon.
Not that I own a lot of hats to begin with, and I wasn't looking to *buy* two hats in any event, but it's the principle, isn't it, Mary Jane?
And then these little people from Venus showed up and not only did they cut in line, they bought up all the pink hats when everyone *knows* it's not pink hat season on Venus. That's the rule: no white shoes on Earth after Labor Day, and no pink hats on Venus after July.
Isn't that right?
Uh, huh... I...

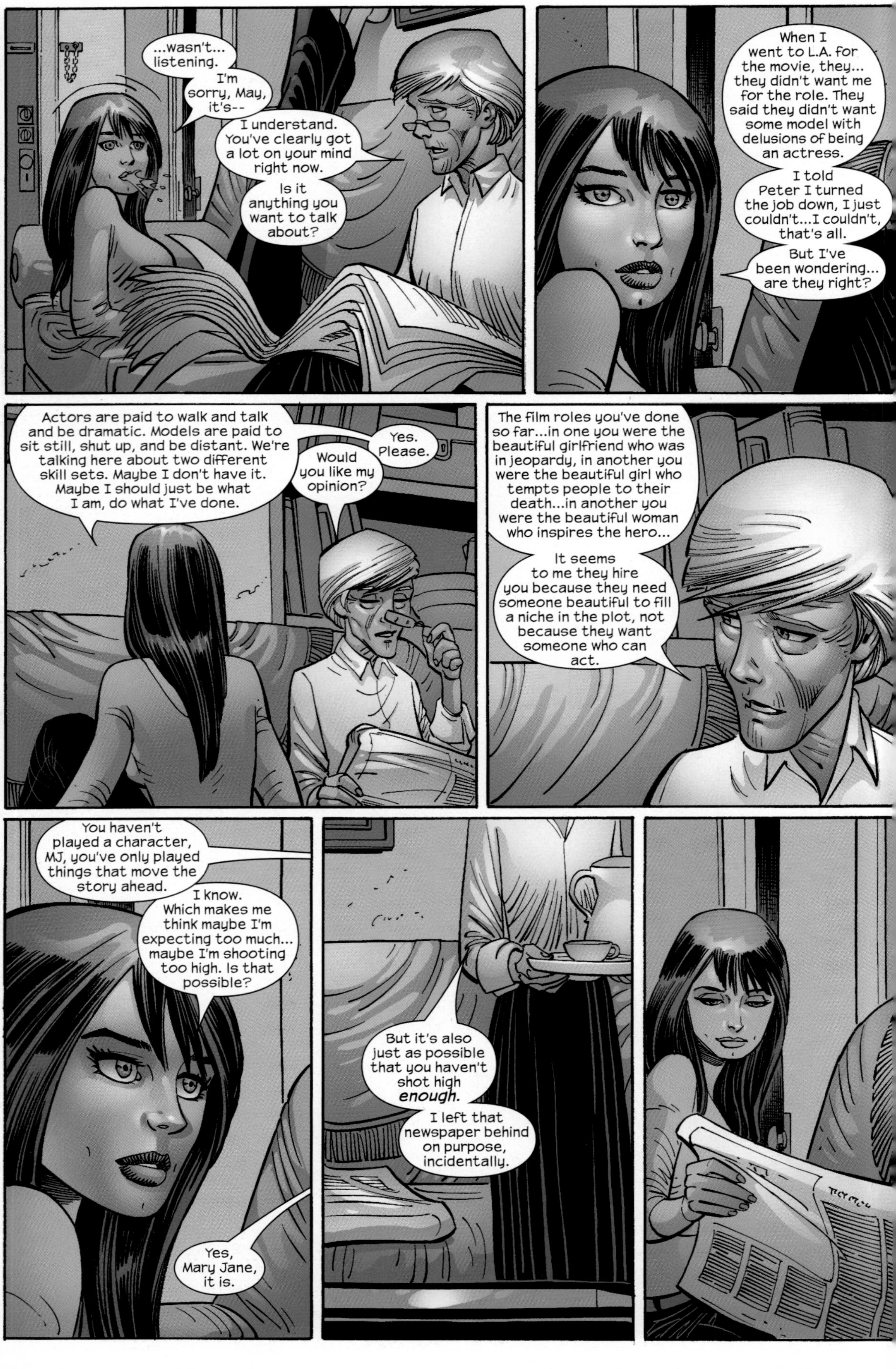
...wasn't... listening.
I'm sorry, May, it's--
I understand. You've clearly got a lot on your mind right now.
Is it anything you want to talk about?
When I went to L.A. for the movie, they... they didn't want me for the role. They said they didn't want some model with delusions of being an actress.
I told Peter I turned the job down, I just couldn't...I couldn't, that's all.
But I've been wondering... are they right?
Actors are paid to walk and talk and be dramatic. Models are paid to sit still, shut up, and be distant. We're talking here about two different skill sets. Maybe I don't have it. Maybe I should just be what I am, do what I've done.
Would you like my opinion?
Yes. Please.
The film roles you've done so far...in one you were the beautiful girlfriend who was in jeopardy, in another you were the beautiful girl who tempts people to their death...in another you were the beautiful woman who inspires the hero...
It seems to me they hire you because they need someone beautiful to fill a niche in the plot, not because they want someone who can act.
You haven't played a character, MJ, you've only played things that move the story ahead.
I know. Which makes me think maybe I'm expecting too much... maybe I'm shooting too high. Is that possible?
Yes, Mary Jane, it is.
But it's also just as possible that you haven't shot high enough.
I left that newspaper behind on purpose, incidentally.

THEATER DIRECTORY

OFF-BROADWAY AUDITIONS

"I have to say, this is quite a surprise..."

...I mean, I often hear about the people Peter meets, but he doesn't usually bring his work home with him, because--

Well, he can't, really.

Secret identity and all that.

Exactly. So this is... nice.

So. Peter tells me you think he got his powers from Slappy the Spider Fairy.

That's *not* what I said.

Actually, it is.

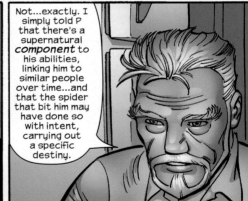

Not...exactly. I simply told P that there's a supernatural *component* to his abilities, linking him to similar people over time...and that the spider that bit him may have done so with intent, carrying out a specific destiny.

Look, I know the source of my abilities--

--and they're all clearly based on the scientific extrapolation of a spider's natural abilities.

The *how*, yes, but not the *why*.

Yep.

That so?

Then what about your spider-sense?

Spiders can see all around them, they know when--

Yes, but you don't. But you are able to sense things behind you. Not just objects behind you, but you can sense danger--a concept--from some distance, even blocks away, sometimes even before it happens.

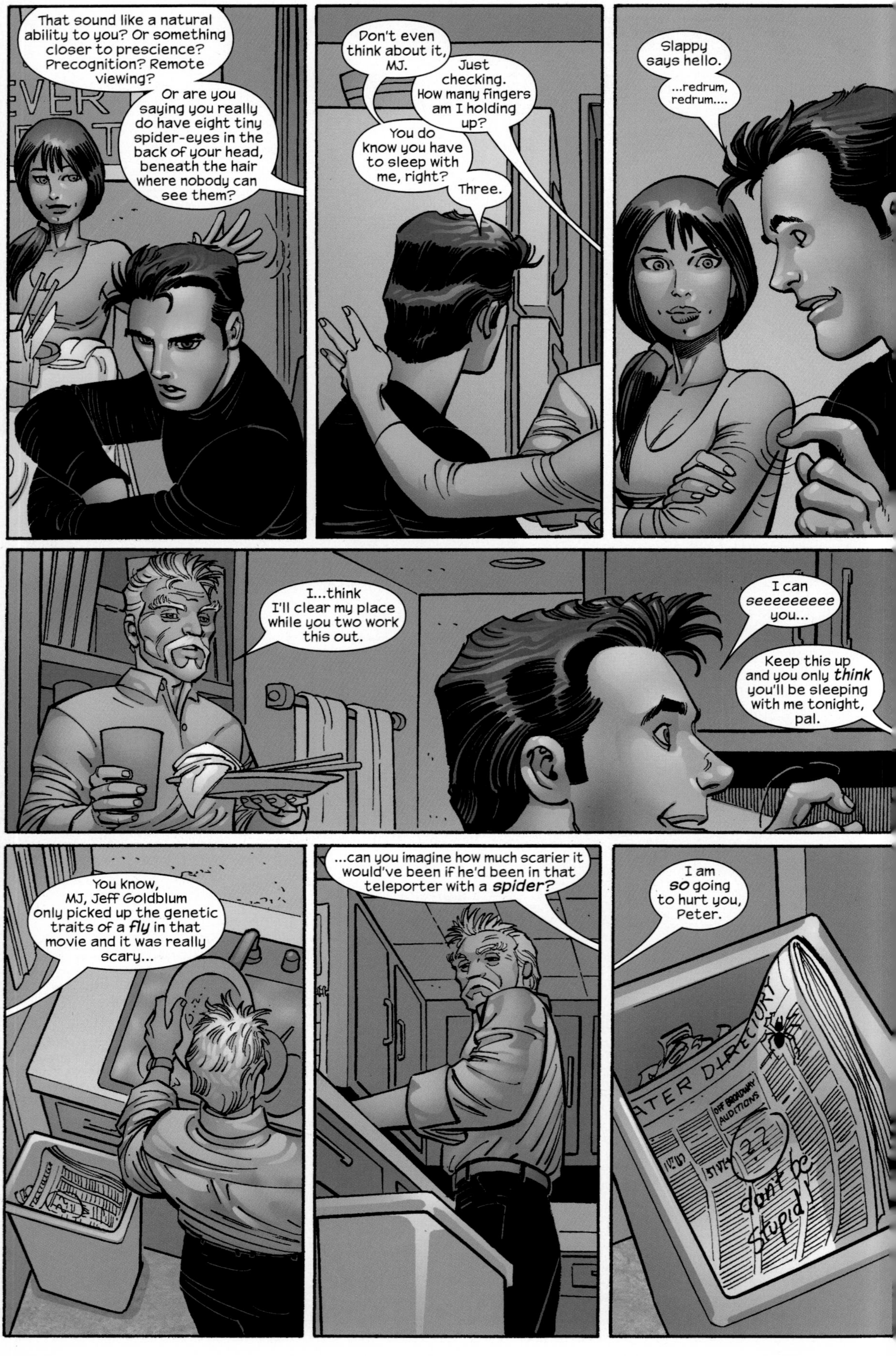
That sound like a natural ability to you? Or something closer to prescience? Precognition? Remote viewing?
Or are you saying you really do have eight tiny spider-eyes in the back of your head, beneath the hair where nobody can see them?
Don't even think about it, MJ.
Just checking. How many fingers am I holding up?
You do know you have to sleep with me, right?
Three.
Slappy says hello.
...redrum, redrum....
I...think I'll clear my place while you two work this out.
I can seeeeeeeee you...
Keep this up and you only think you'll be sleeping with me tonight, pal.
You know, MJ, Jeff Goldblum only picked up the genetic traits of a fly in that movie and it was really scary...
...can you imagine how much scarier it would've been if he'd been in that teleporter with a spider?
I am so going to hurt you, Peter.
OFF BROADWAY AUDITIONS
don't be stupid!

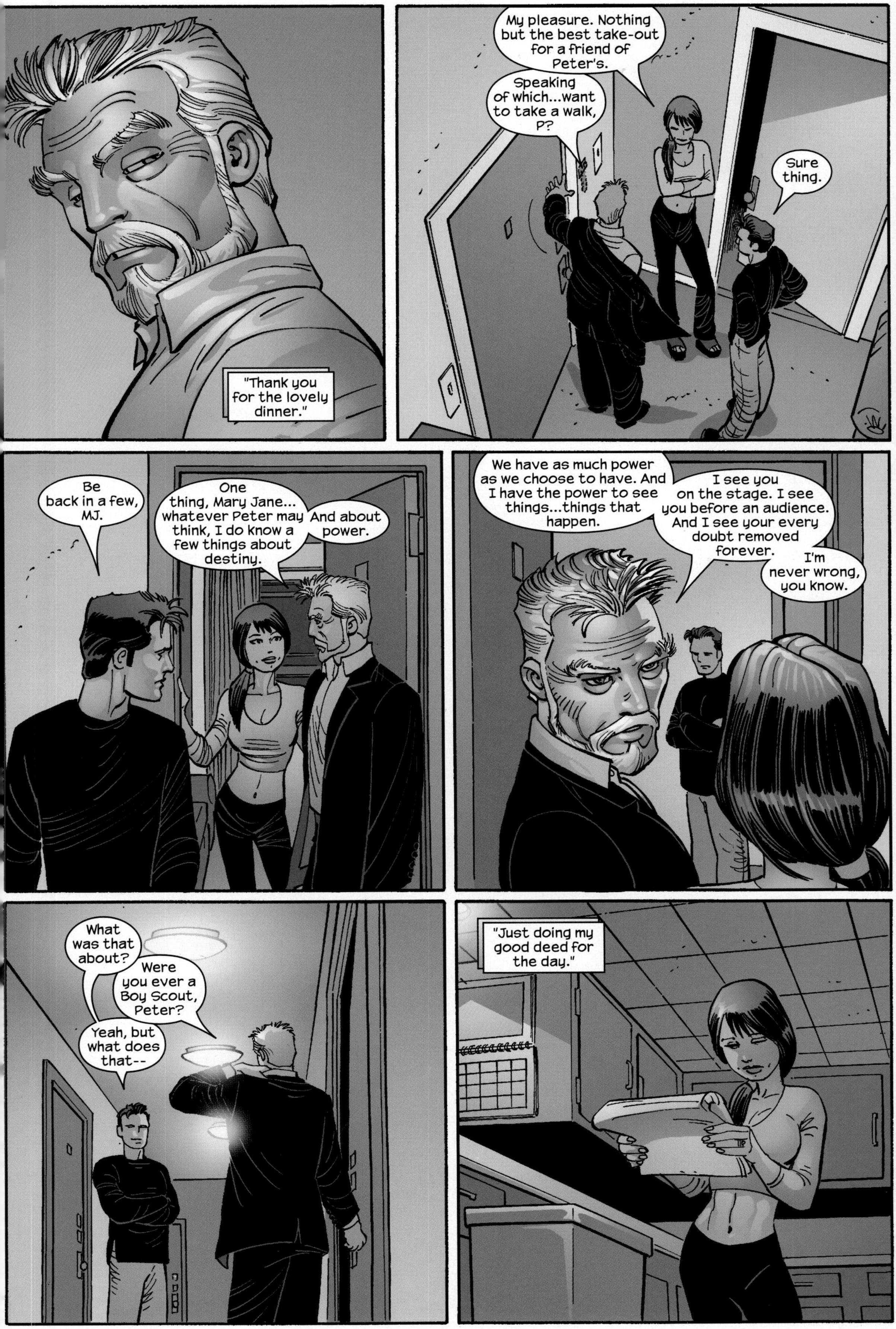
"Thank you for the lovely dinner."
My pleasure. Nothing but the best take-out for a friend of Peter's.
Speaking of which...want to take a walk, P?
Sure thing.
Be back in a few, MJ.
One thing, Mary Jane... whatever Peter may think, I do know a few things about destiny.
And about power.
We have as much power as we choose to have. And I have the power to see things...things that happen.
I see you on the stage. I see you before an audience. And I see your every doubt removed forever.
I'm never wrong, you know.
What was that about?
Were you ever a Boy Scout, Peter?
Yeah, but what does that--
"Just doing my good deed for the day."

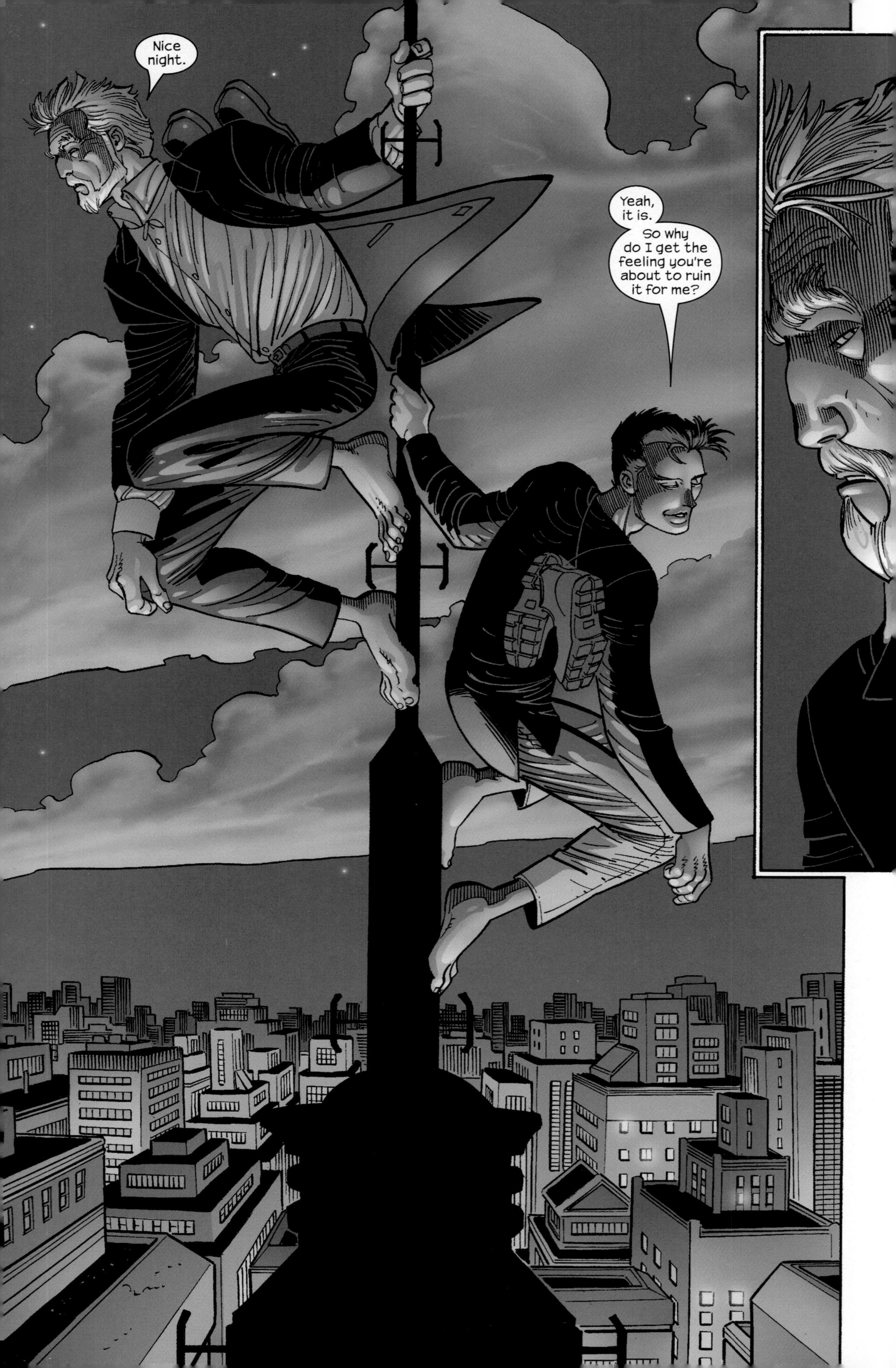
Nice night.
Yeah, it is.
So why do I get the feeling you're about to ruin it for me?

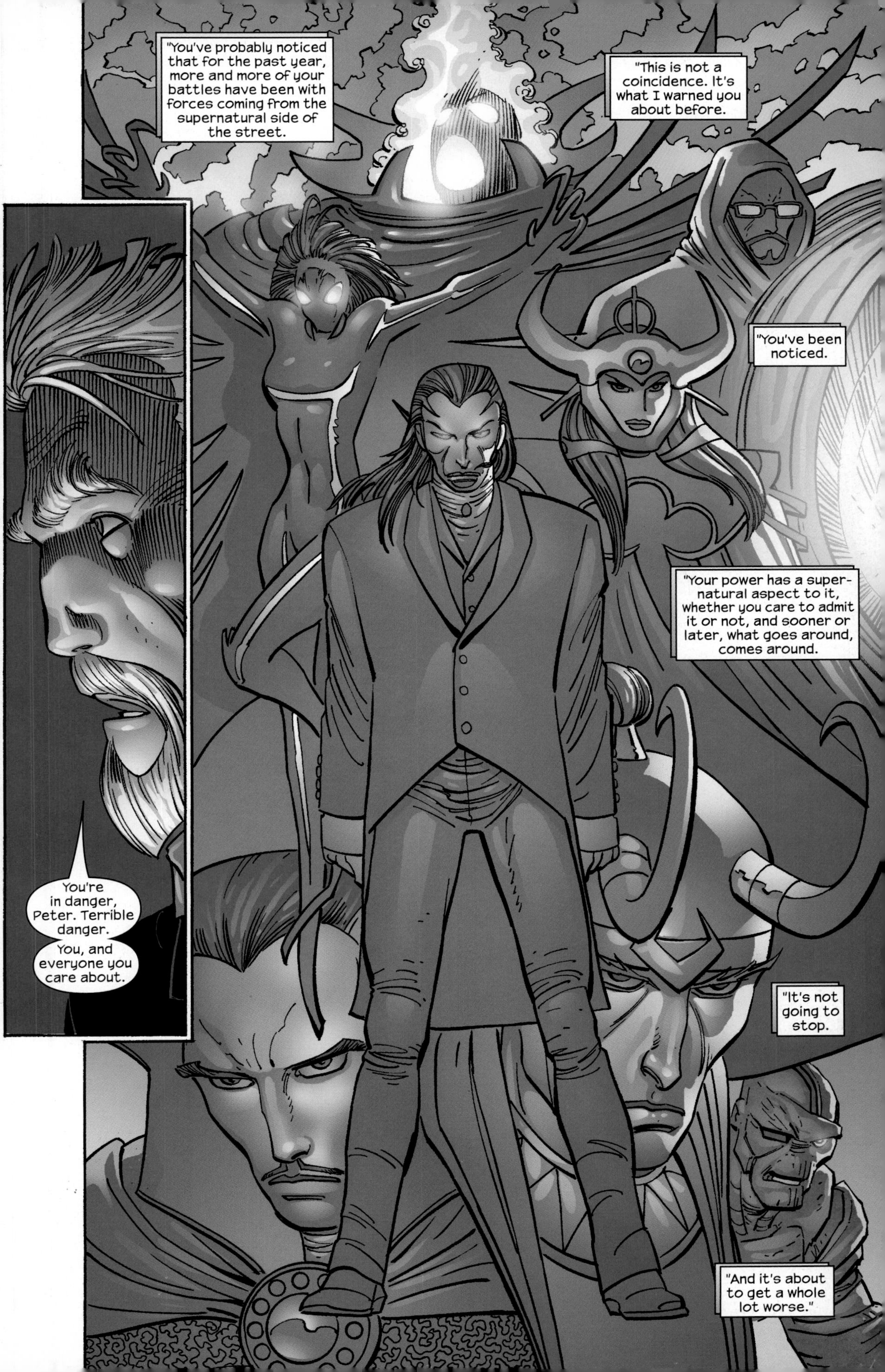
"You've probably noticed that for the past year, more and more of your battles have been with forces coming from the supernatural side of the street.
"This is not a coincidence. It's what I warned you about before.
"You've been noticed.
You're in danger, Peter. Terrible danger.
You, and everyone you care about.
"Your power has a super-natural aspect to it, whether you care to admit it or not, and sooner or later, what goes around, comes around.
"It's not going to stop.
"And it's about to get a whole lot worse."

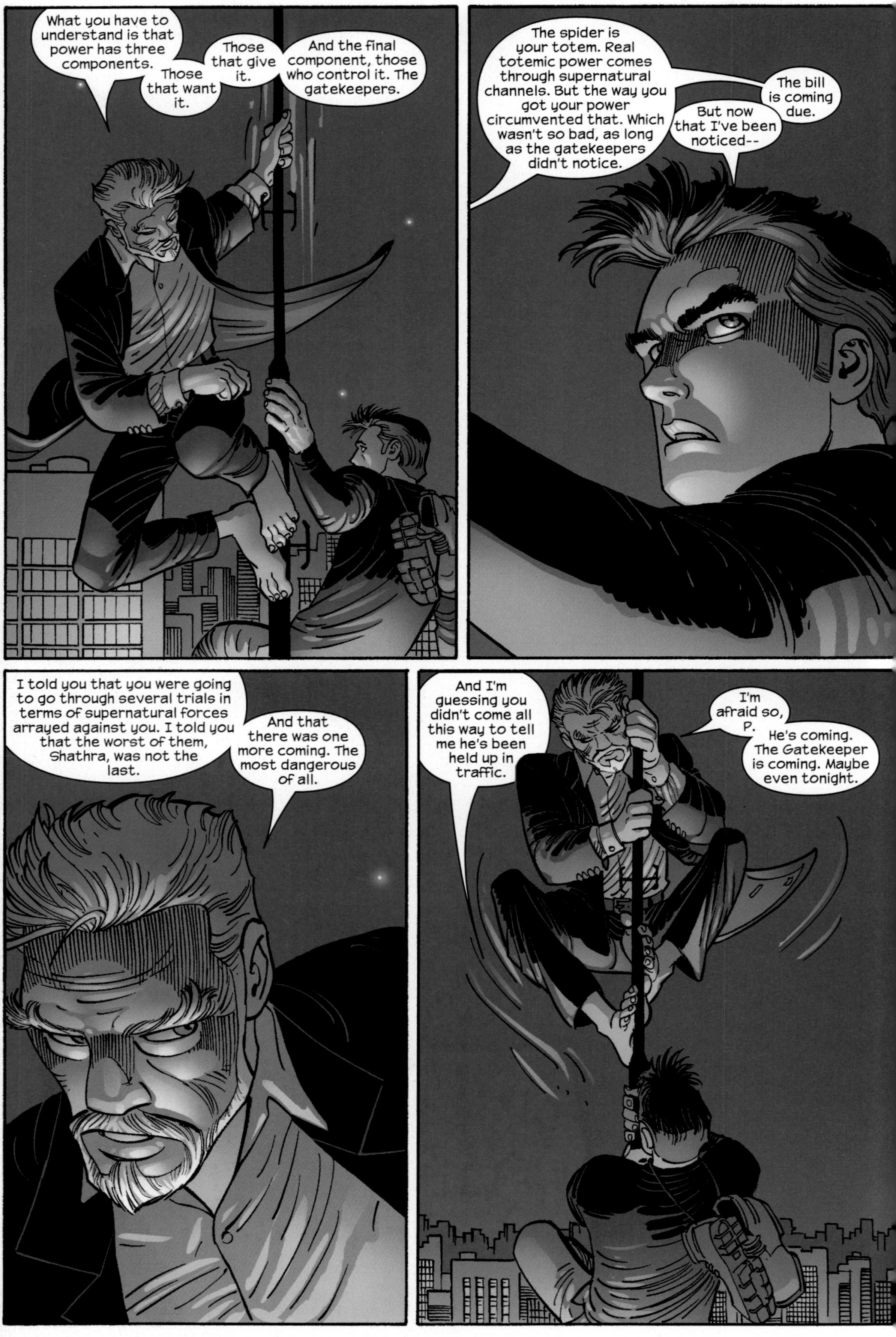
What you have to understand is that power has three components.
Those that want it.
Those that give it.
And the final component, those who control it. The gatekeepers.
The spider is your totem. Real totemic power comes through supernatural channels. But the way you got your power circumvented that. Which wasn't so bad, as long as the gatekeepers didn't notice.
But now that I've been noticed--
The bill is coming due.
I told you that you were going to go through several trials in terms of supernatural forces arrayed against you. I told you that the worst of them, Shathra, was not the last.
And that there was one more coming. The most dangerous of all.
And I'm guessing you didn't come all this way to tell me he's been held up in traffic.
I'm afraid so, P.
He's coming. The Gatekeeper is coming. Maybe even tonight.

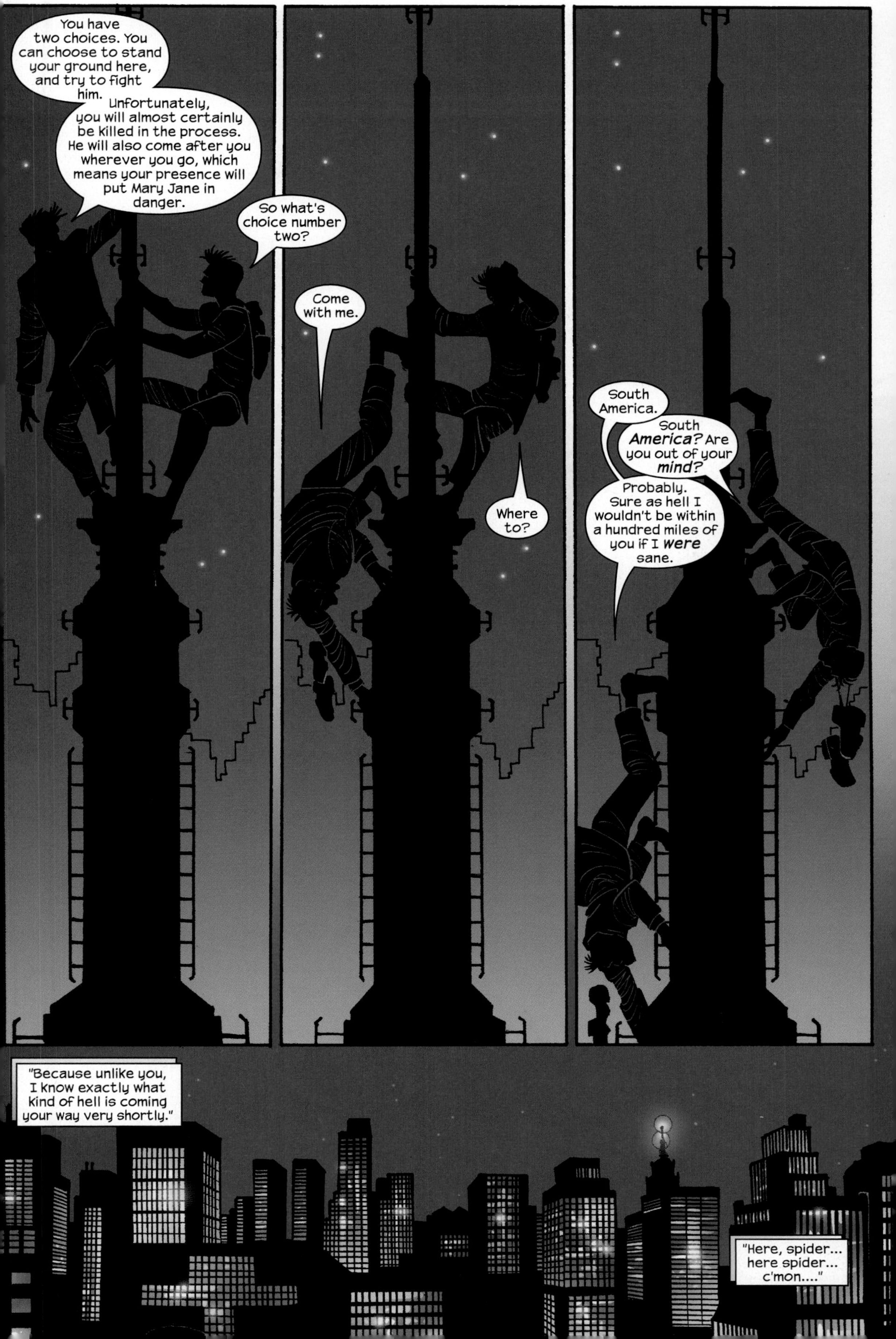
You have two choices. You can choose to stand your ground here, and try to fight him.
Unfortunately, you will almost certainly be killed in the process. He will also come after you wherever you go, which means your presence will put Mary Jane in danger.
So what's choice number two?
Come with me.
Where to?
South America.
South *America?* Are you out of your *mind?*
Probably. Sure as hell I wouldn't be within a hundred miles of you if I *were* sane.
"Because unlike you, I know exactly what kind of hell is coming your way very shortly."
"Here, spider... here spider... c'mon...."

Gotcha!

Heh...*that'll* teach you ta mess around with Lightnin' Jack, fastest spider-smasher in this part of--

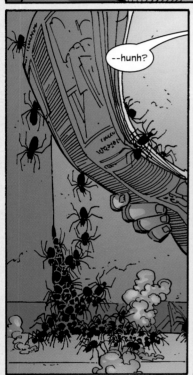

--hunh?

WHAM!
WHAM!
WHAM!
WHAM!

Holy...

LEMMEOUTTAHERE!

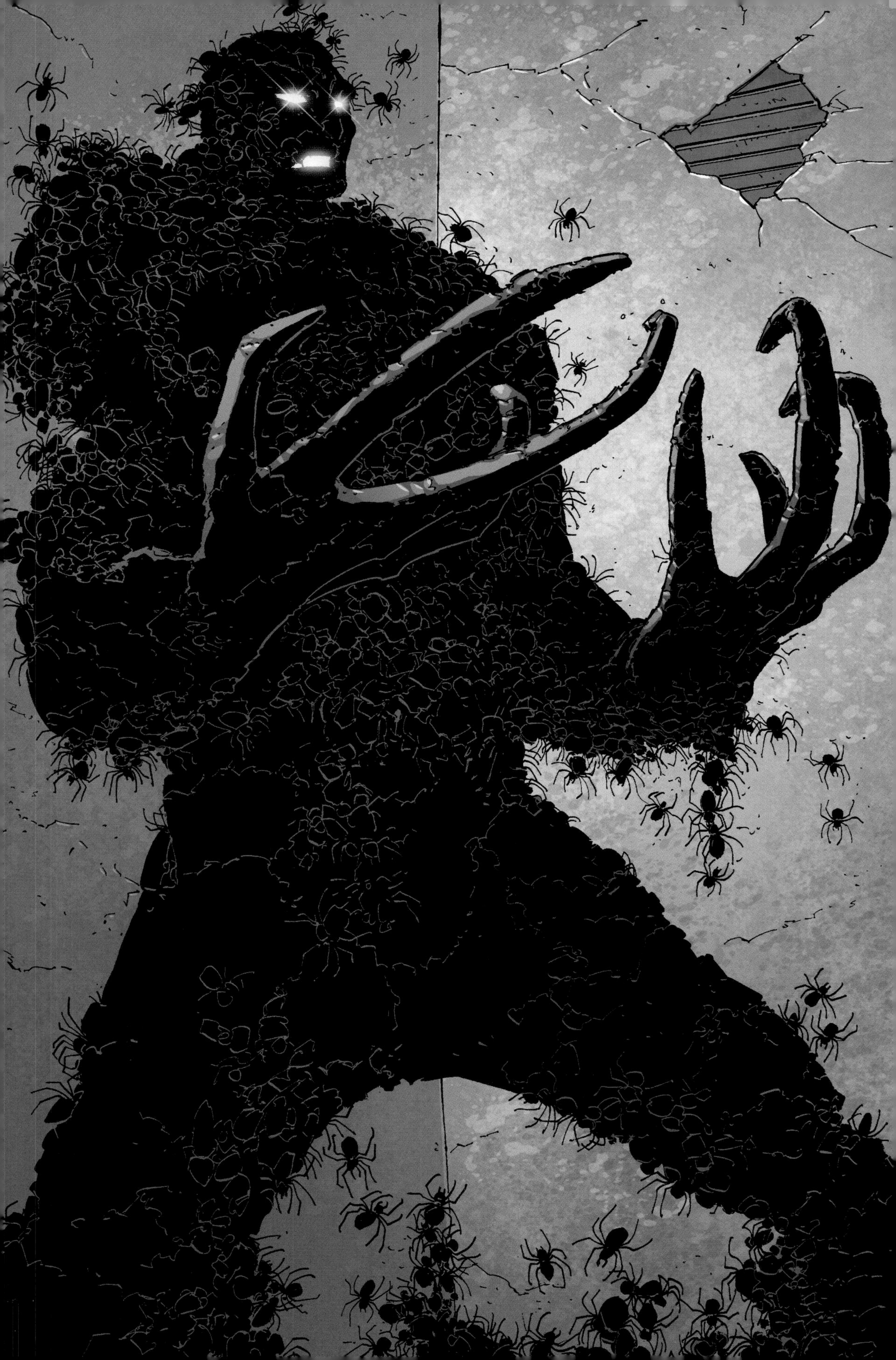

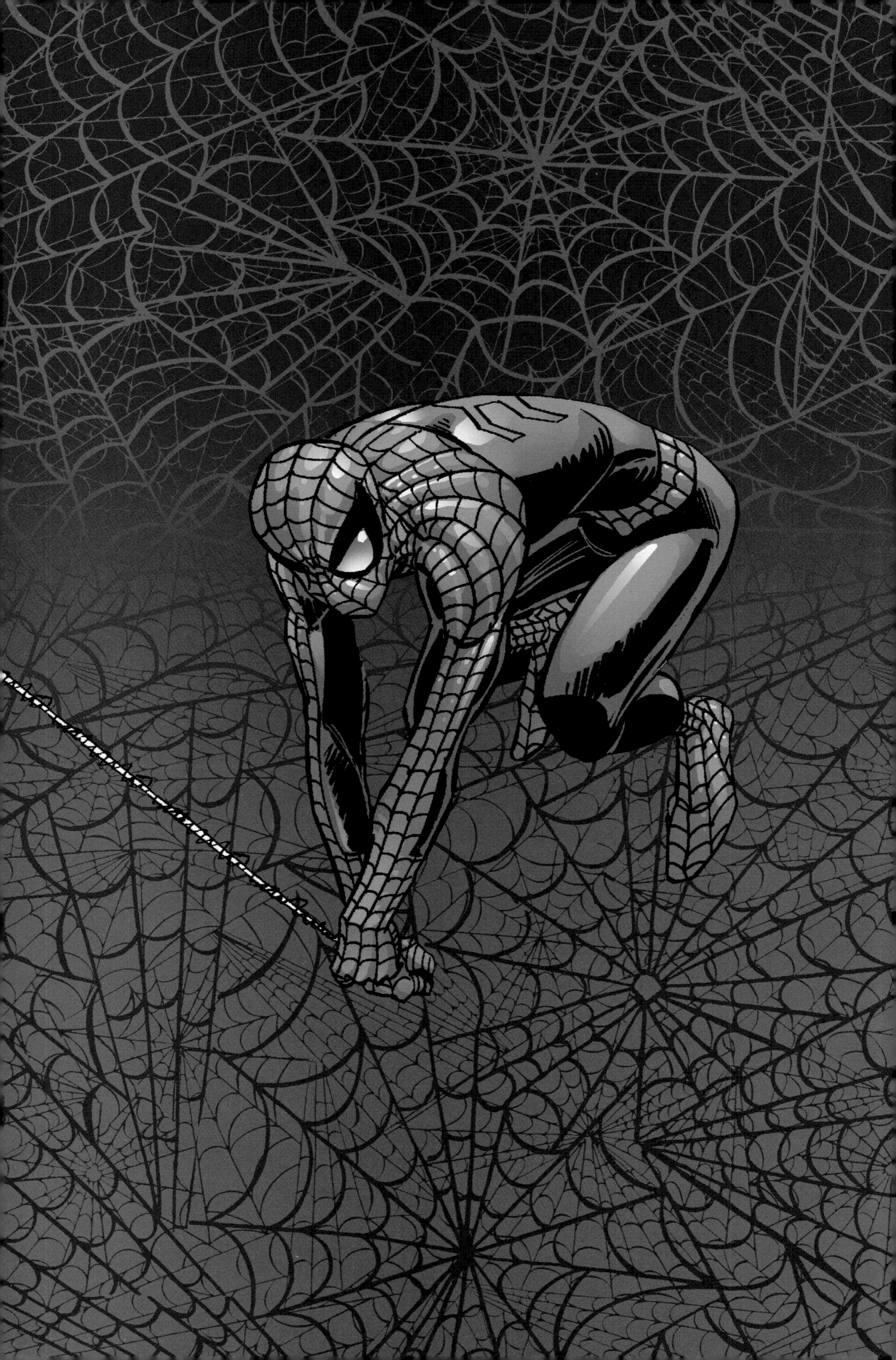

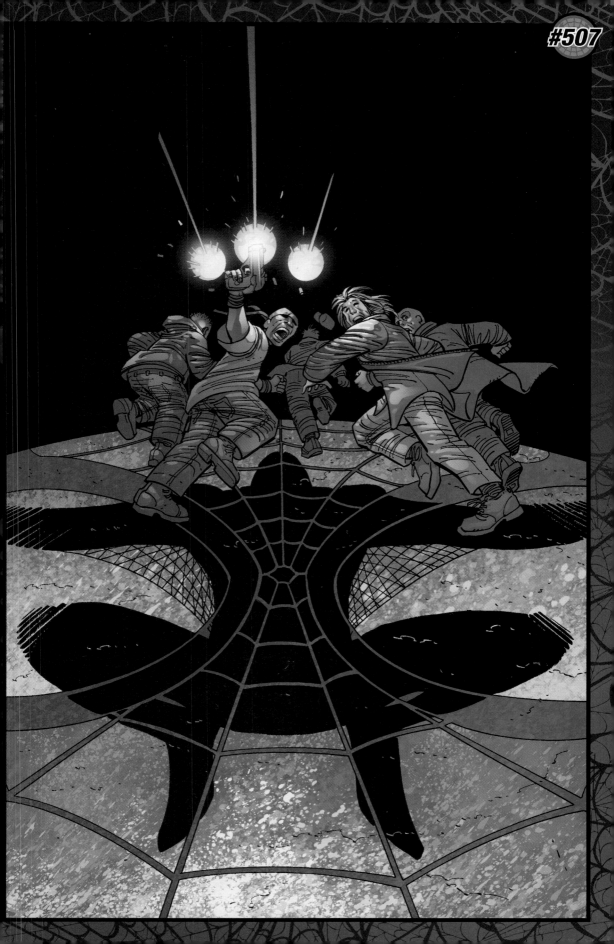

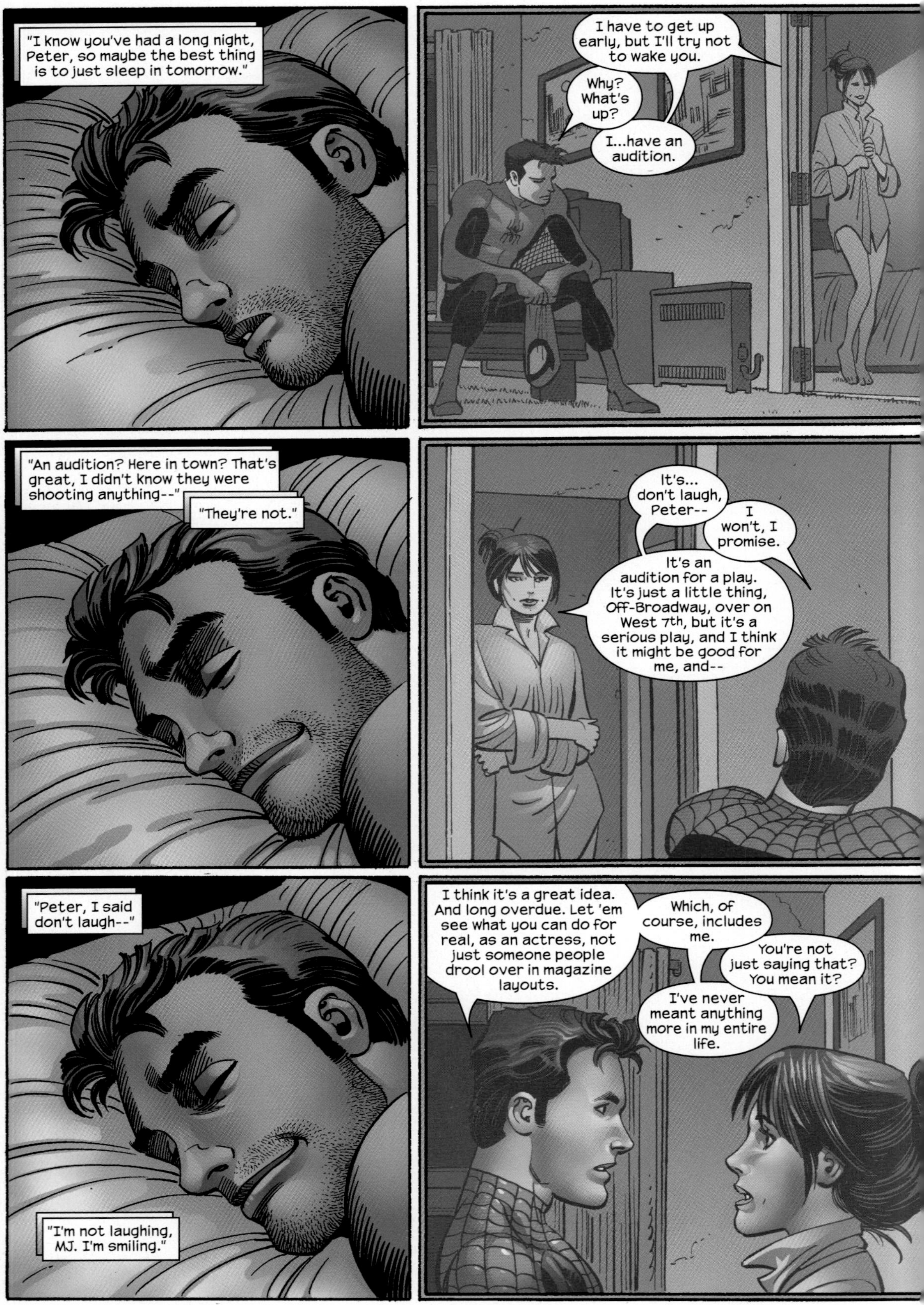
"I know you've had a long night, Peter, so maybe the best thing is to just sleep in tomorrow."
I have to get up early, but I'll try not to wake you.
Why? What's up?
I...have an audition.
"An audition? Here in town? That's great, I didn't know they were shooting anything--"
"They're not."
It's... don't laugh, Peter--
I won't, I promise.
It's an audition for a play. It's just a little thing, Off-Broadway, over on West 7th, but it's a serious play, and I think it might be good for me, and--
"Peter, I said don't laugh--"
"I'm not laughing, MJ. I'm smiling."
I think it's a great idea. And long overdue. Let 'em see what you can do for real, as an actress, not just someone people drool over in magazine layouts.
Which, of course, includes me.
You're not just saying that? You mean it?
I've never meant anything more in my entire life.

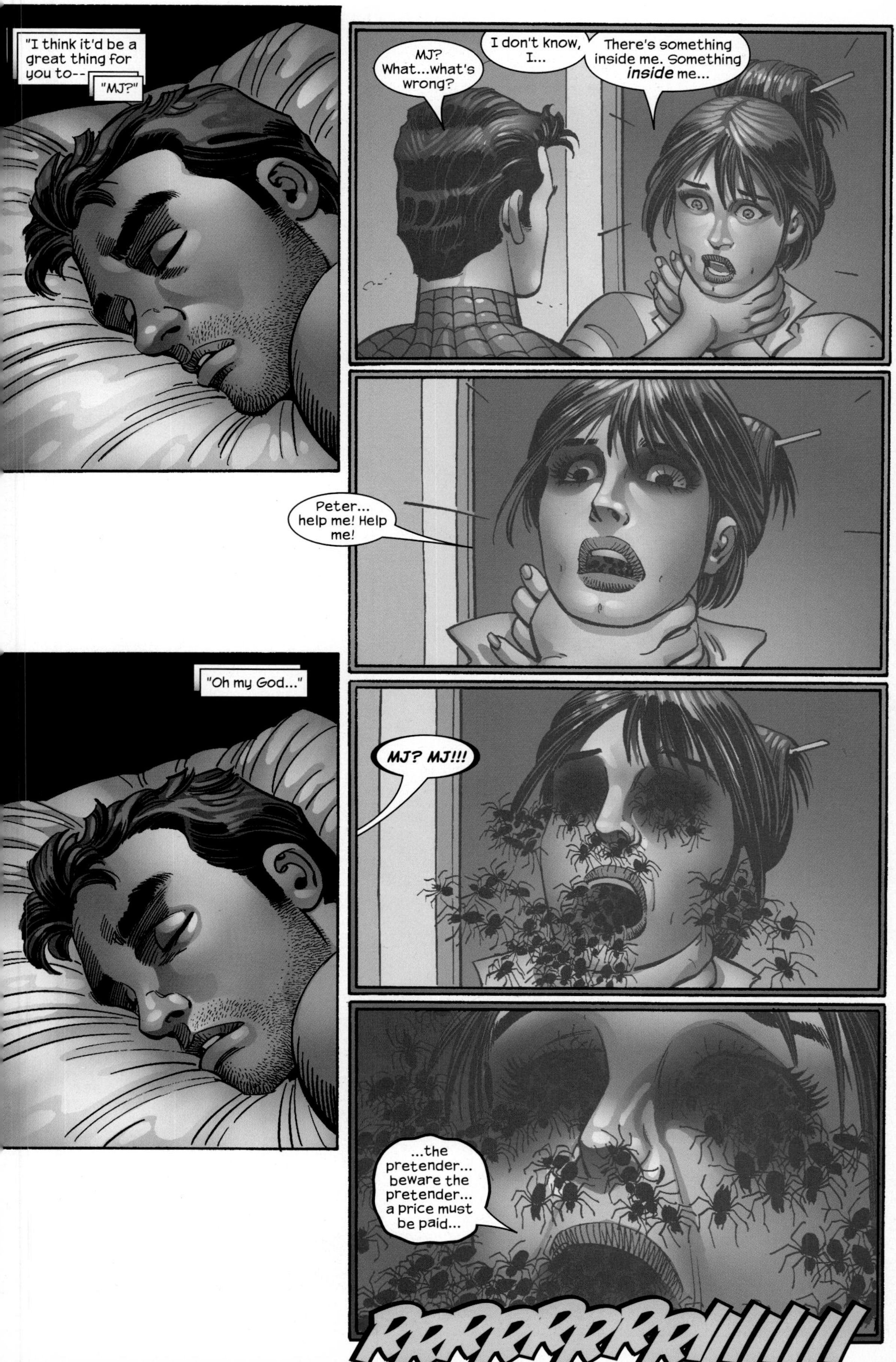
"I think it'd be a great thing for you to--
"MJ?"
MJ? What...what's wrong?
I don't know, I...
There's something inside me. Something *inside* me...
Peter... help me! Help me!
"Oh my God..."
MJ? MJ!!!
...the pretender... beware the pretender... a price must be paid...
RRRRRRRRRI!!!!!!!!

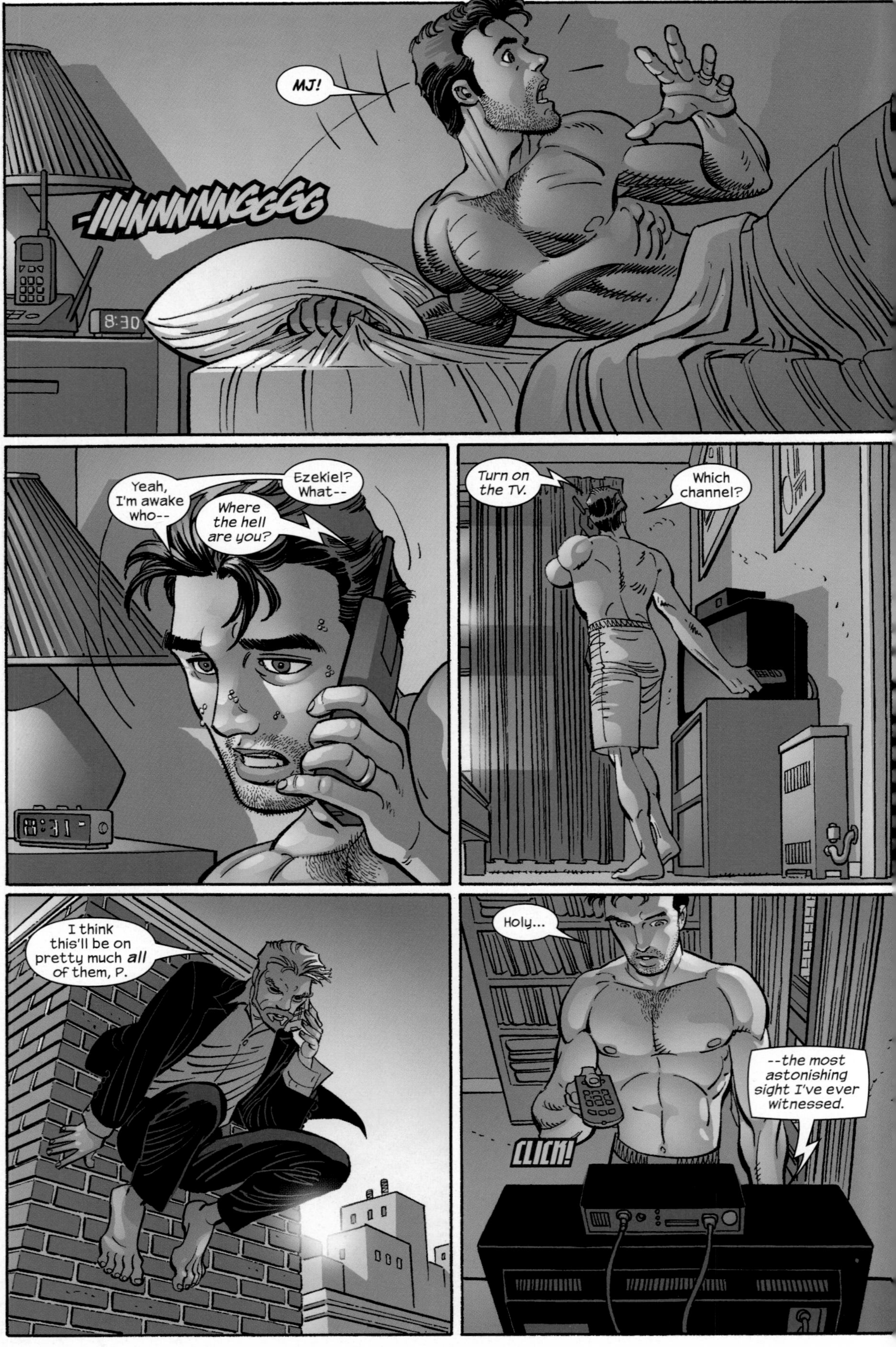
MJ!
-IIIINNNNNGGGG
8:30
Yeah, I'm awake who--
Ezekiel? What--
Where the hell are you?
Turn on the TV.
Which channel?
I think this'll be on pretty much *all* of them, P.
Holy...
CLICK!
--the most astonishing sight I've ever witnessed.

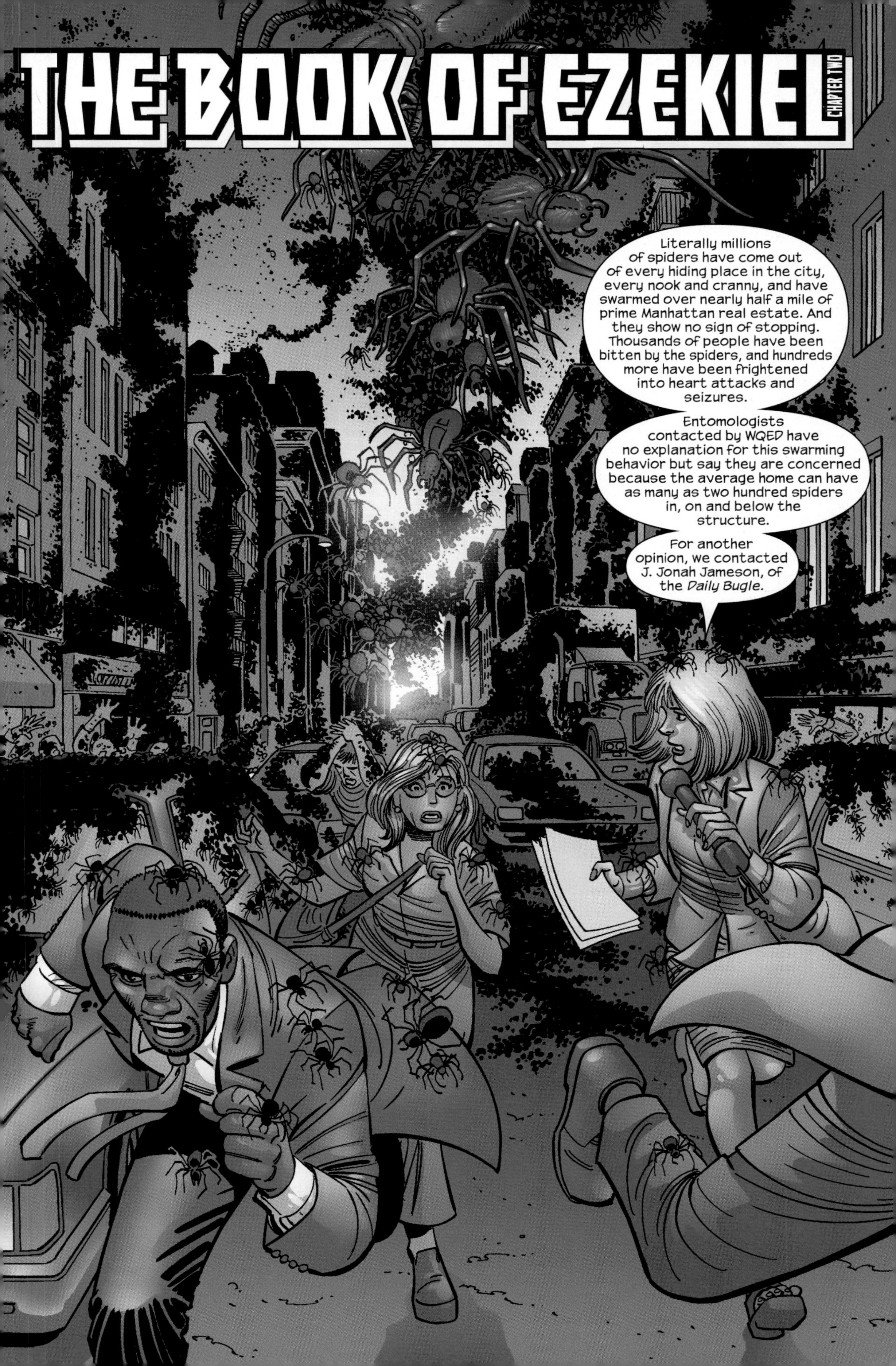
THE BOOK OF EZEKIEL
CHAPTER TWO
Literally millions of spiders have come out of every hiding place in the city, every nook and cranny, and have swarmed over nearly half a mile of prime Manhattan real estate. And they show no sign of stopping. Thousands of people have been bitten by the spiders, and hundreds more have been frightened into heart attacks and seizures.
Entomologists contacted by WQED have no explanation for this swarming behavior but say they are concerned because the average home can have as many as two hundred spiders in, on and below the structure.
For another opinion, we contacted J. Jonah Jameson, of the *Daily Bugle*.

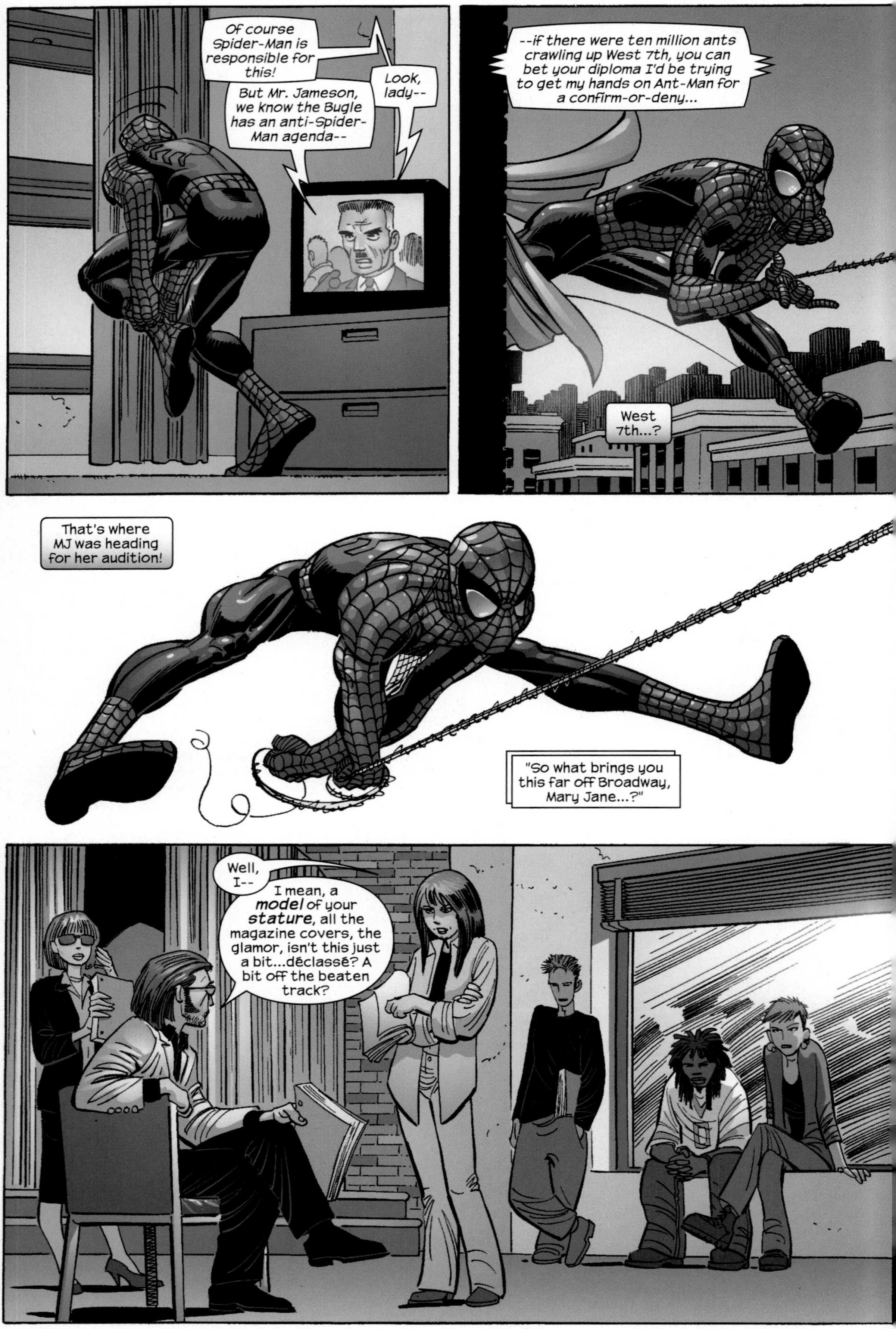

Of course Spider-Man is responsible for this!
But Mr. Jameson, we know the Bugle has an anti-Spider-Man agenda--
Look, lady--
--if there were ten million ants crawling up West 7th, you can bet your diploma I'd be trying to get my hands on Ant-Man for a confirm-or-deny...
West 7th...?
That's where MJ was heading for her audition!
"So what brings you this far off Broadway, Mary Jane...?"
Well, I--
I mean, a *model* of your *stature*, all the magazine covers, the glamor, isn't this just a bit...déclassé? A bit off the beaten track?

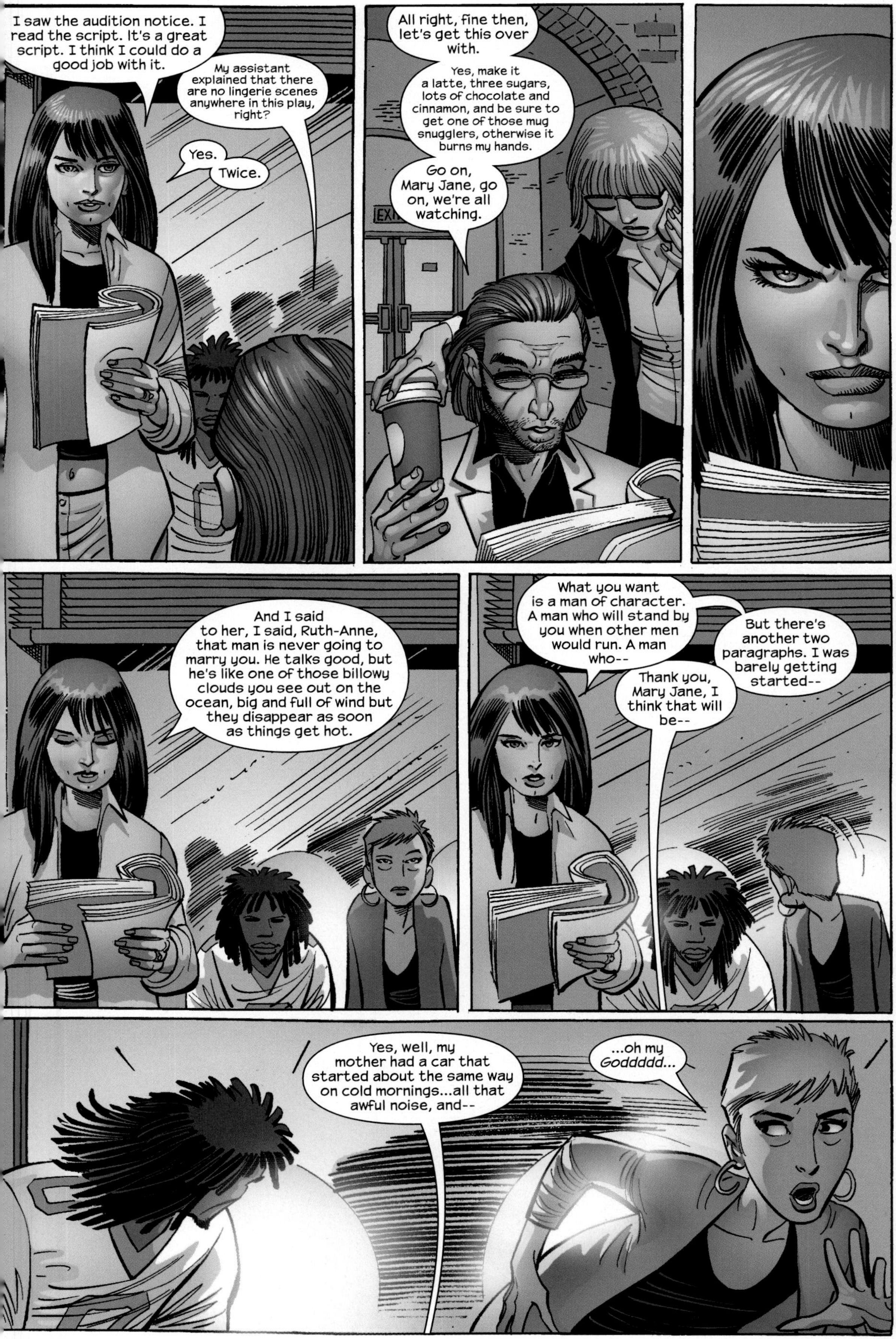

I saw the audition notice. I read the script. It's a great script. I think I could do a good job with it.
My assistant explained that there are no lingerie scenes anywhere in this play, right?
Yes.
Twice.
All right, fine then, let's get this over with.
Yes, make it a latte, three sugars, lots of chocolate and cinnamon, and be sure to get one of those mug snugglers, otherwise it burns my hands.
Go on, Mary Jane, go on, we're all watching.
And I said to her, I said, Ruth-Anne, that man is never going to marry you. He talks good, but he's like one of those billowy clouds you see out on the ocean, big and full of wind but they disappear as soon as things get hot.
What you want is a man of character. A man who will stand by you when other men would run. A man who--
But there's another two paragraphs. I was barely getting started--
Thank you, Mary Jane, I think that will be--
Yes, well, my mother had a car that started about the same way on cold mornings...all that awful noise, and--
...oh my *Goddddd...*

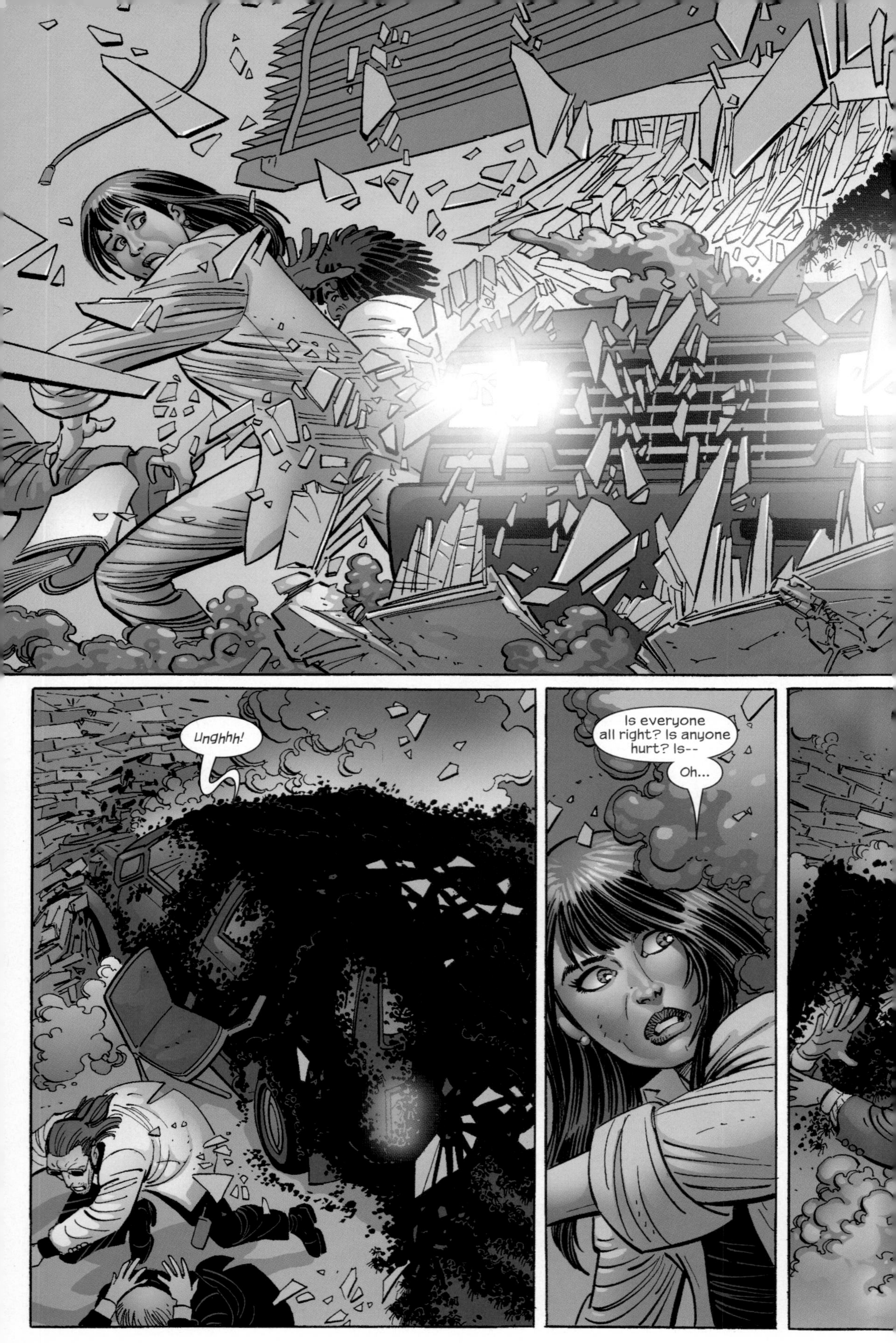
Unghhh!
Is everyone all right? Is anyone hurt? Is--
Oh...

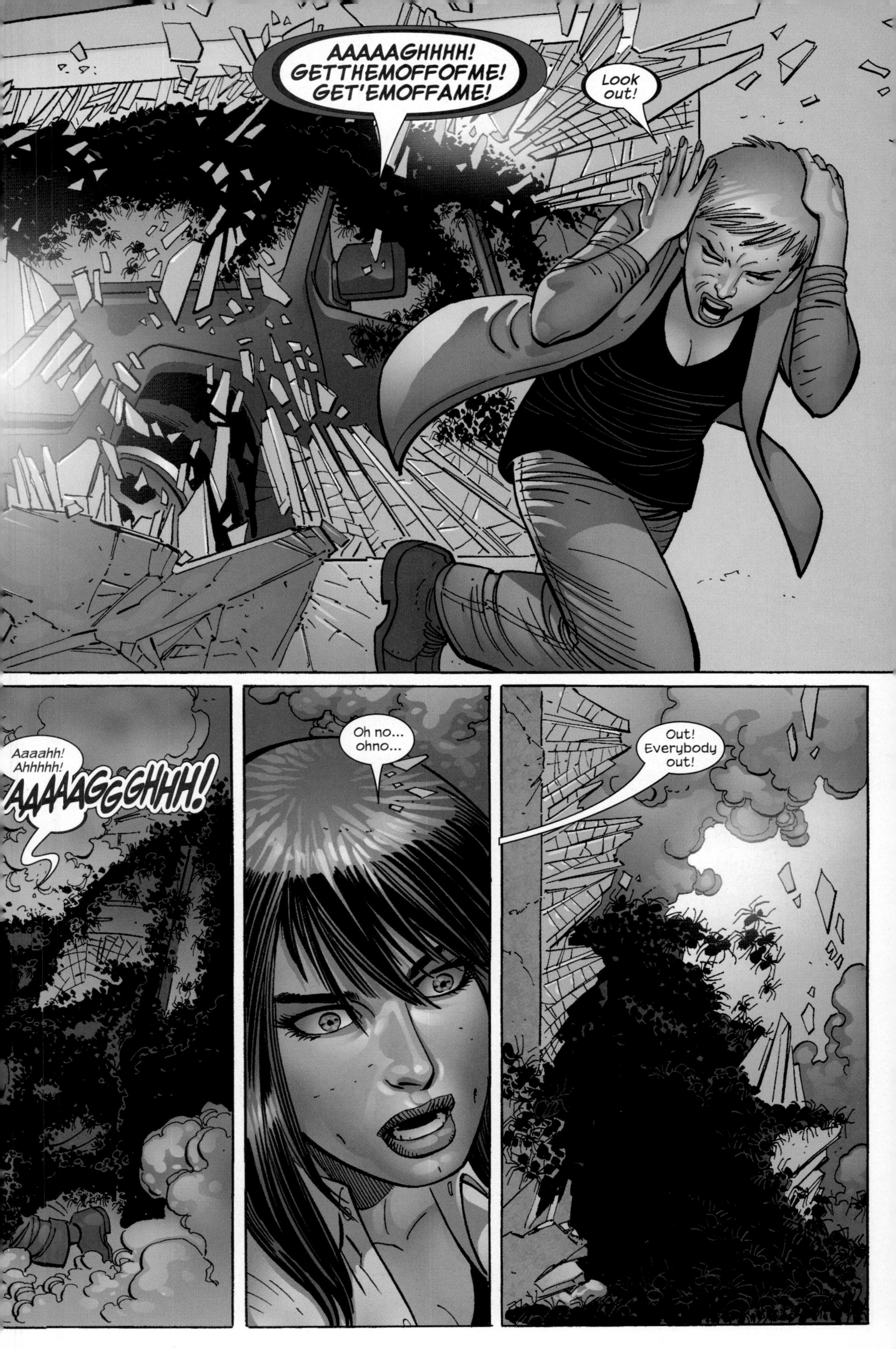
AAAAAGHHHH! GETTHEMOFFOFME! GET'EMOFFAME!
Look out!
Aaaahh! Ahhhhh! AAAAAGGGHHH!
Oh no... ohno...
Out! Everybody out!

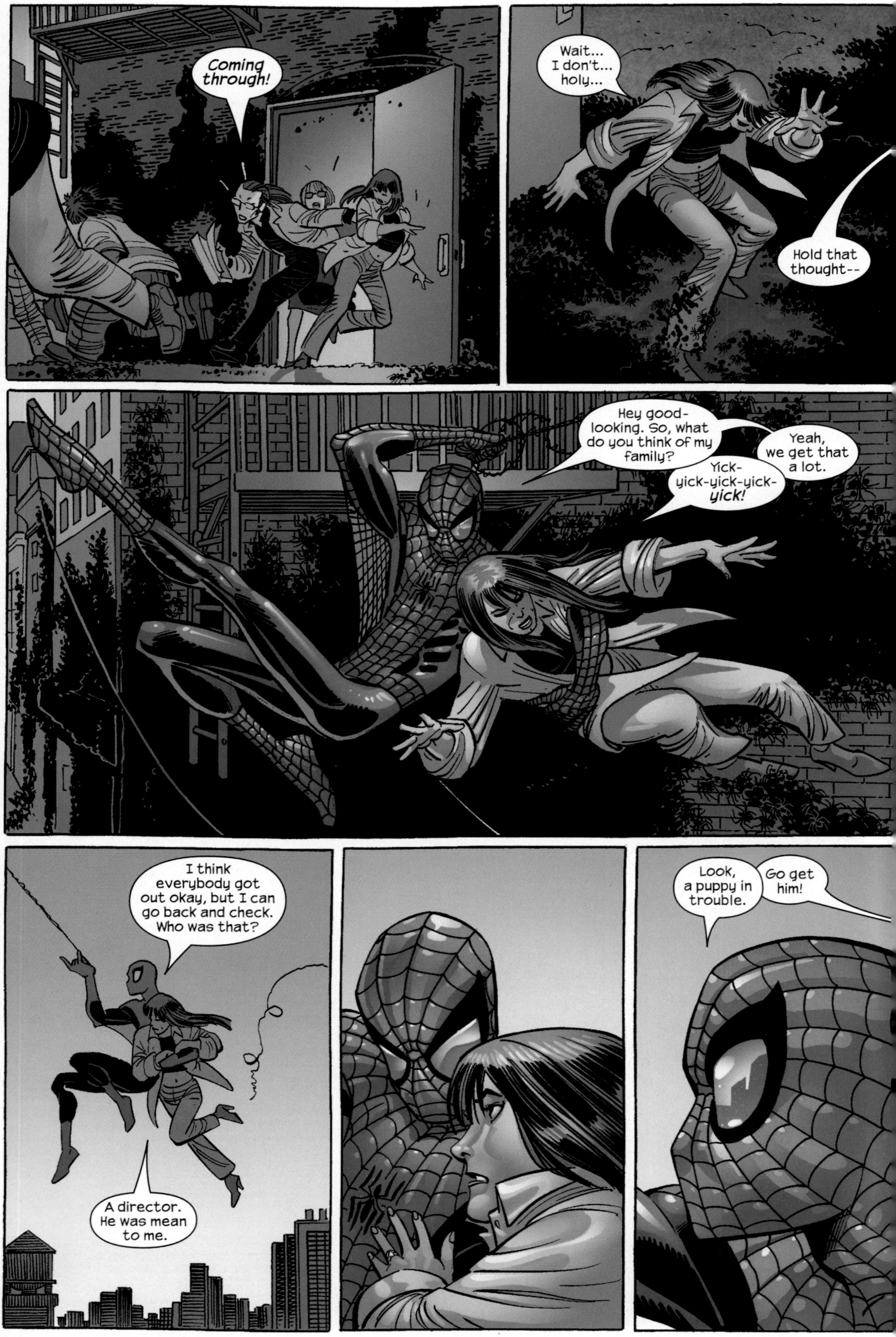
Coming through!
Wait... I don't... holy...
Hold that thought--
Hey good-looking. So, what do you think of my family?
Yeah, we get that a lot.
Yick-yick-yick-yick-yick!
I think everybody got out okay, but I can go back and check. Who was that?
A director. He was mean to me.
Look, a puppy in trouble.
Go get him!

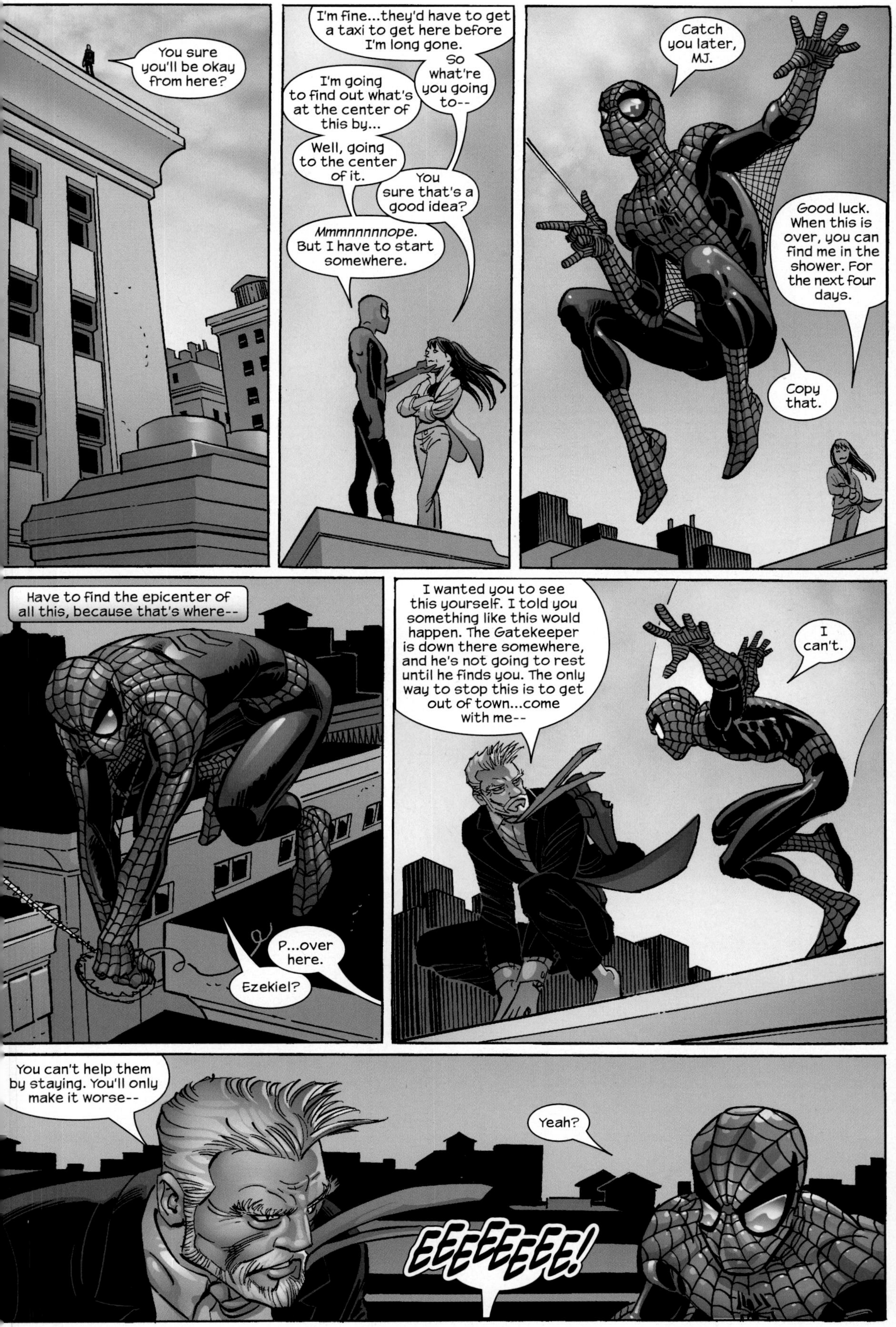

You sure you'll be okay from here?
I'm fine...they'd have to get a taxi to get here before I'm long gone.
So what're you going to--
I'm going to find out what's at the center of this by...
Well, going to the center of it.
You sure that's a good idea?
Mmmnnnnnope. But I have to start somewhere.
Catch you later, MJ.
Good luck. When this is over, you can find me in the shower. For the next four days.
Copy that.
Have to find the epicenter of all this, because that's where--
Ezekiel?
P...over here.
I wanted you to see this yourself. I told you something like this would happen. The Gatekeeper is down there somewhere, and he's not going to rest until he finds you. The only way to stop this is to get out of town...come with me--
I can't.
You can't help them by staying. You'll only make it worse--
Yeah?
EEEEEEEEE!

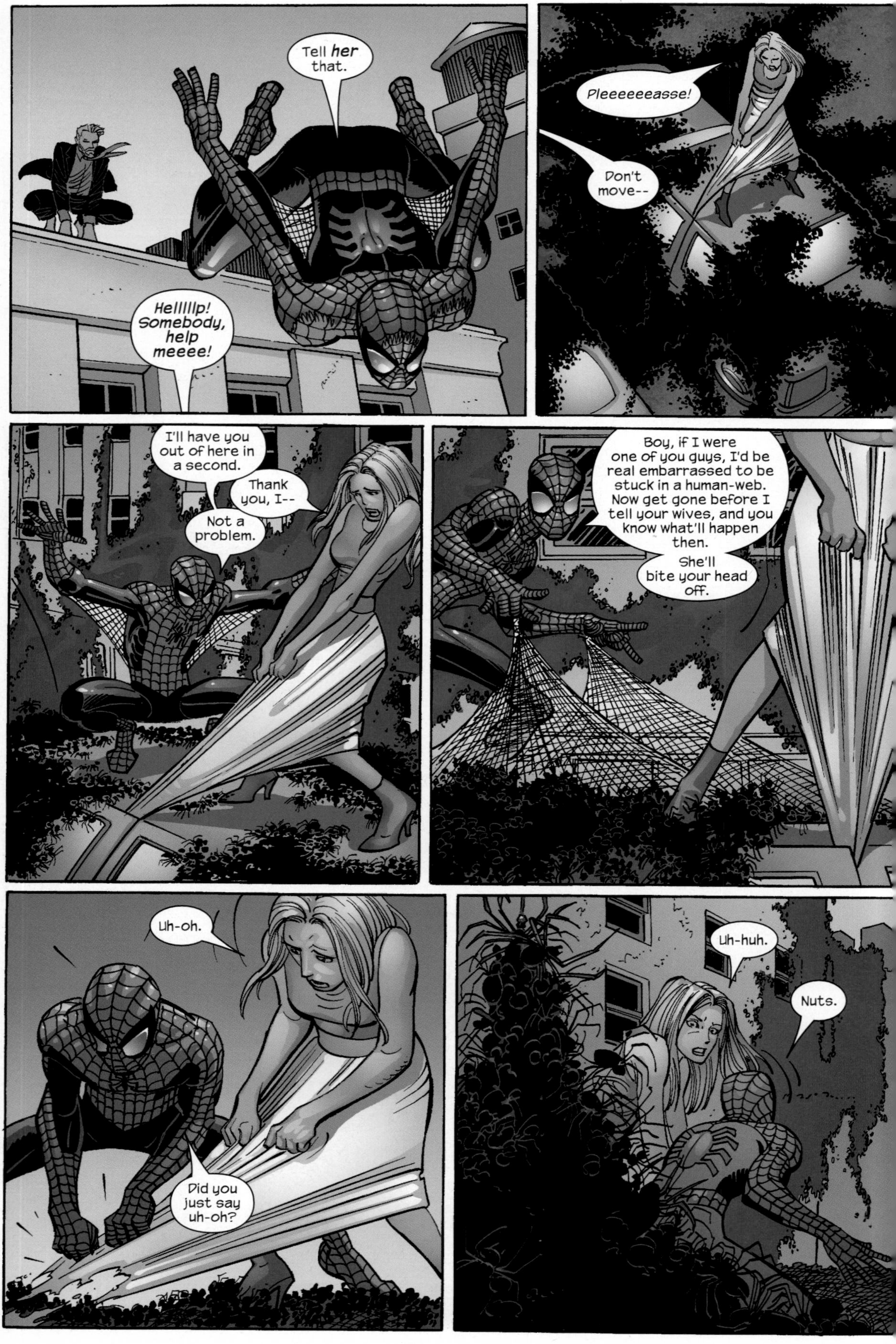

Tell *her* that.
Helllllp! Somebody, help meeee!
Pleeeeeeasse!
Don't move--
I'll have you out of here in a second.
Thank you, I--
Not a problem.
Boy, if I were one of you guys, I'd be real embarrassed to be stuck in a human-web. Now get gone before I tell your wives, and you know what'll happen then.
She'll bite your head off.
Uh-oh.
Did you just say uh-oh?
Uh-huh.
Nuts.

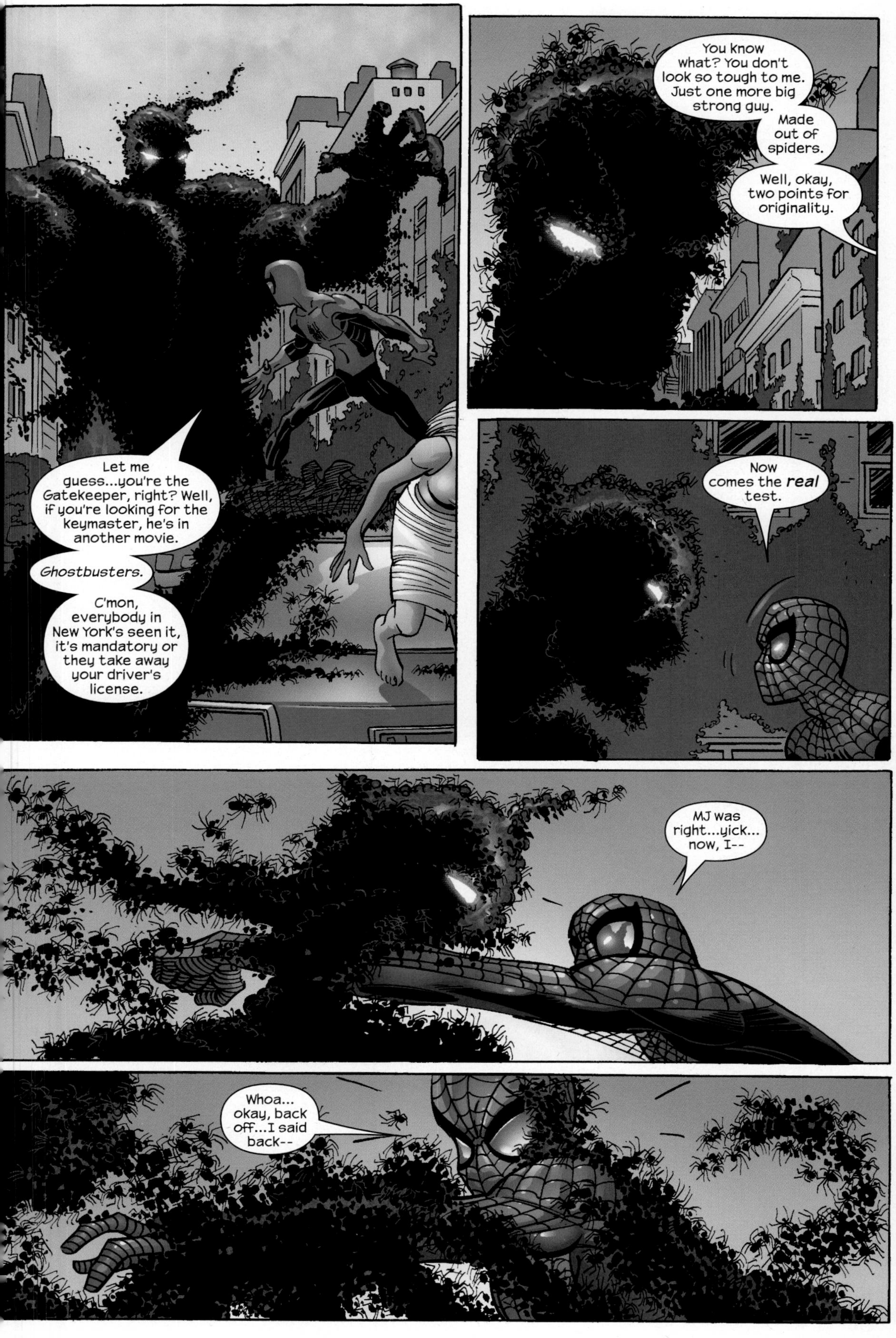
Let me guess...you're the Gatekeeper, right? Well, if you're looking for the keymaster, he's in another movie.
Ghostbusters.
C'mon, everybody in New York's seen it, it's mandatory or they take away your driver's license.
You know what? You don't look so tough to me. Just one more big strong guy.
Made out of spiders.
Well, okay, two points for originality.
Now comes the ***real*** test.
MJ was right...yick... now, I--
Whoa... okay, back off...I said back--

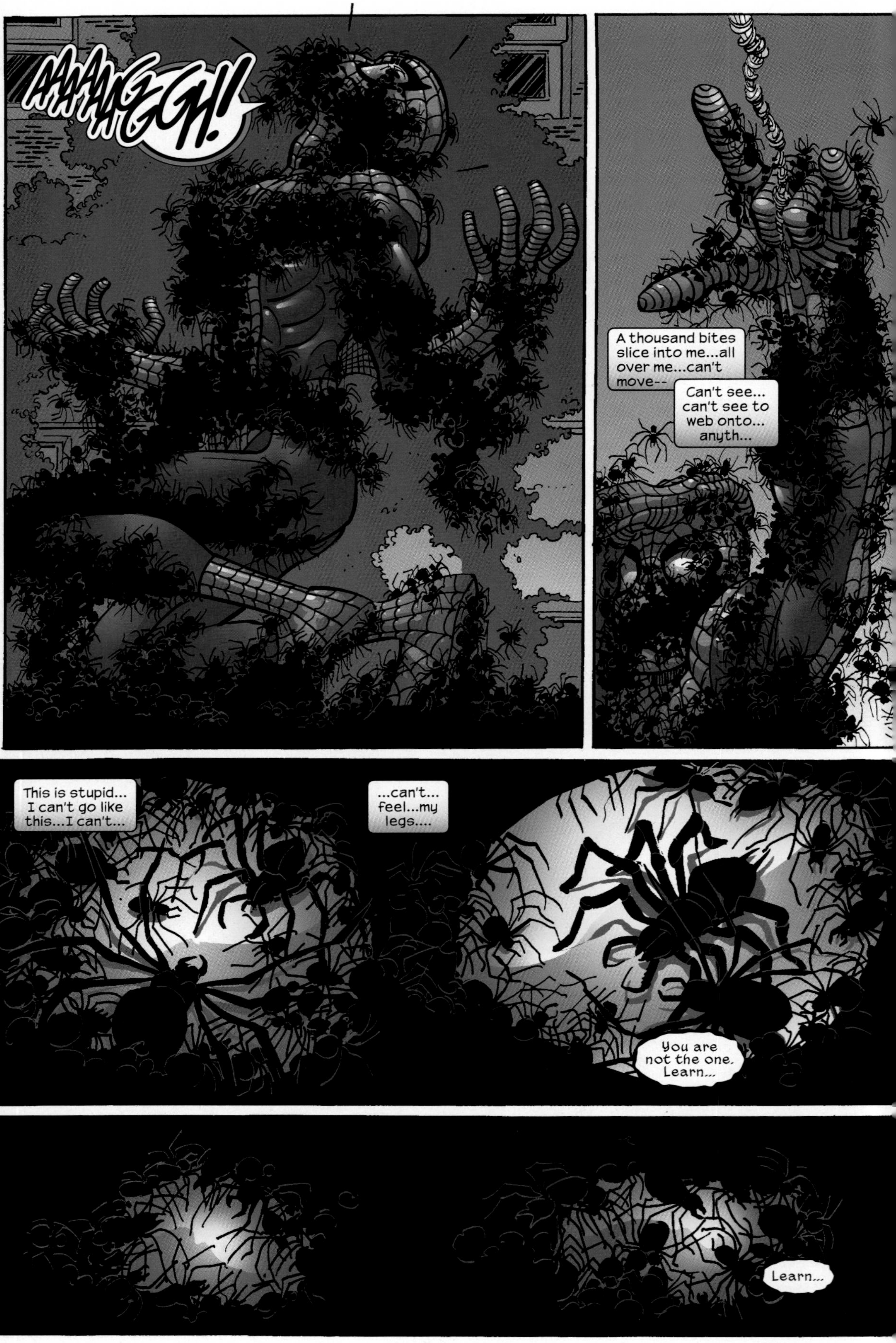
AAAAAAGGGH!
A thousand bites slice into me...all over me...can't move--
Can't see... can't see to web onto... anyth...
This is stupid... I can't go like this...I can't...
...can't... feel...my legs....
You are not the one. Learn...
Learn...

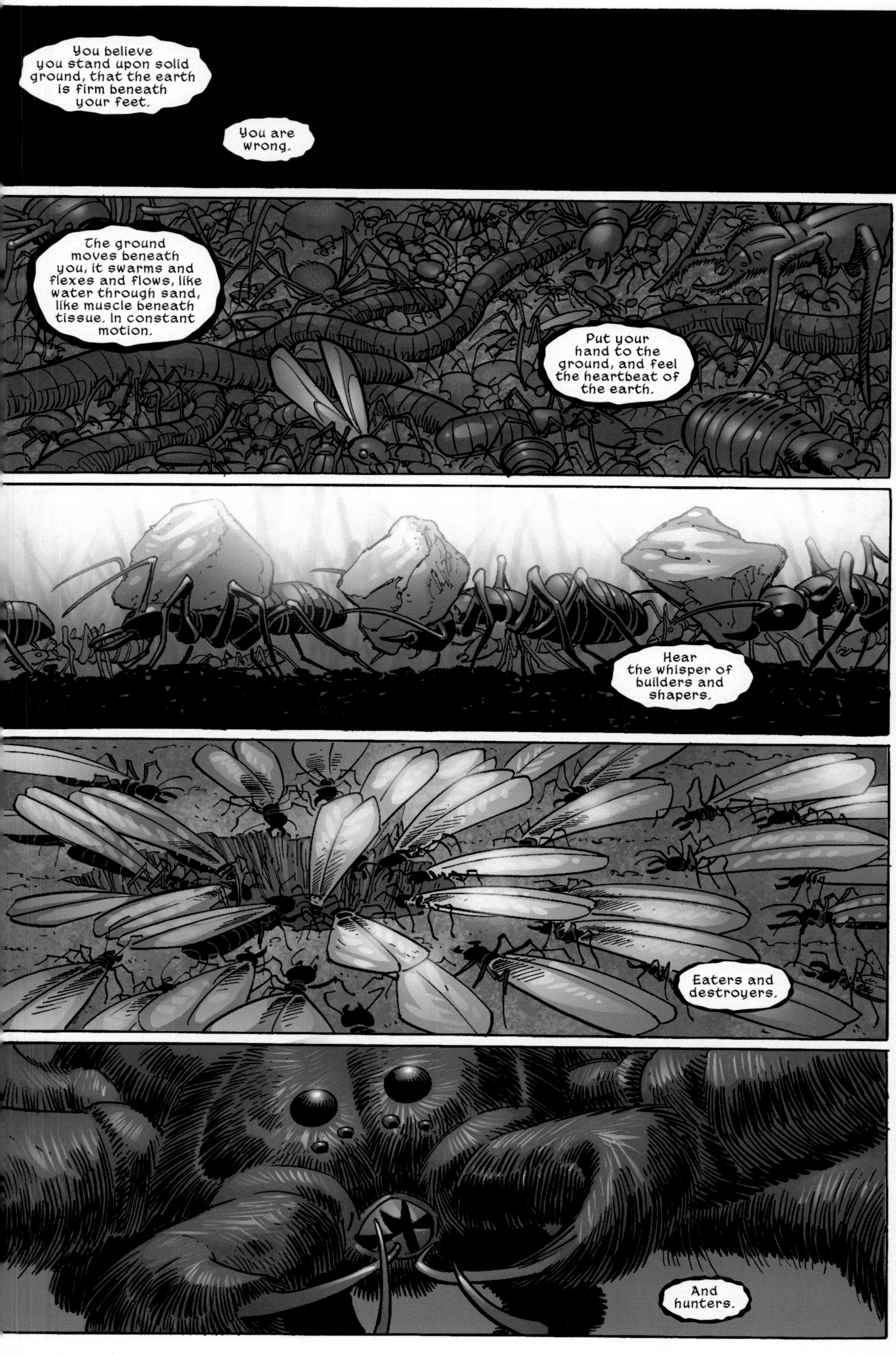
You believe you stand upon solid ground, that the earth is firm beneath your feet.
You are wrong.
The ground moves beneath you, it swarms and flexes and flows, like water through sand, like muscle beneath tissue. In constant motion.
Put your hand to the ground, and feel the heartbeat of the earth.
Hear the whisper of builders and shapers.
Eaters and destroyers.
And hunters.

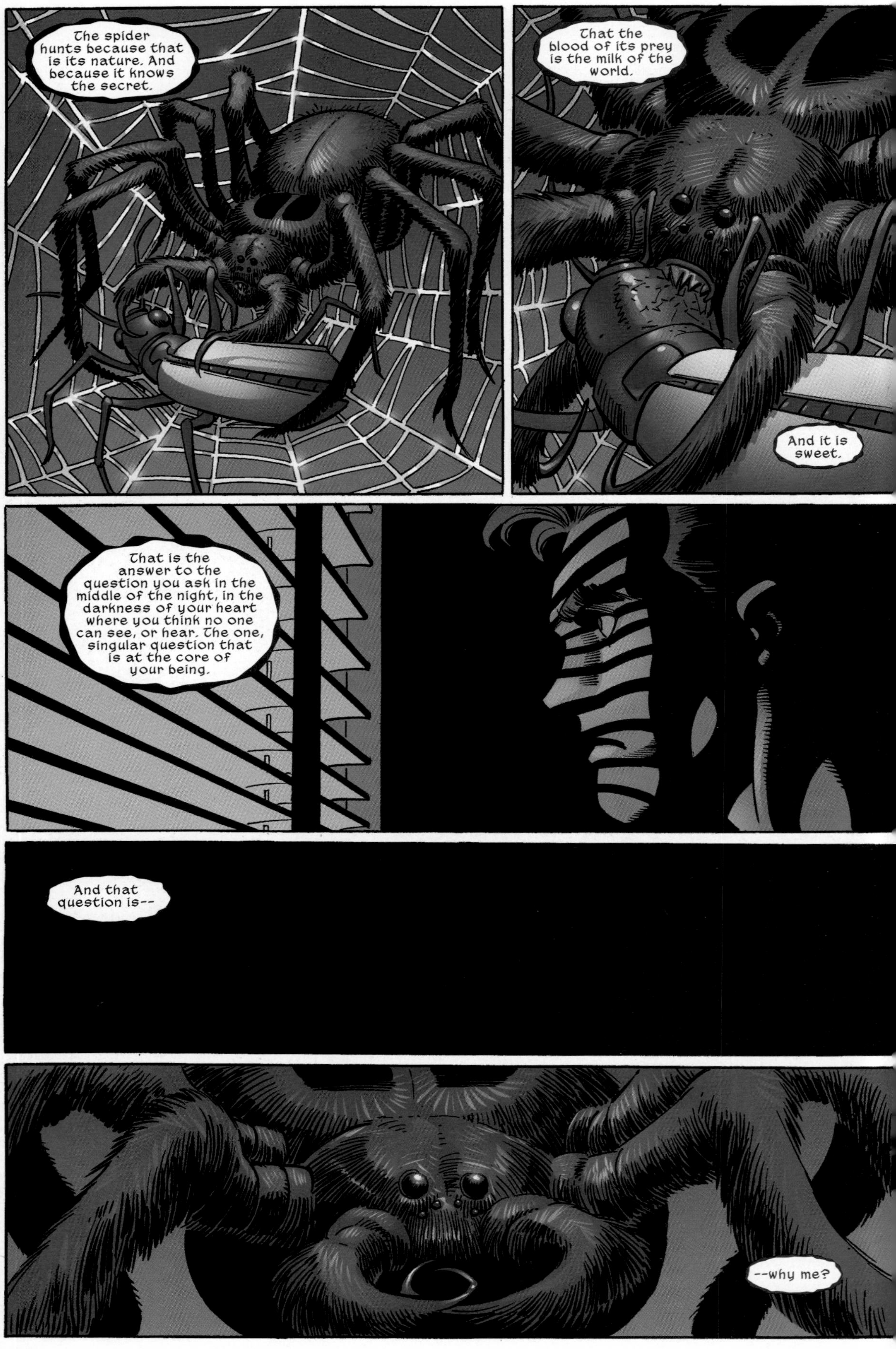
The spider hunts because that is its nature. And because it knows the secret.
That the blood of its prey is the milk of the world.
And it is sweet.
That is the answer to the question you ask in the middle of the night, in the darkness of your heart where you think no one can see, or hear. The one, singular question that is at the core of your being.
And that question is--
--why me?

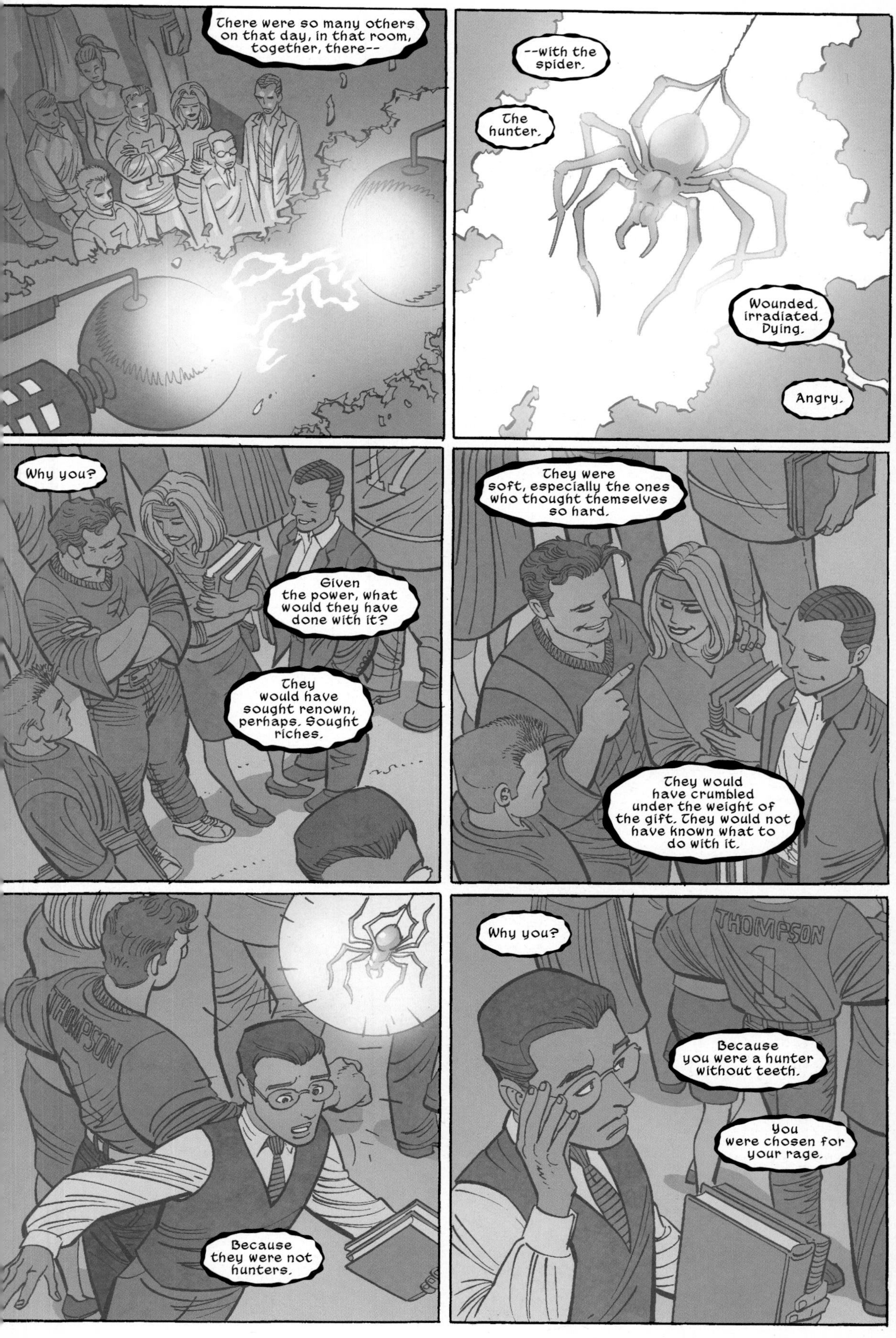
There were so many others on that day, in that room, together, there--
--with the spider.
The hunter.
Wounded, irradiated. Dying.
Angry.
Why you?
Given the power, what would they have done with it?
They would have sought renown, perhaps. Sought riches.
They were soft, especially the ones who thought themselves so hard.
They would have crumbled under the weight of the gift. They would not have known what to do with it.
THOMPSON
Because they were not hunters.
Why you?
THOMPSON
Because you were a hunter without teeth.
You were chosen for your rage.

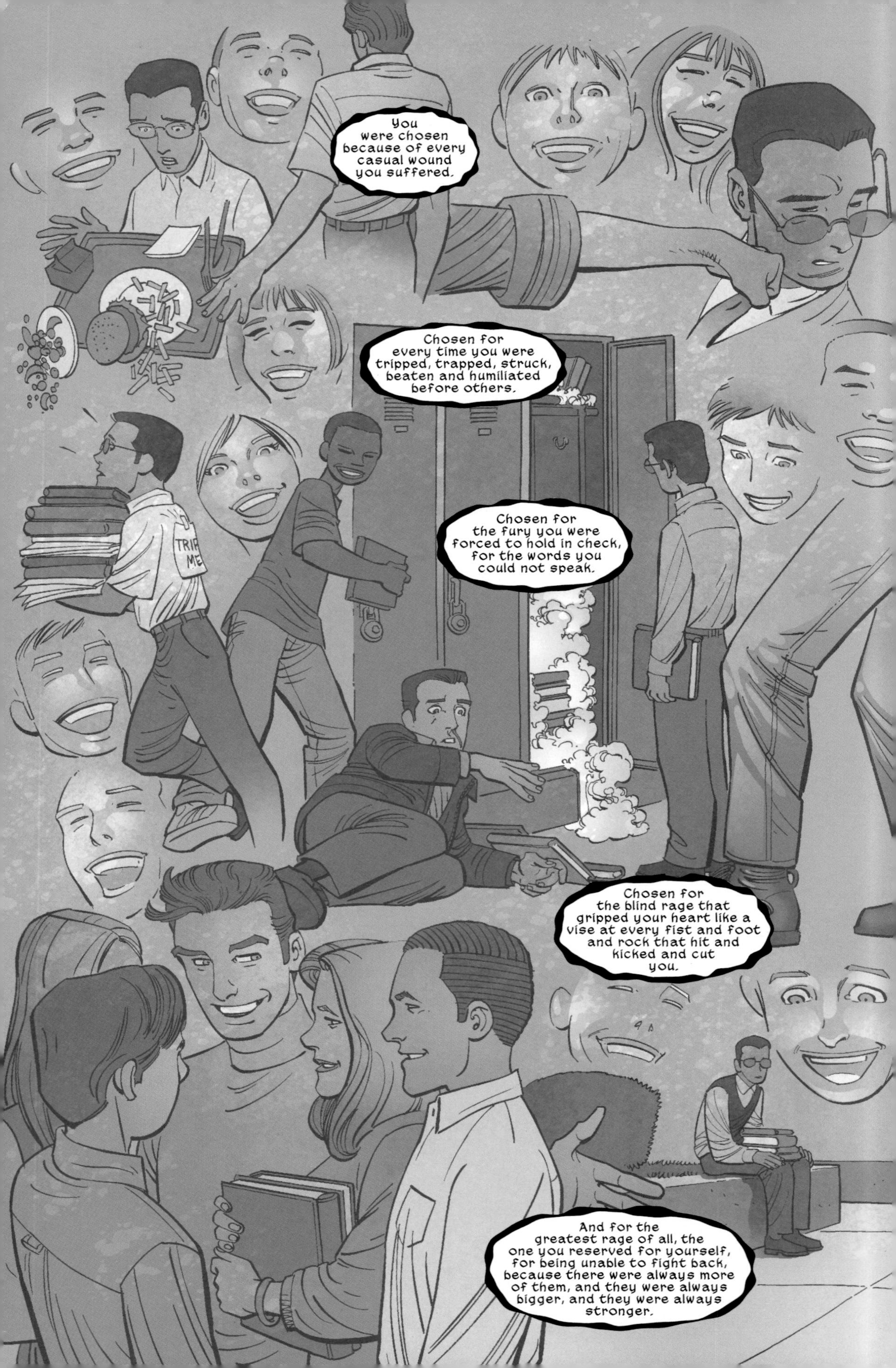

You were chosen because of every casual wound you suffered.
Chosen for every time you were tripped, trapped, struck, beaten and humiliated before others.
TRIP ME
Chosen for the fury you were forced to hold in check, for the words you could not speak.
Chosen for the blind rage that gripped your heart like a vise at every fist and foot and rock that hit and kicked and cut you.
And for the greatest rage of all, the one you reserved for yourself, for being unable to fight back, because there were always more of them, and they were always bigger, and they were always stronger.

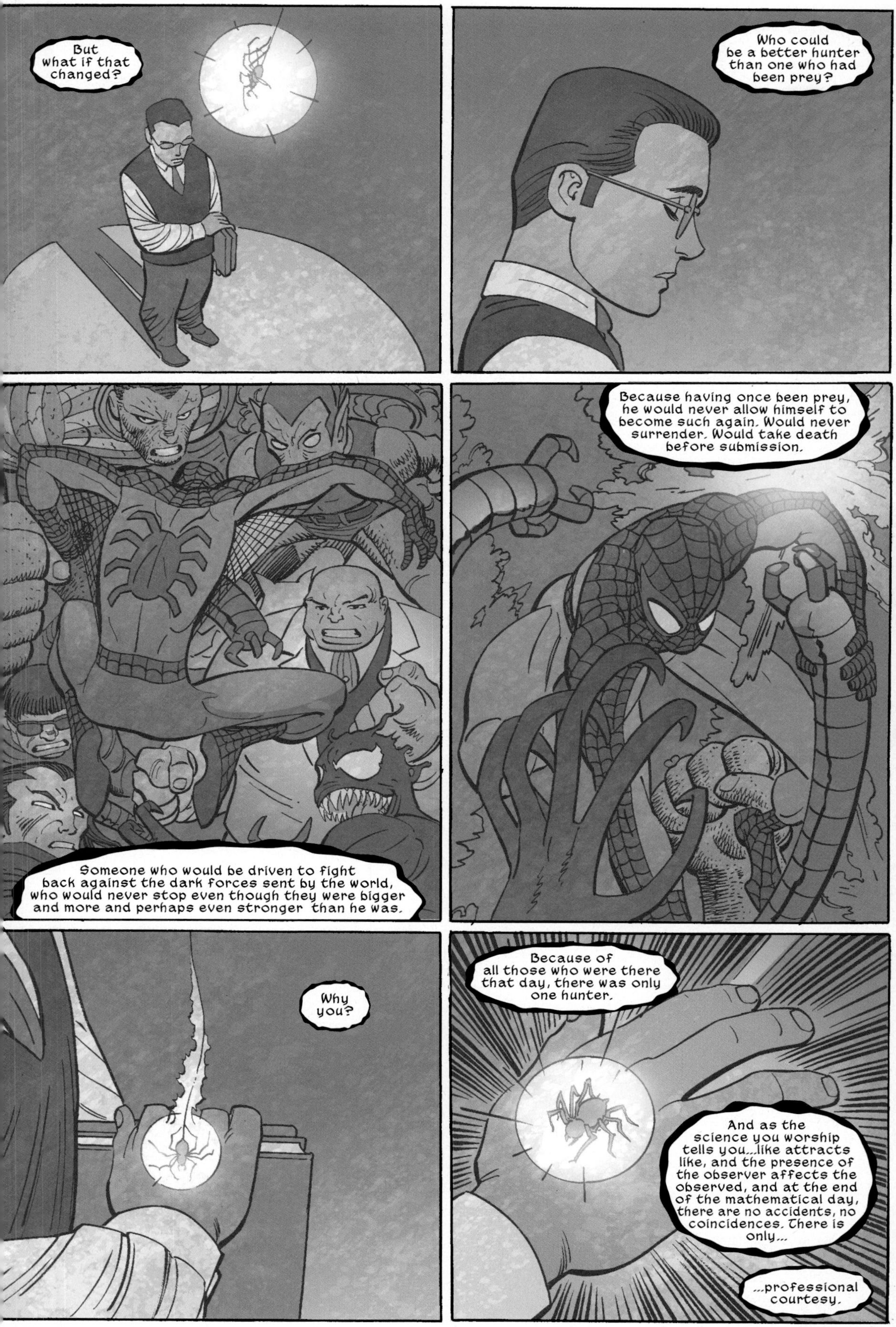
But what if that changed?
Who could be a better hunter than one who had been prey?
Someone who would be driven to fight back against the dark forces sent by the world, who would never stop even though they were bigger and more and perhaps even stronger than he was.
Because having once been prey, he would never allow himself to become such again. Would never surrender. Would take death before submission.
Why you?
Because of all those who were there that day, there was only one hunter.
And as the science you worship tells you...like attracts like, and the presence of the observer affects the observed, and at the end of the mathematical day, there are no accidents, no coincidences. There is only...
...professional courtesy.

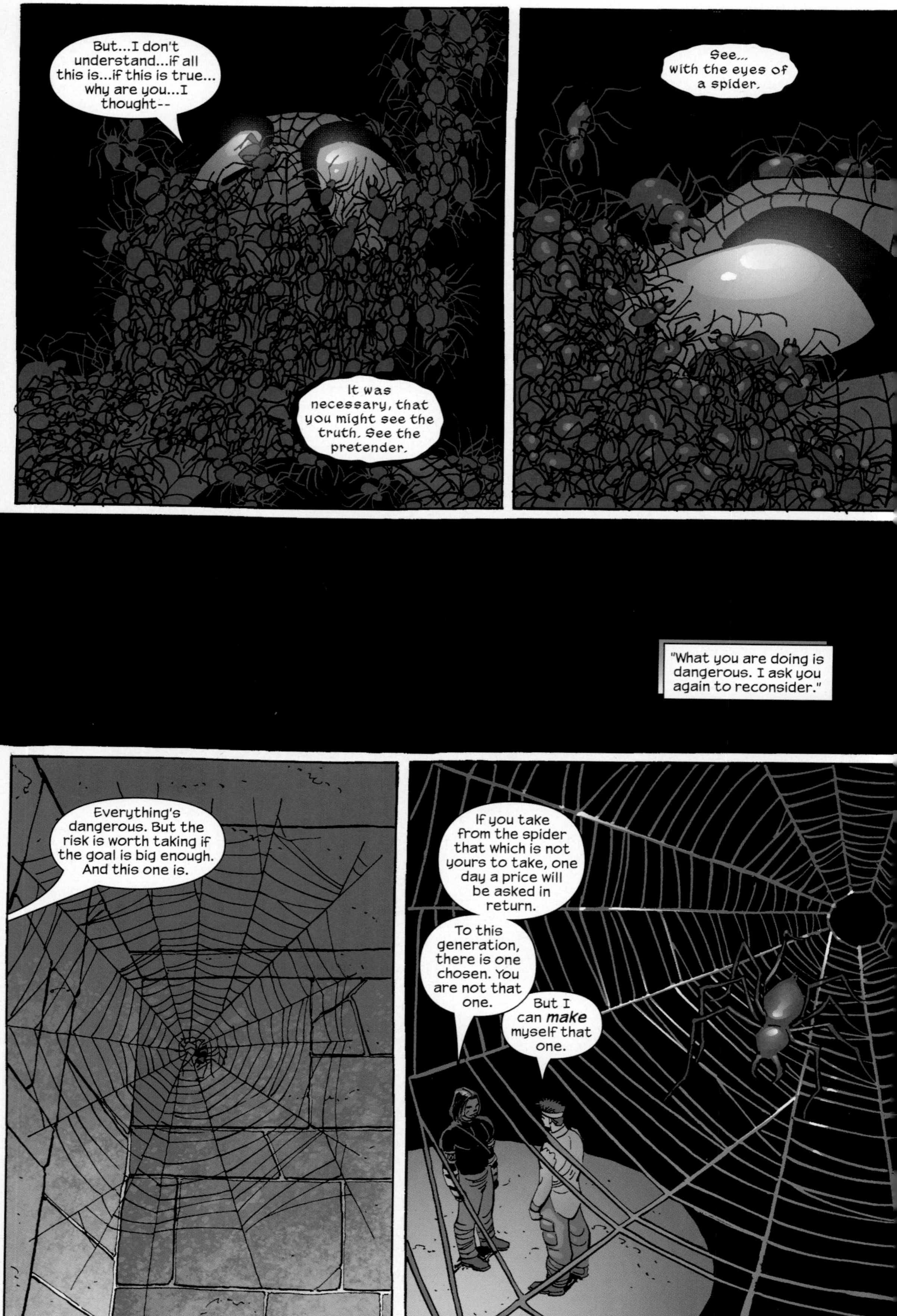
But...I don't understand...if all this is...if this is true... why are you...I thought--
It was necessary, that you might see the truth. See the pretender.
See... with the eyes of a spider.
"What you are doing is dangerous. I ask you again to reconsider."
Everything's dangerous. But the risk is worth taking if the goal is big enough. And this one is.
If you take from the spider that which is not yours to take, one day a price will be asked in return.
To this generation, there is one chosen. You are not that one.
But I can *make* myself that one.

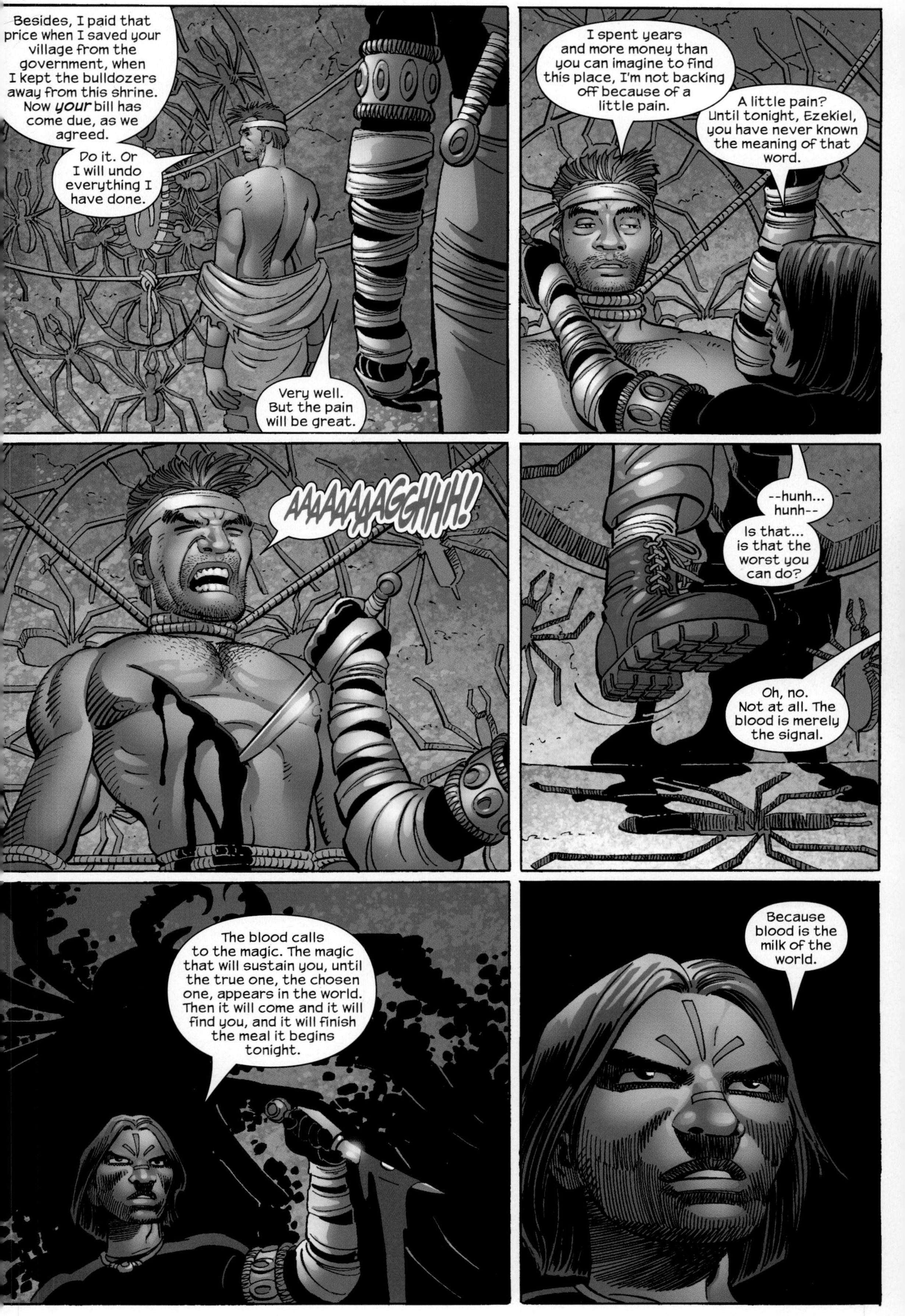

Besides, I paid that price when I saved your village from the government, when I kept the bulldozers away from this shrine. Now *your* bill has come due, as we agreed.
Do it. Or I will undo everything I have done.
Very well. But the pain will be great.
I spent years and more money than you can imagine to find this place, I'm not backing off because of a little pain.
A little pain? Until tonight, Ezekiel, you have never known the meaning of that word.
AAAAAAAAGGHHH!
--hunh... hunh--
Is that... is that the worst you can do?
Oh, no. Not at all. The blood is merely the signal.
The blood calls to the magic. The magic that will sustain you, until the true one, the chosen one, appears in the world. Then it will come and it will find you, and it will finish the meal it begins tonight.
Because blood is the milk of the world.

AAAAAIIIIEEEE!

"When that time comes, Ezekiel, your only hope is to divert the powers you have bargained with, to bring them to attack the chosen, and in so doing eliminate your competition."

"Or, failing that, to convince him to fight them on your behalf...and bring him here, to the beginning, to this place...that his blood may take the place of your own when the madness, and the death, follows..."

Unhhhh... unhhhhhHHHHHHH--

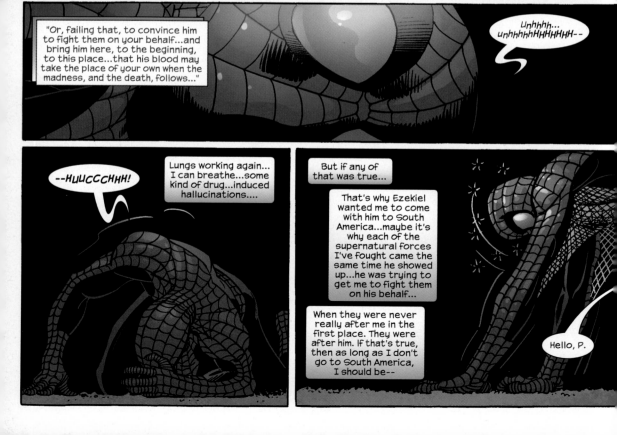

--HUUCCCHHH!

Lungs working again... I can breathe...some kind of drug...induced hallucinations....

But if any of that was true...

That's why Ezekiel wanted me to come with him to South America...maybe it's why each of the supernatural forces I've fought came the same time he showed up...he was trying to get me to fight them on his behalf...

When they were never really after me in the first place. They were after him. If that's true, then as long as I don't go to South America, I should be--

Hello, P.

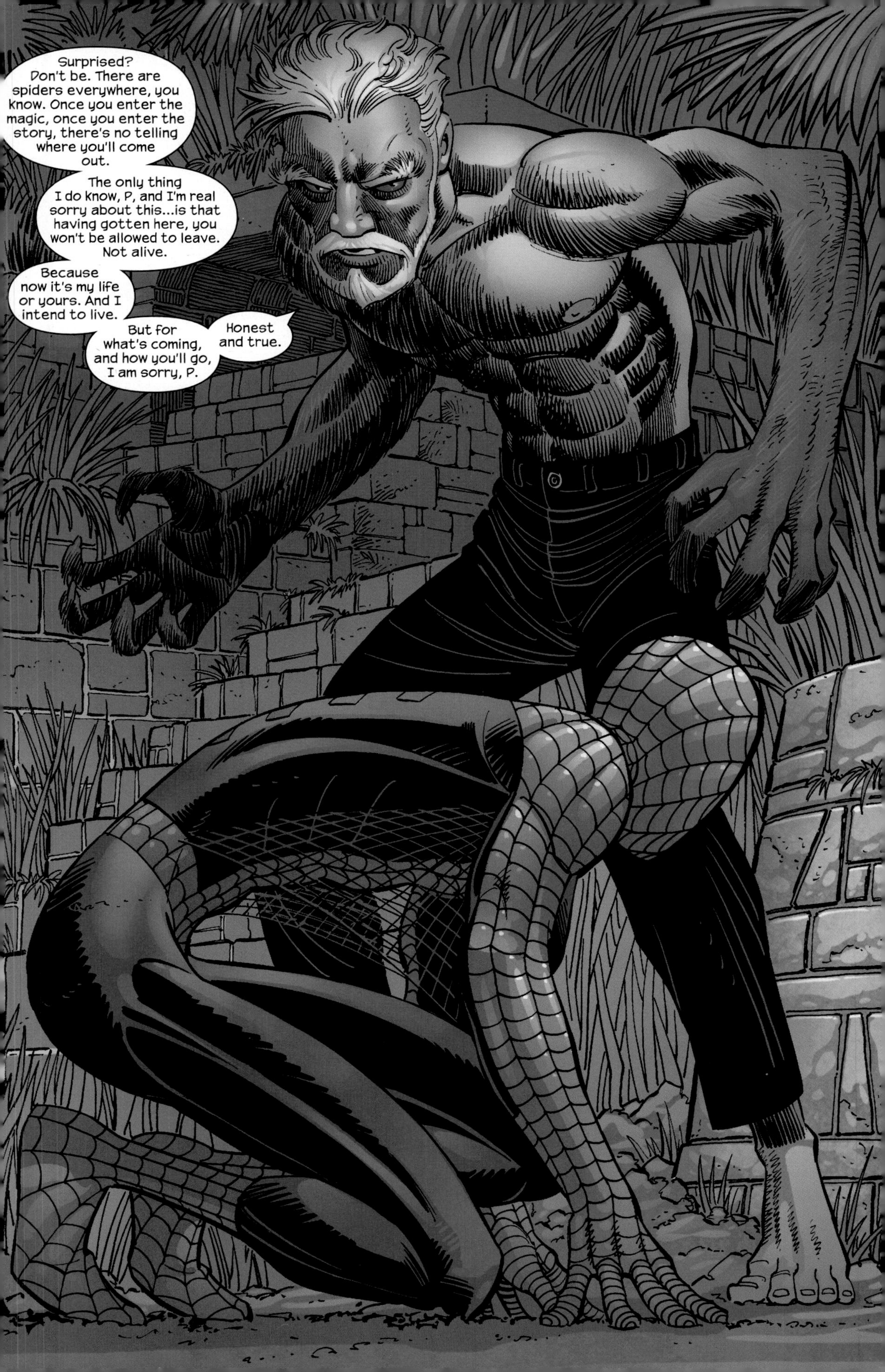
Surprised? Don't be. There are spiders everywhere, you know. Once you enter the magic, once you enter the story, there's no telling where you'll come out.
The only thing I do know, P, and I'm real sorry about this...is that having gotten here, you won't be allowed to leave. Not alive.
Because now it's my life or yours. And I intend to live.
But for what's coming, and how you'll go, I am sorry, P.
Honest and true.

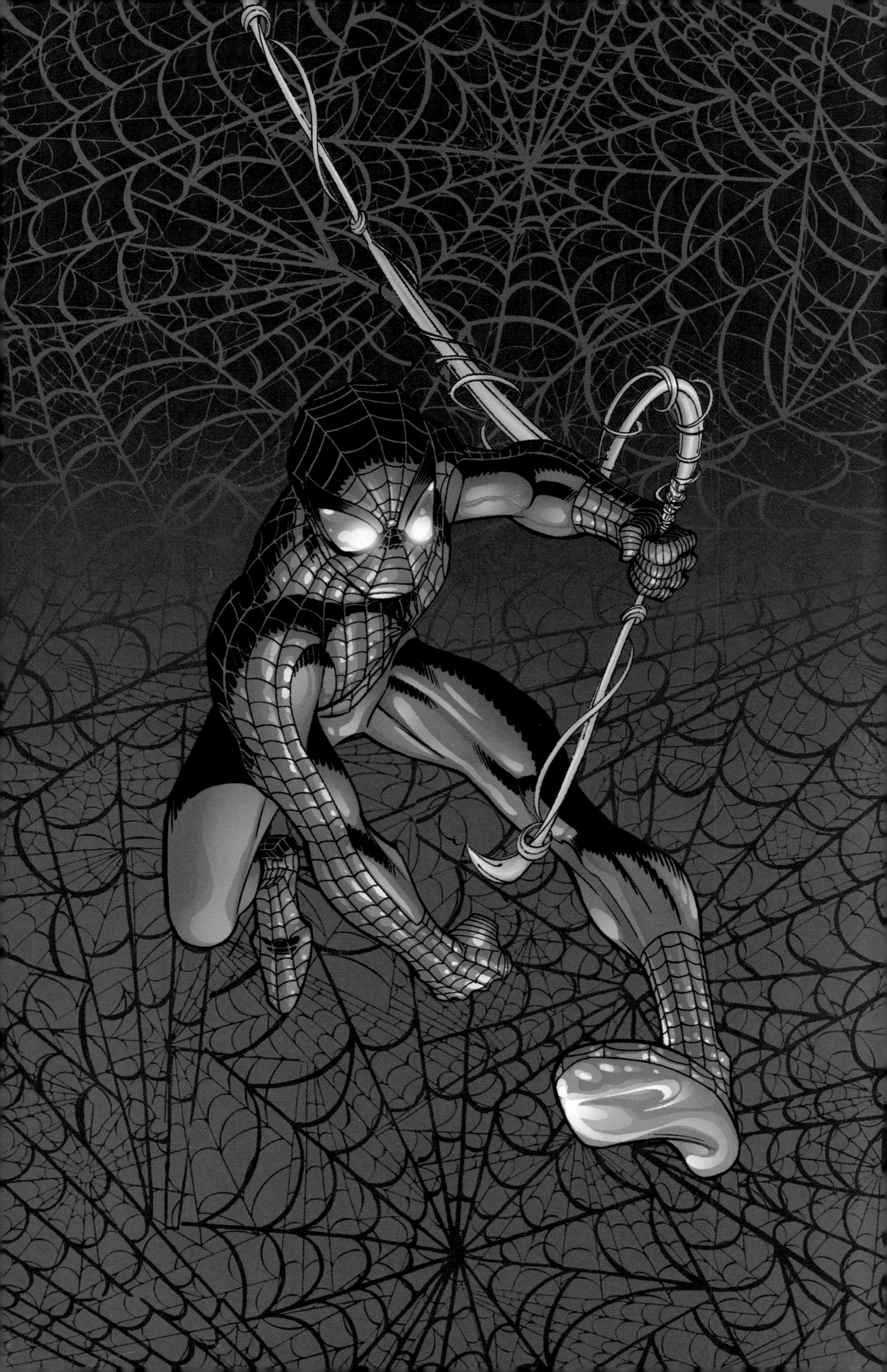

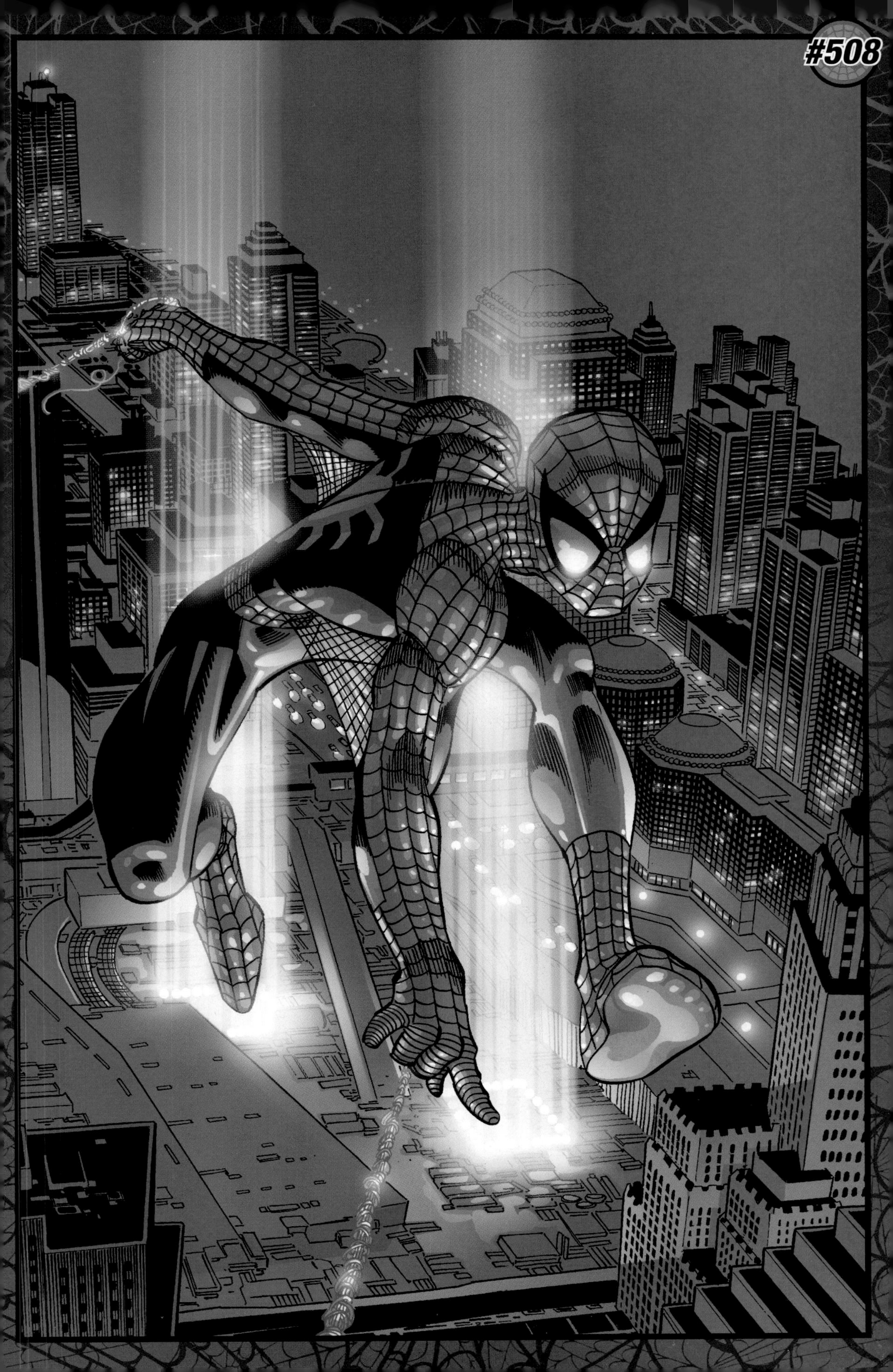
#508

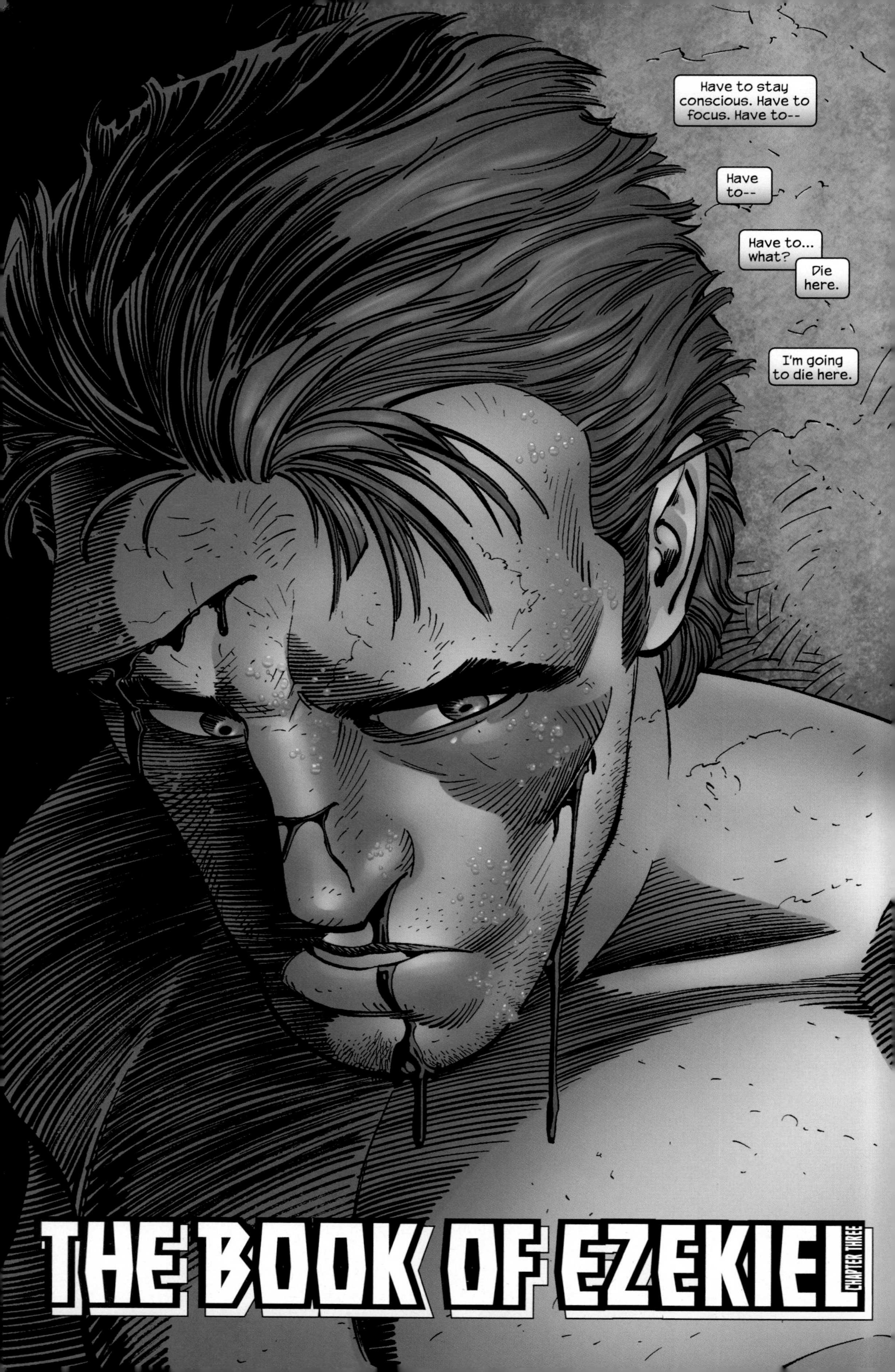

Have to stay conscious. Have to focus. Have to--
Have to--
Have to... what?
Die here.
I'm going to die here.
THE BOOK OF EZEKIEL
CHAPTER THREE

How did I-- Yes--

Ezekiel.

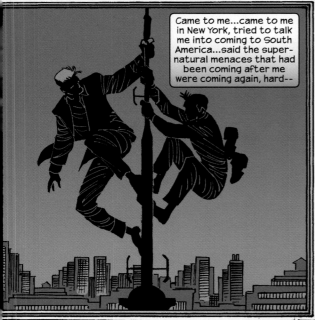

Came to me...came to me in New York, tried to talk me into coming to South America...said the supernatural menaces that had been coming after me were coming again, hard--

--but he was lying. They weren't coming after me. They were coming after him. He used--

--used me.

And then--

--then darkness, and the voice--

--the voice, old, so old--

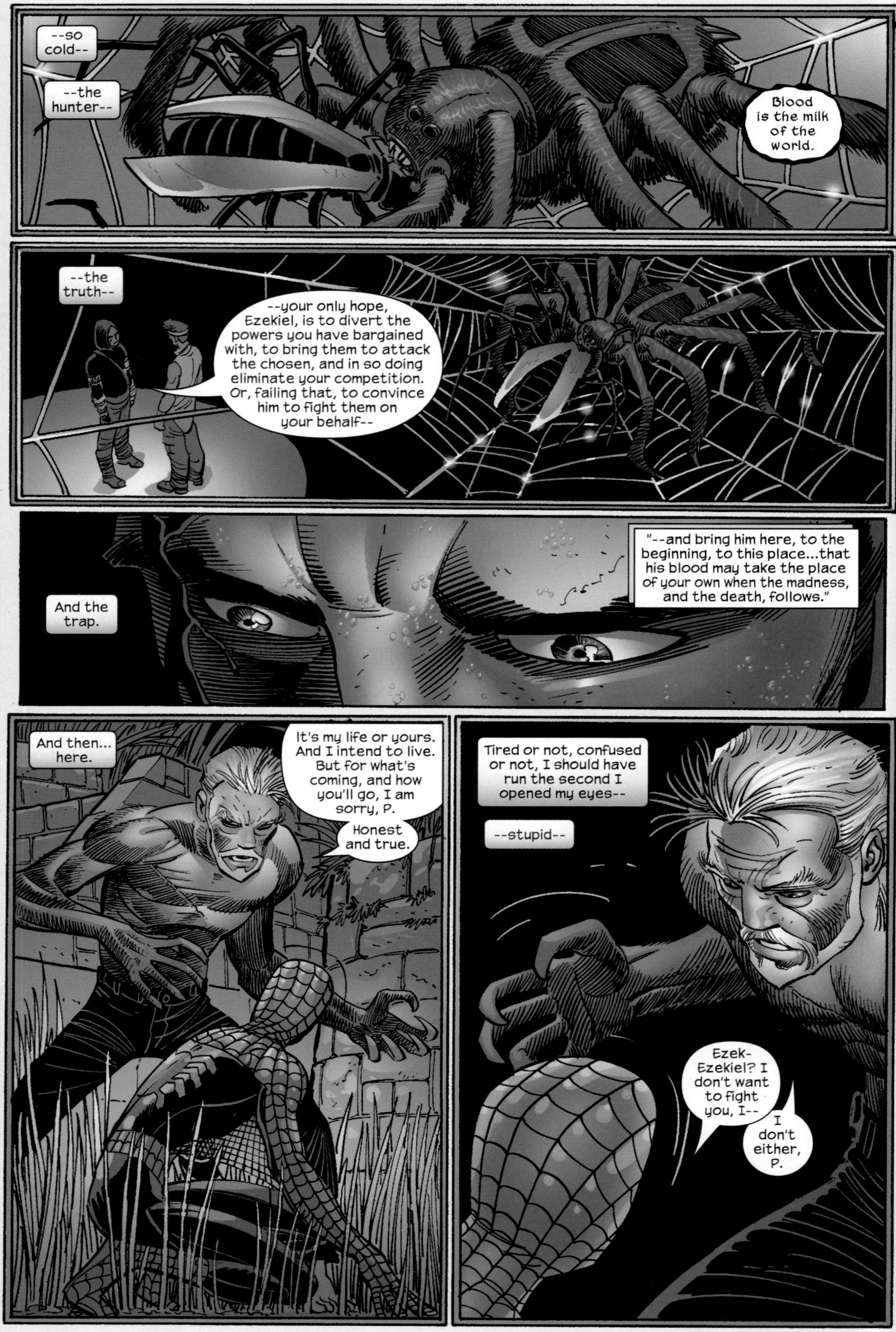

--so cold--
--the hunter--
Blood is the milk of the world.
--the truth--
--your only hope, Ezekiel, is to divert the powers you have bargained with, to bring them to attack the chosen, and in so doing eliminate your competition. Or, failing that, to convince him to fight them on your behalf--
And the trap.
"--and bring him here, to the beginning, to this place...that his blood may take the place of your own when the madness, and the death, follows."
And then... here.
It's my life or yours. And I intend to live. But for what's coming, and how you'll go, I am sorry, P.
Honest and true.
Tired or not, confused or not, I should have run the second I opened my eyes--
--stupid--
Ezek- Ezekiel? I don't want to fight you, I--
I don't either, P.

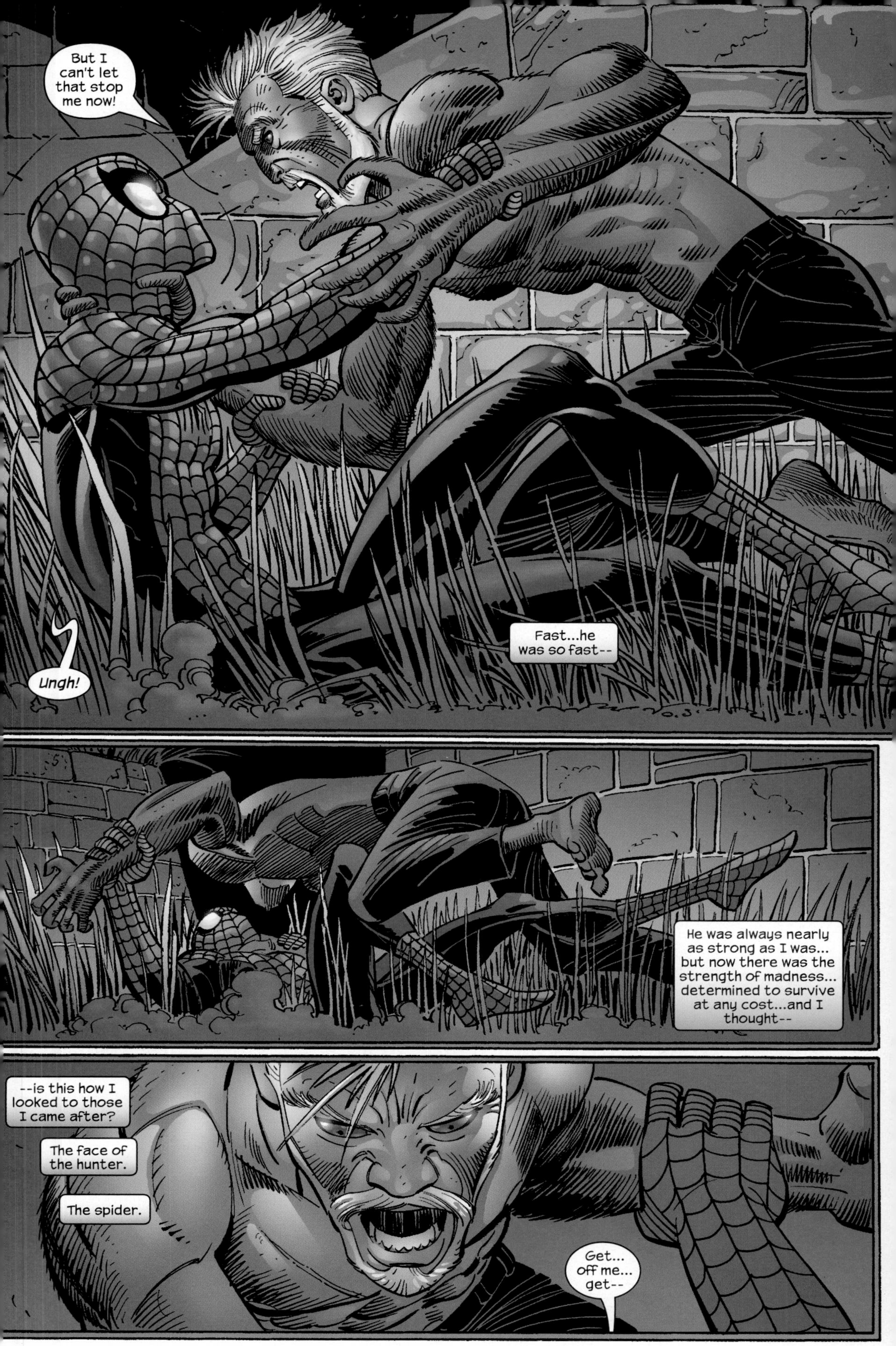
But I can't let that stop me now!
Ungh!
Fast...he was so fast--
He was always nearly as strong as I was... but now there was the strength of madness... determined to survive at any cost...and I thought--
--is this how I looked to those I came after?
The face of the hunter.
The spider.
Get... off me... get--

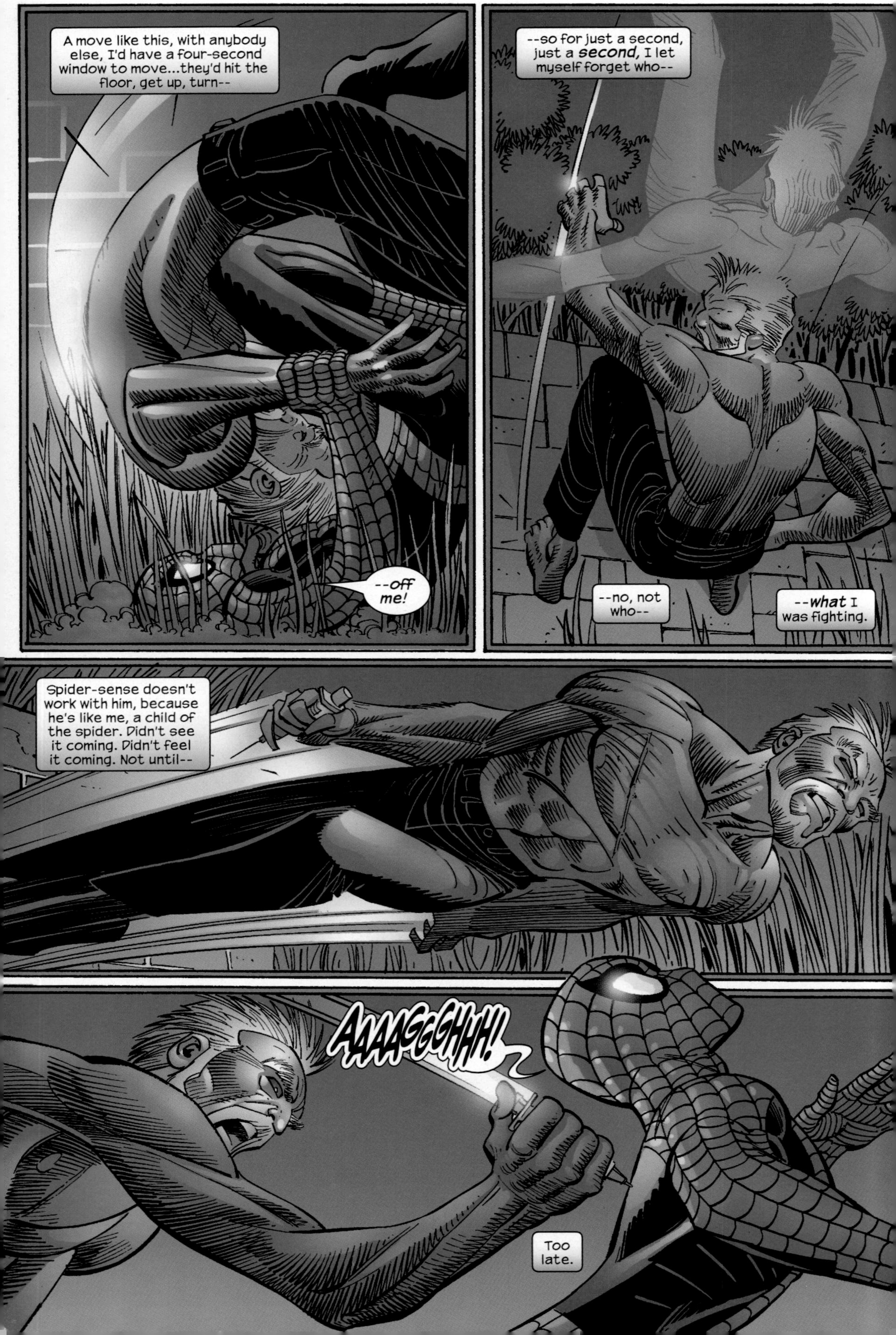
A move like this, with anybody else, I'd have a four-second window to move...they'd hit the floor, get up, turn--
--off me!
--so for just a second, just a *second,* I let myself forget who--
--no, not who--
--*what* I was fighting.
Spider-sense doesn't work with him, because he's like me, a child of the spider. Didn't see it coming. Didn't feel it coming. Not until--
AAAAGGHHH!
Too late.

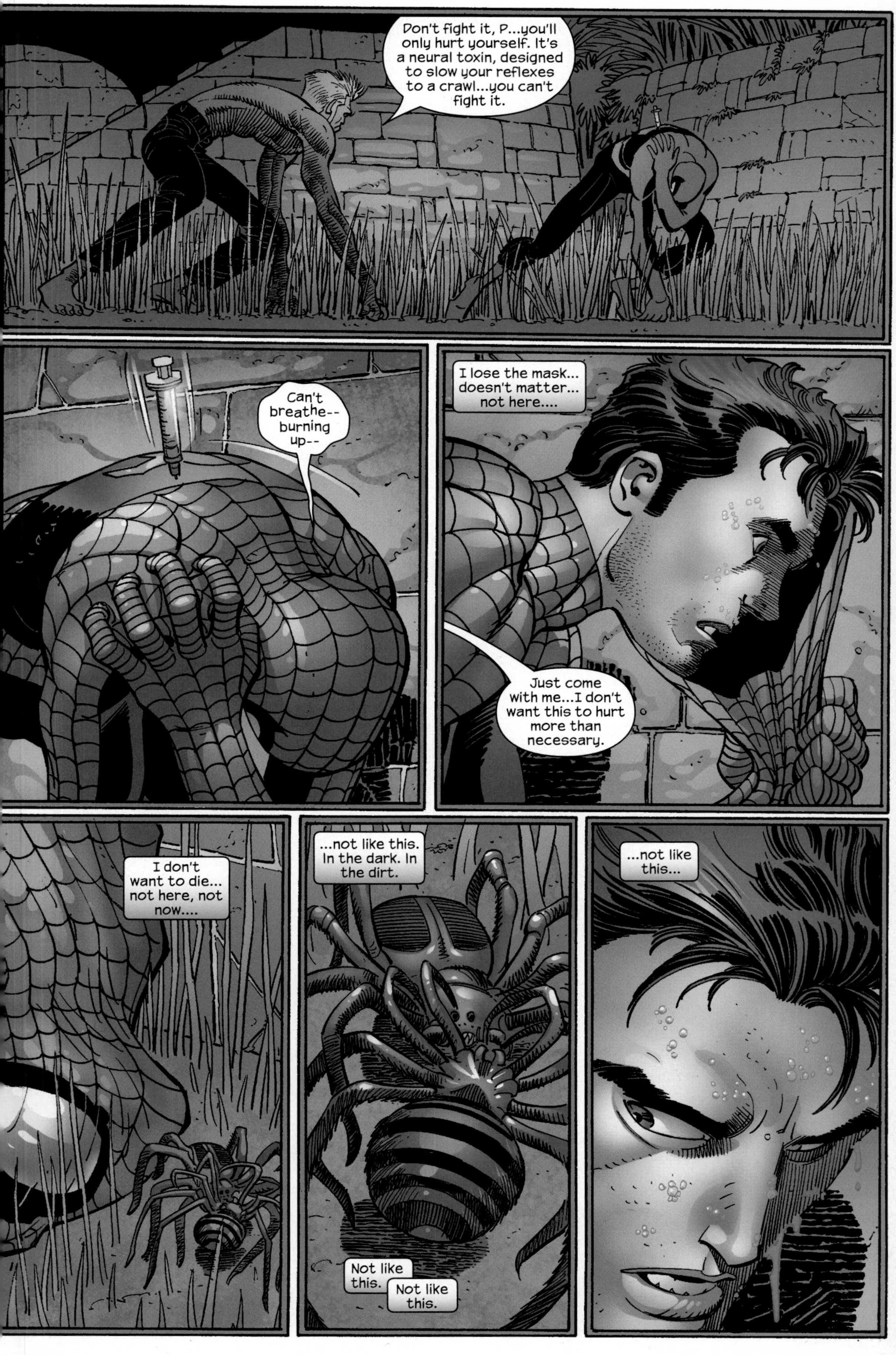
Don't fight it, P...you'll only hurt yourself. It's a neural toxin, designed to slow your reflexes to a crawl...you can't fight it.
Can't breathe-- burning up--
I lose the mask... doesn't matter... not here....
Just come with me...I don't want this to hurt more than necessary.
I don't want to die... not here, not now....
...not like this. In the dark. In the dirt.
Not like this.
Not like this.
...not like this...

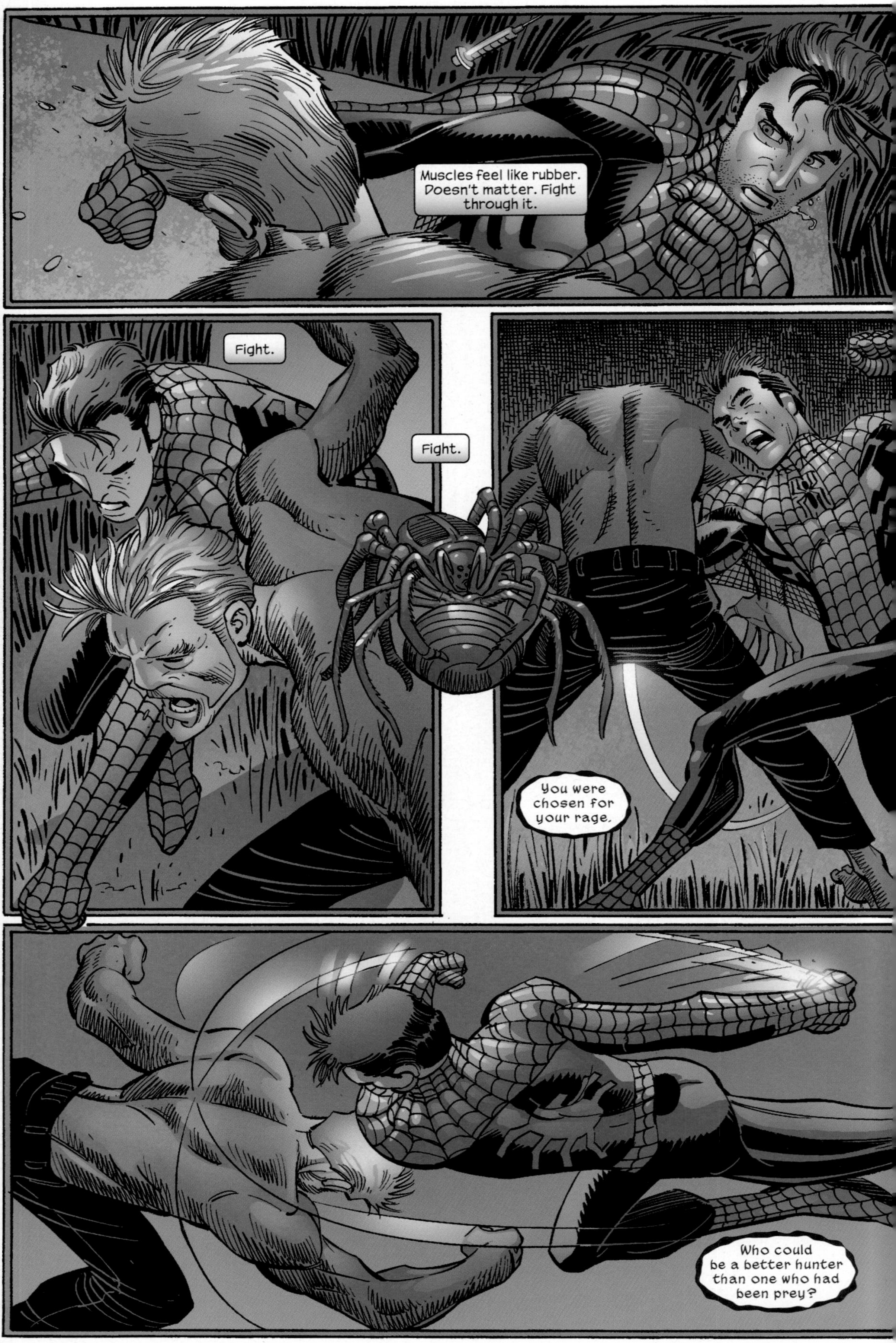
Muscles feel like rubber. Doesn't matter. Fight through it.
Fight.
Fight.
You were chosen for your rage.
Who could be a better hunter than one who had been prey?

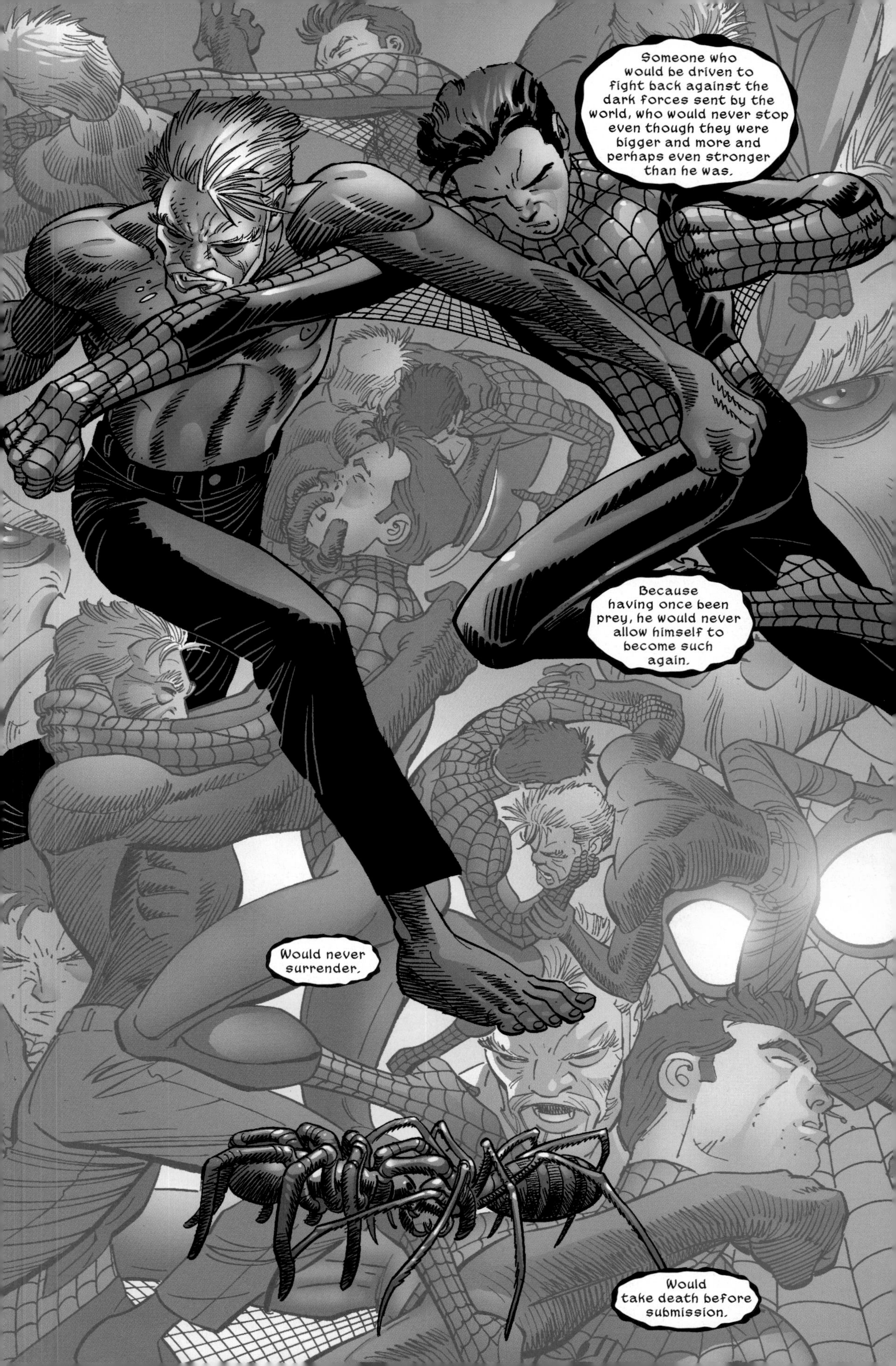
Someone who would be driven to fight back against the dark forces sent by the world, who would never stop even though they were bigger and more and perhaps even stronger than he was.
Because having once been prey, he would never allow himself to become such again.
Would never surrender.
Would take death before submission.

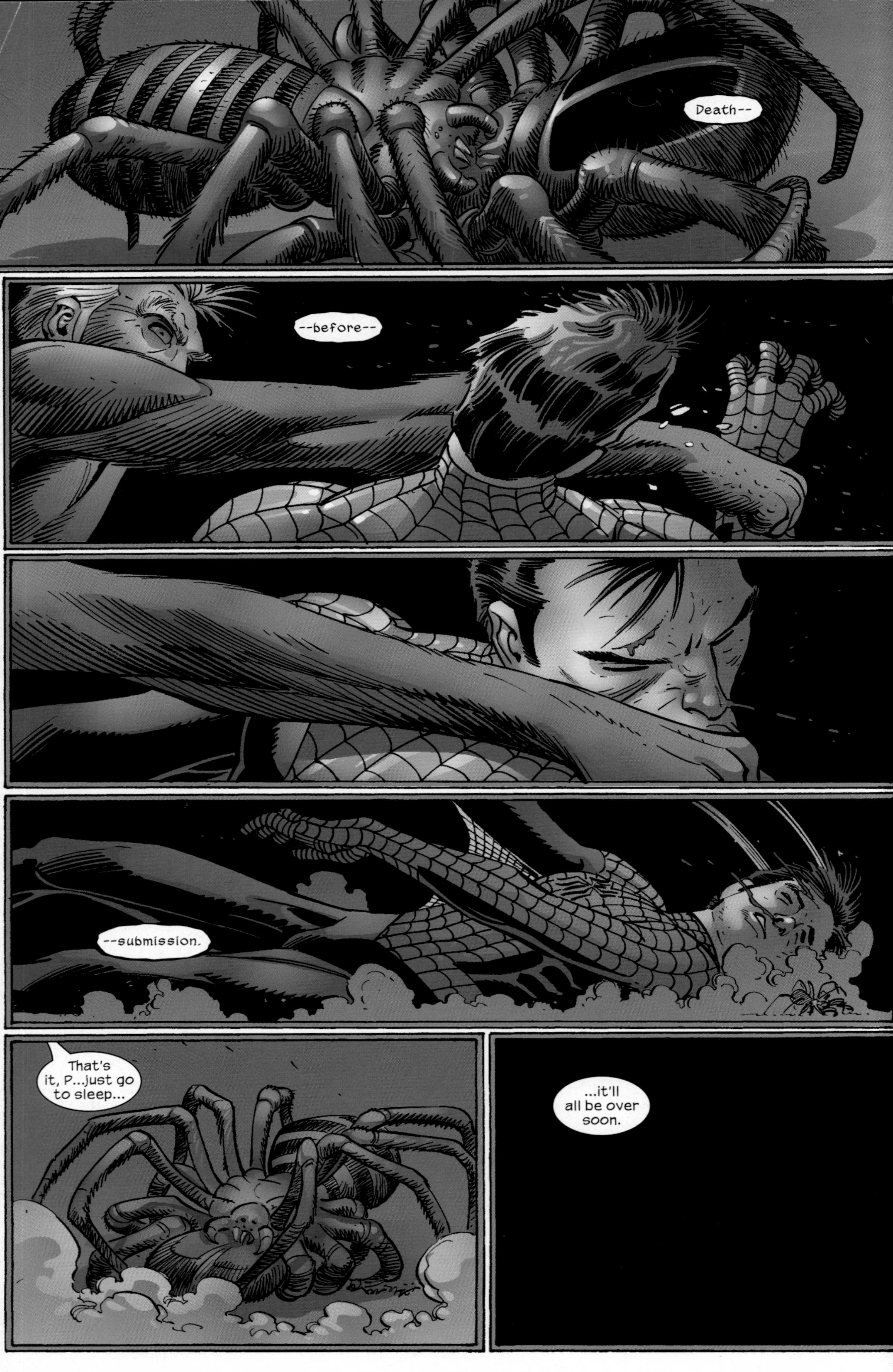
Death--
--before--
--submission.
That's it, P...just go to sleep...
...it'll all be over soon.

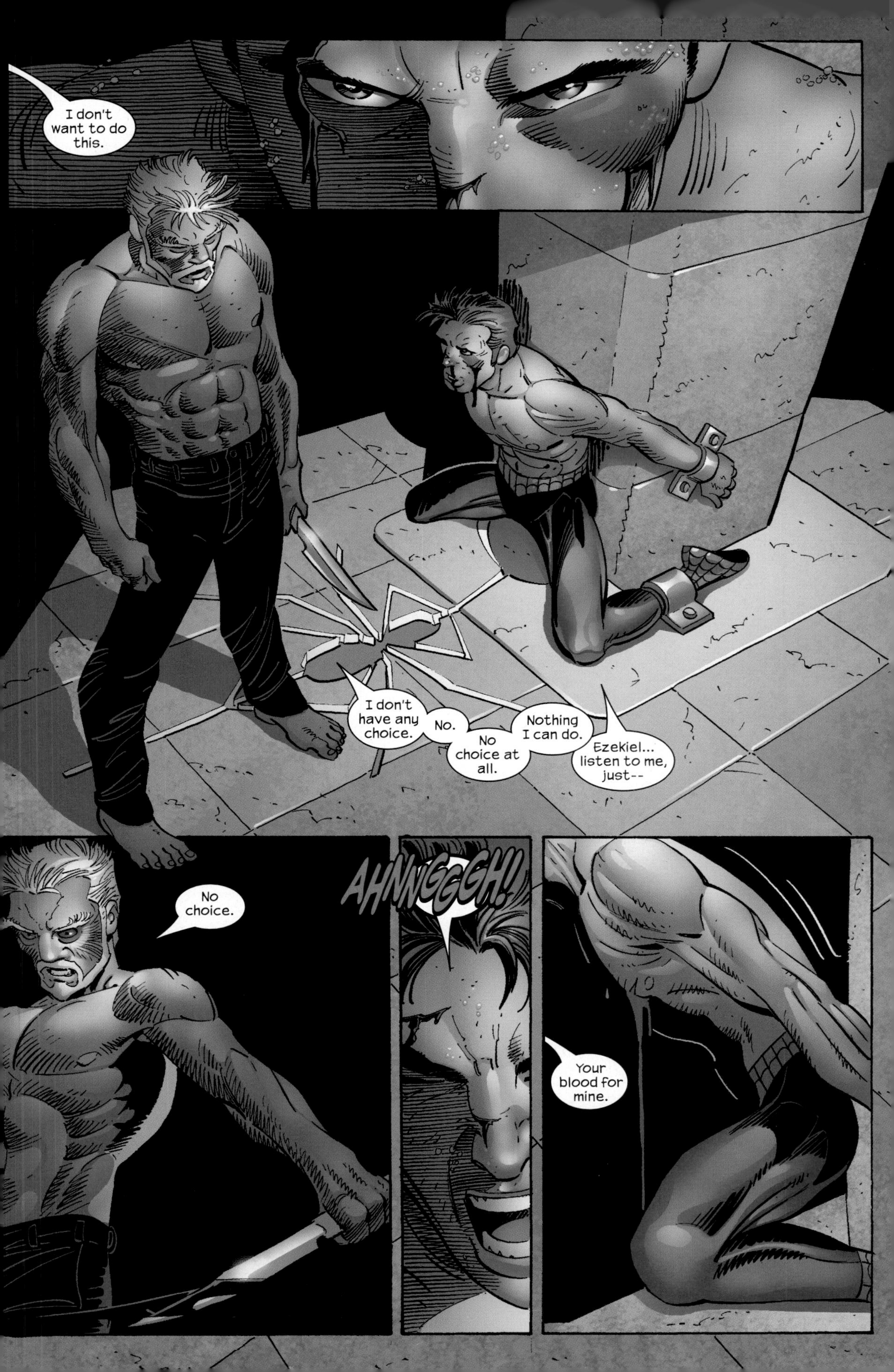
I don't want to do this.
I don't have any choice.
No.
No choice at all.
Nothing I can do.
Ezekiel... listen to me, just--
No choice.
AHNNGGGH!
Your blood for mine.

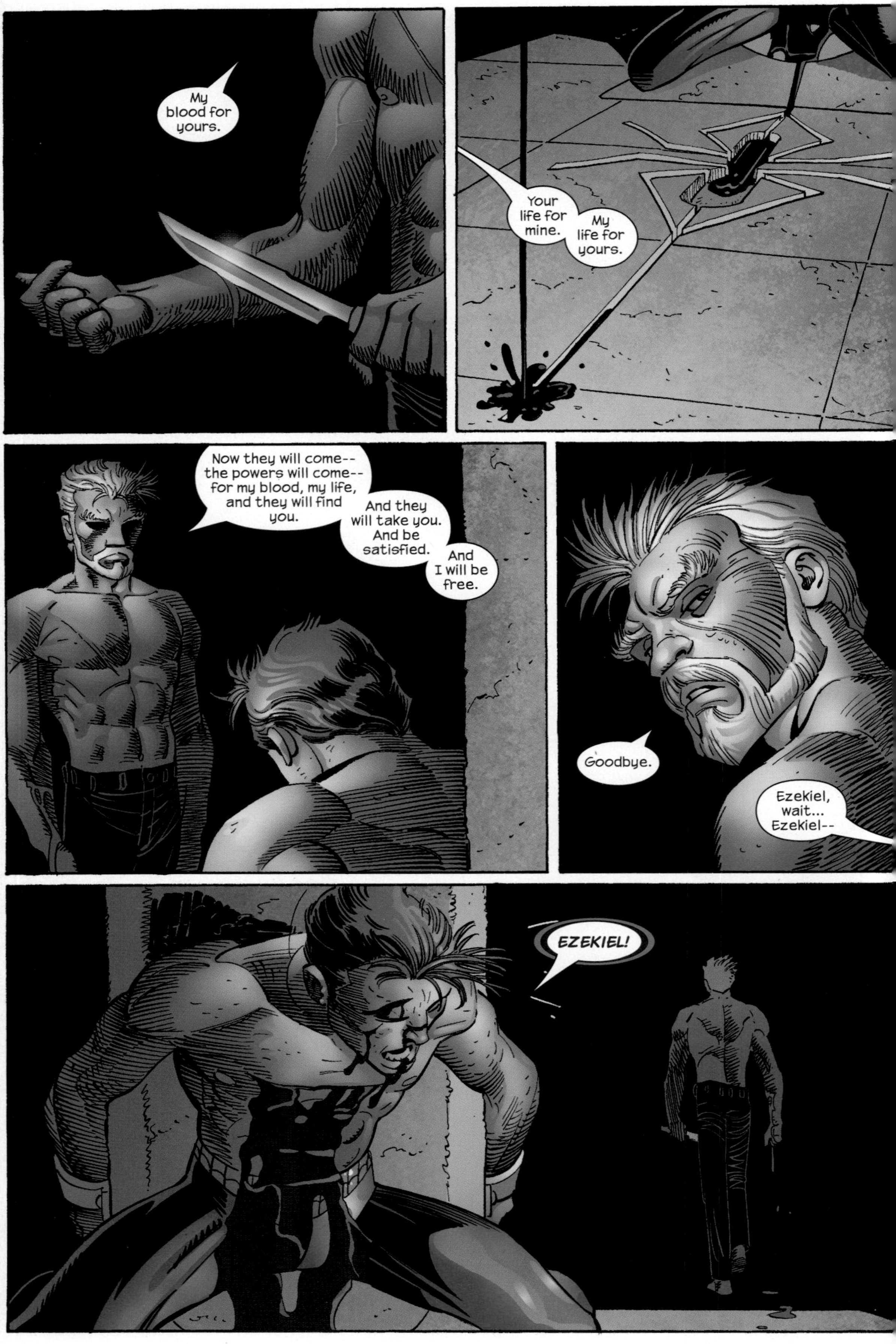
My blood for yours.
Your life for mine.
My life for yours.
Now they will come-- the powers will come-- for my blood, my life, and they will find you.
And they will take you. And be satisfied.
And I will be free.
Goodbye.
Ezekiel, wait... Ezekiel--
EZEKIEL!

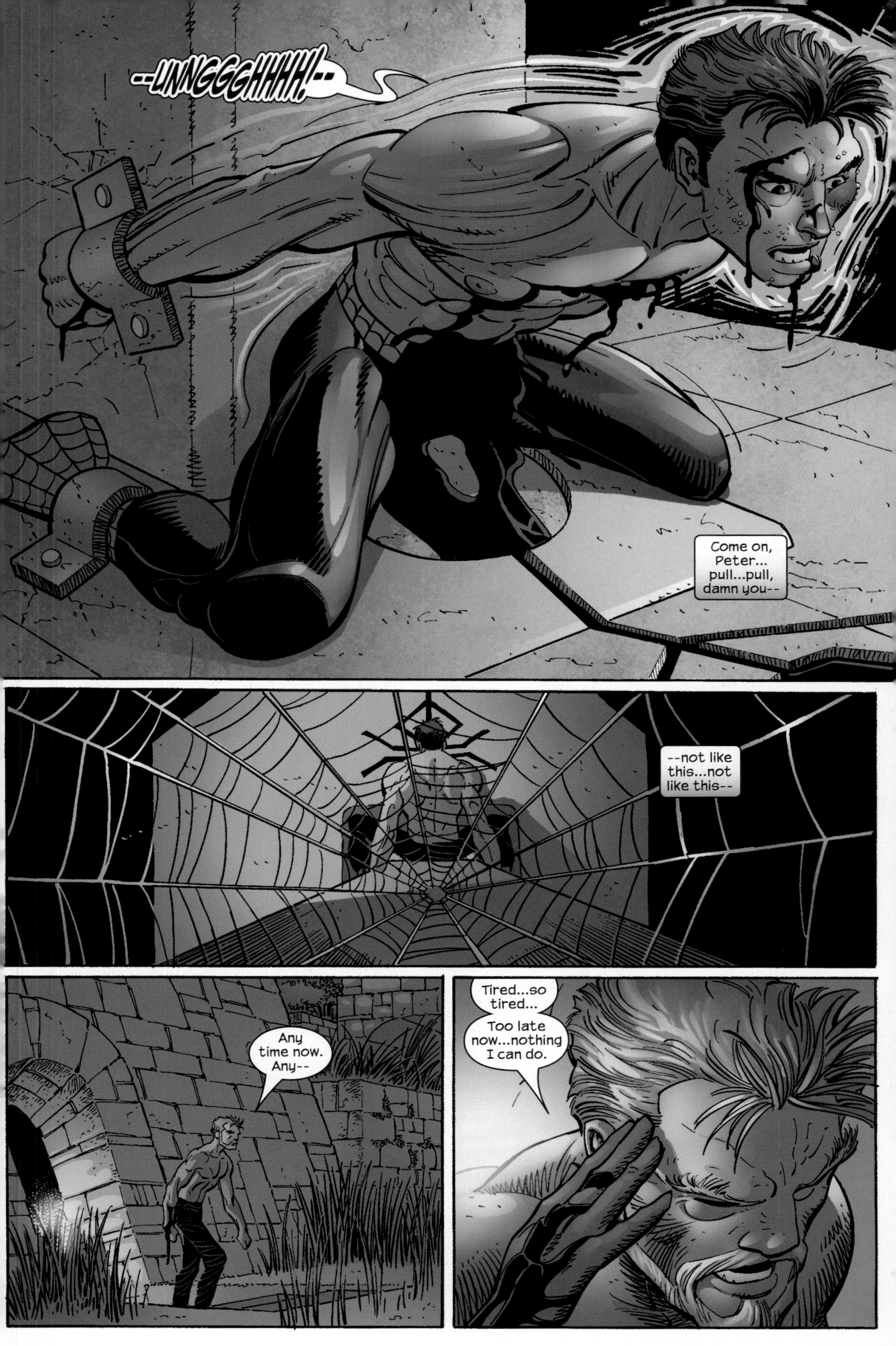
--UNNGGGHHHH!--
Come on, Peter... pull...pull, damn you--
--not like this...not like this--
Any time now. Any--
Tired...so tired...
Too late now...nothing I can do.

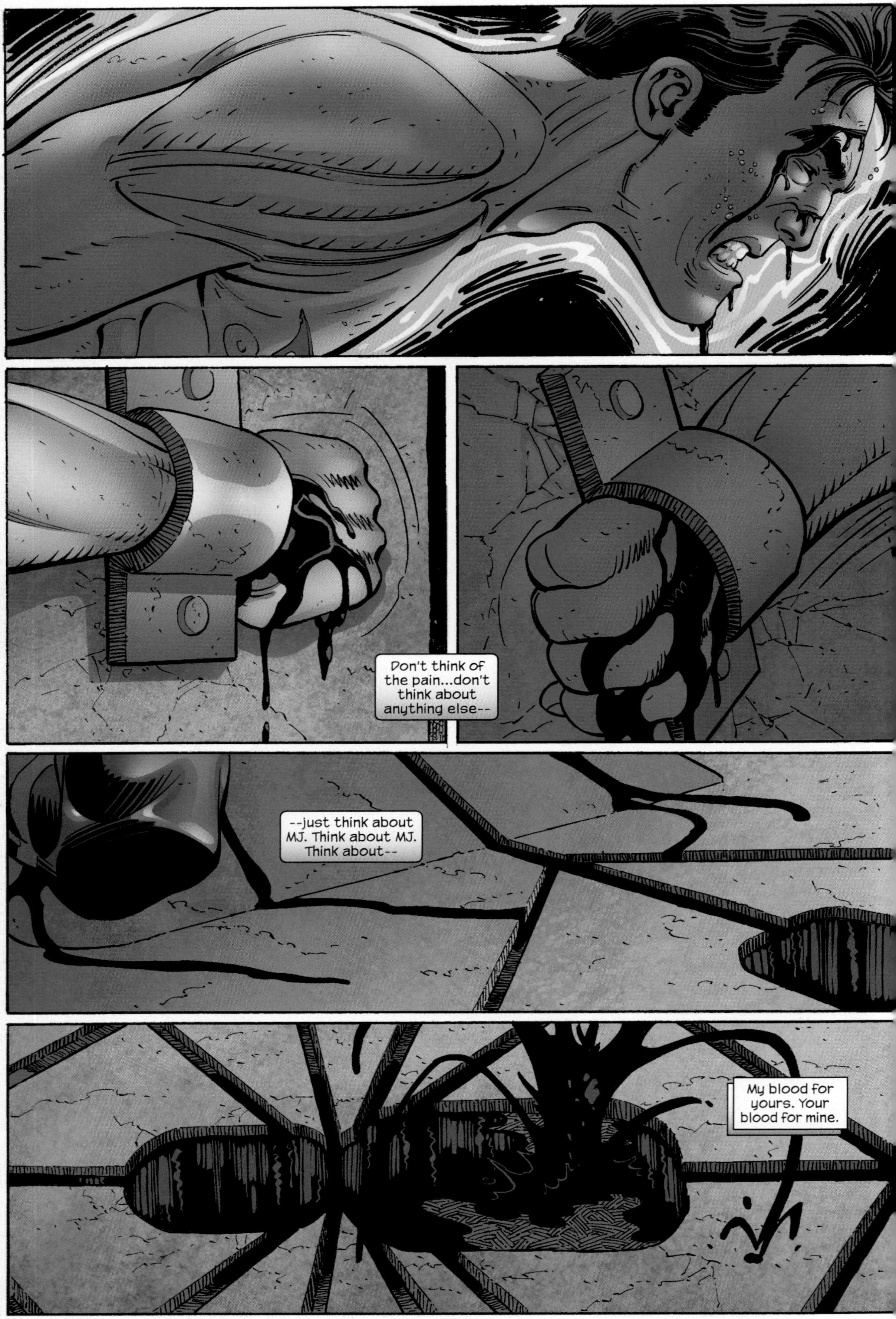
Don't think of the pain...don't think about anything else--
--just think about MJ. Think about MJ. Think about--
My blood for yours. Your blood for mine.

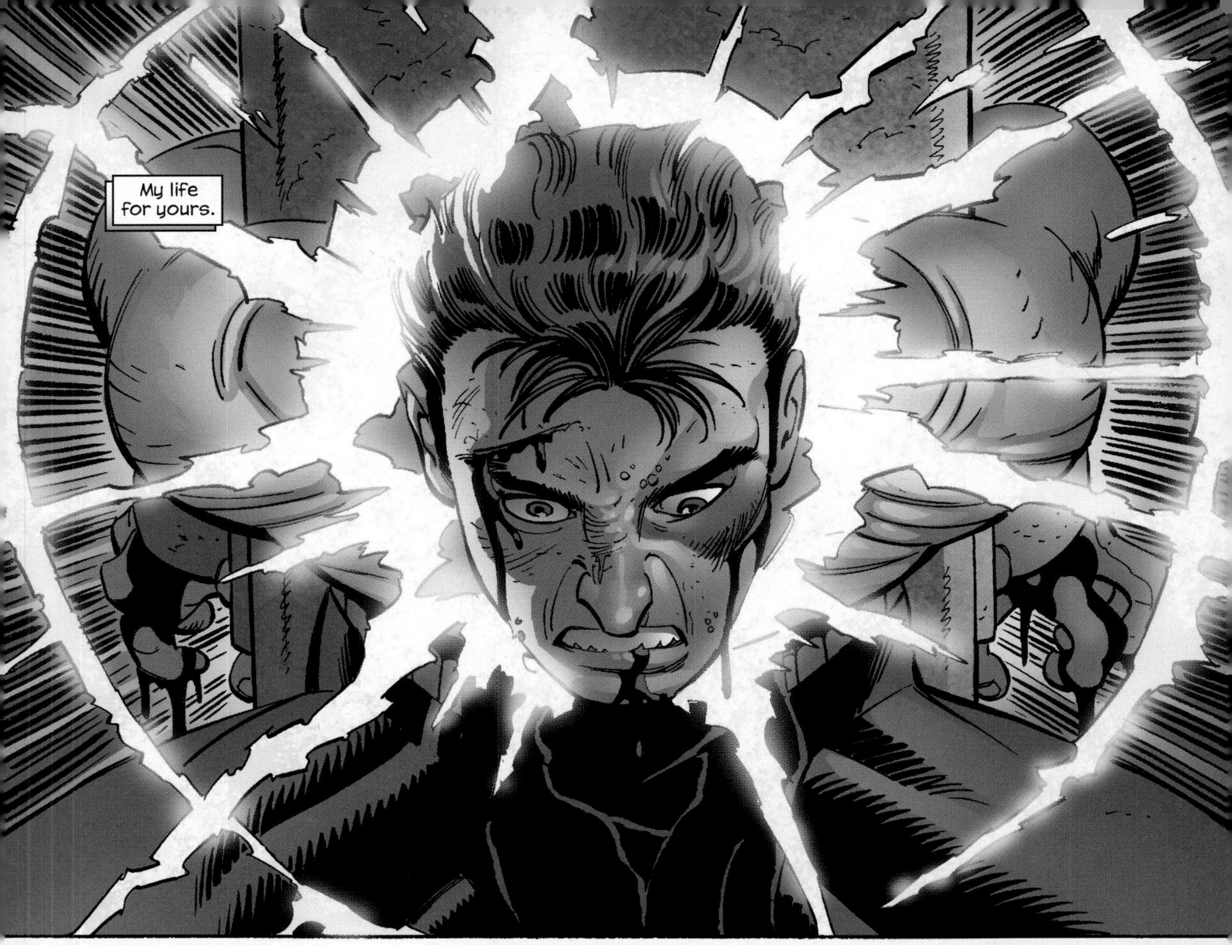
My life for yours.

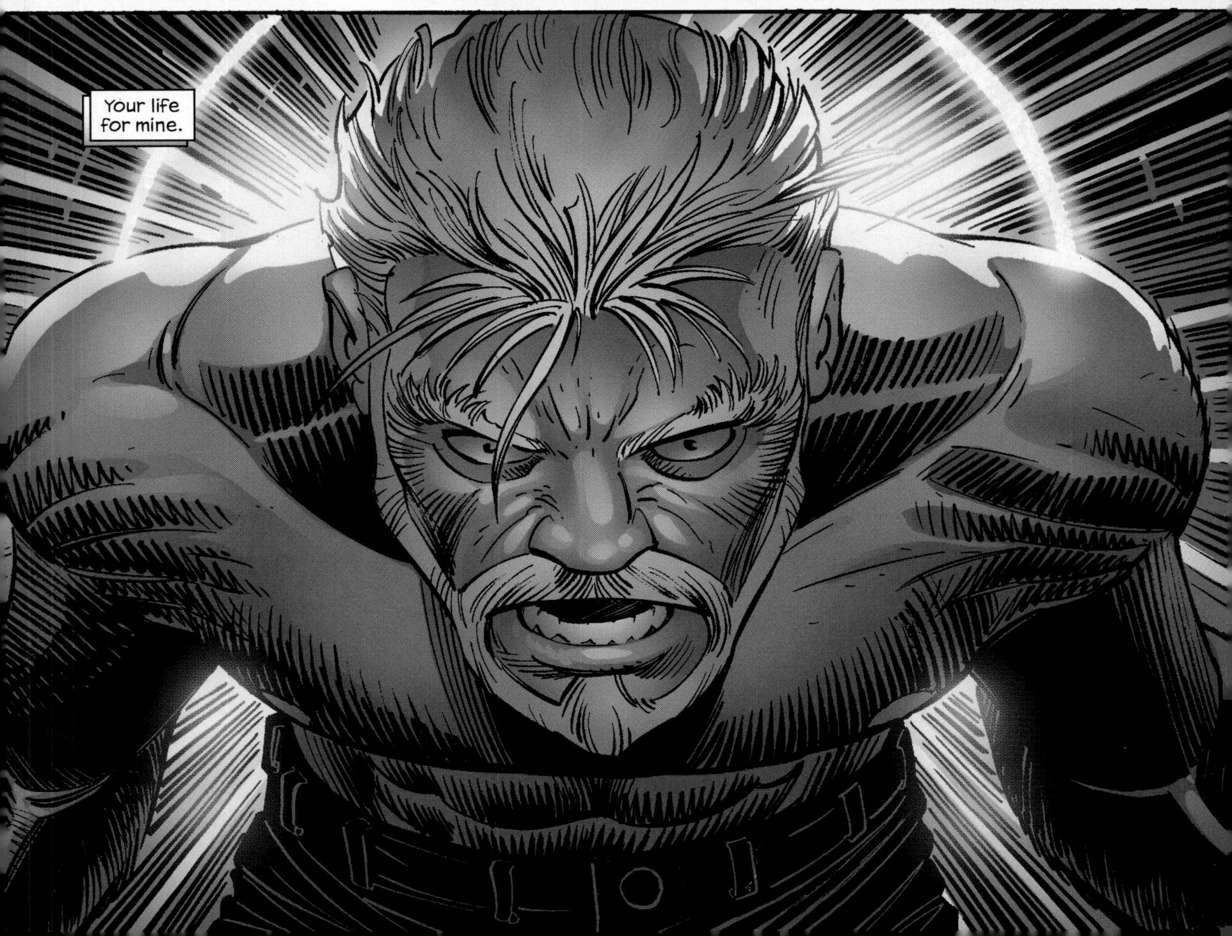
Your life for mine.

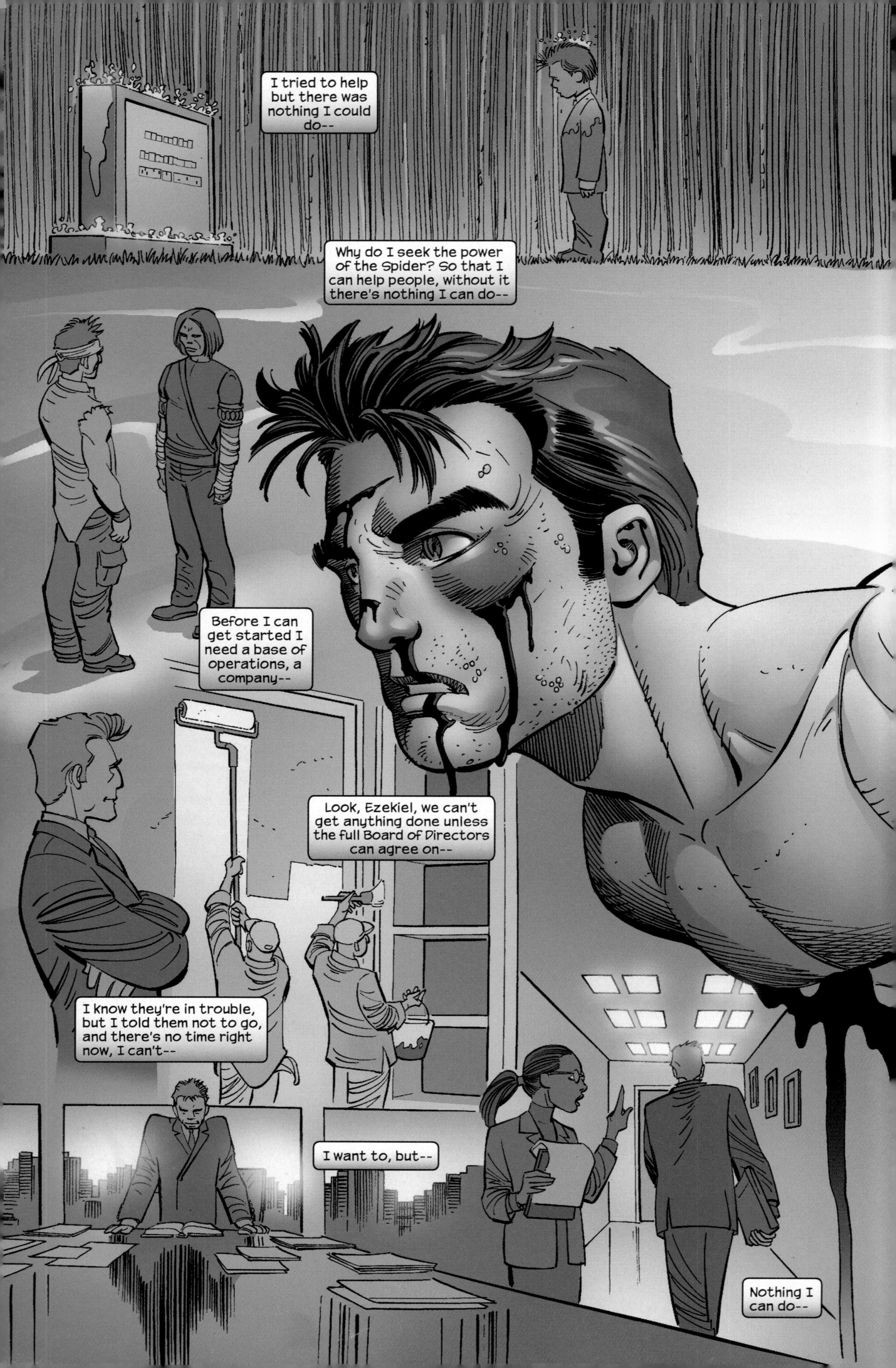
I tried to help but there was nothing I could do--
Why do I seek the power of the Spider? So that I can help people, without it there's nothing I can do--
Before I can get started I need a base of operations, a company--
Look, Ezekiel, we can't get anything done unless the full Board of Directors can agree on--
I know they're in trouble, but I told them not to go, and there's no time right now, I can't--
I want to, but--
Nothing I can do--

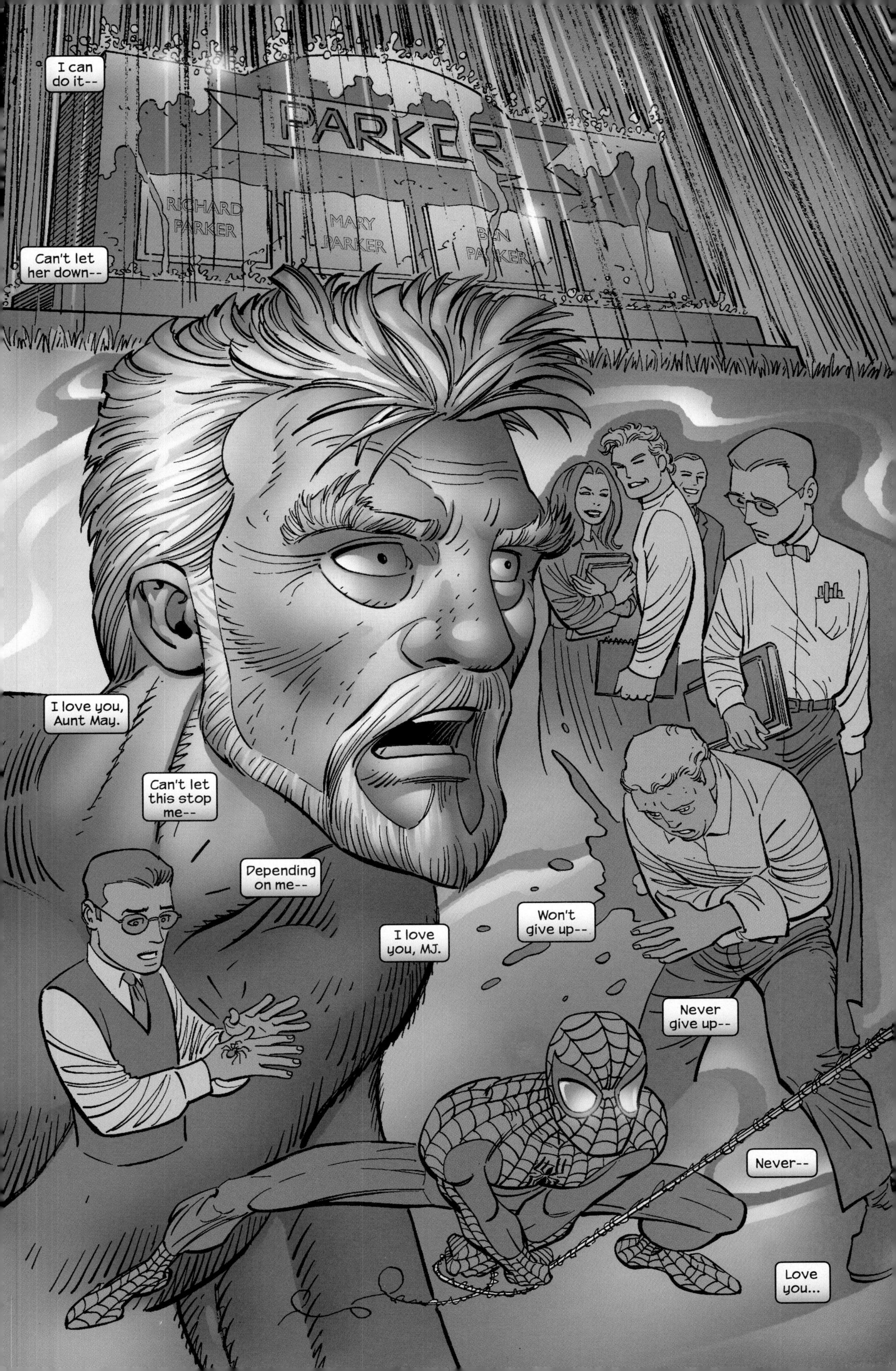
I can do it--
PARKER
RICHARD PARKER
MARY PARKER
BEN PARKER
Can't let her down--
I love you, Aunt May.
Can't let this stop me--
Depending on me--
I love you, MJ.
Won't give up--
Never give up--
Never--
Love you...

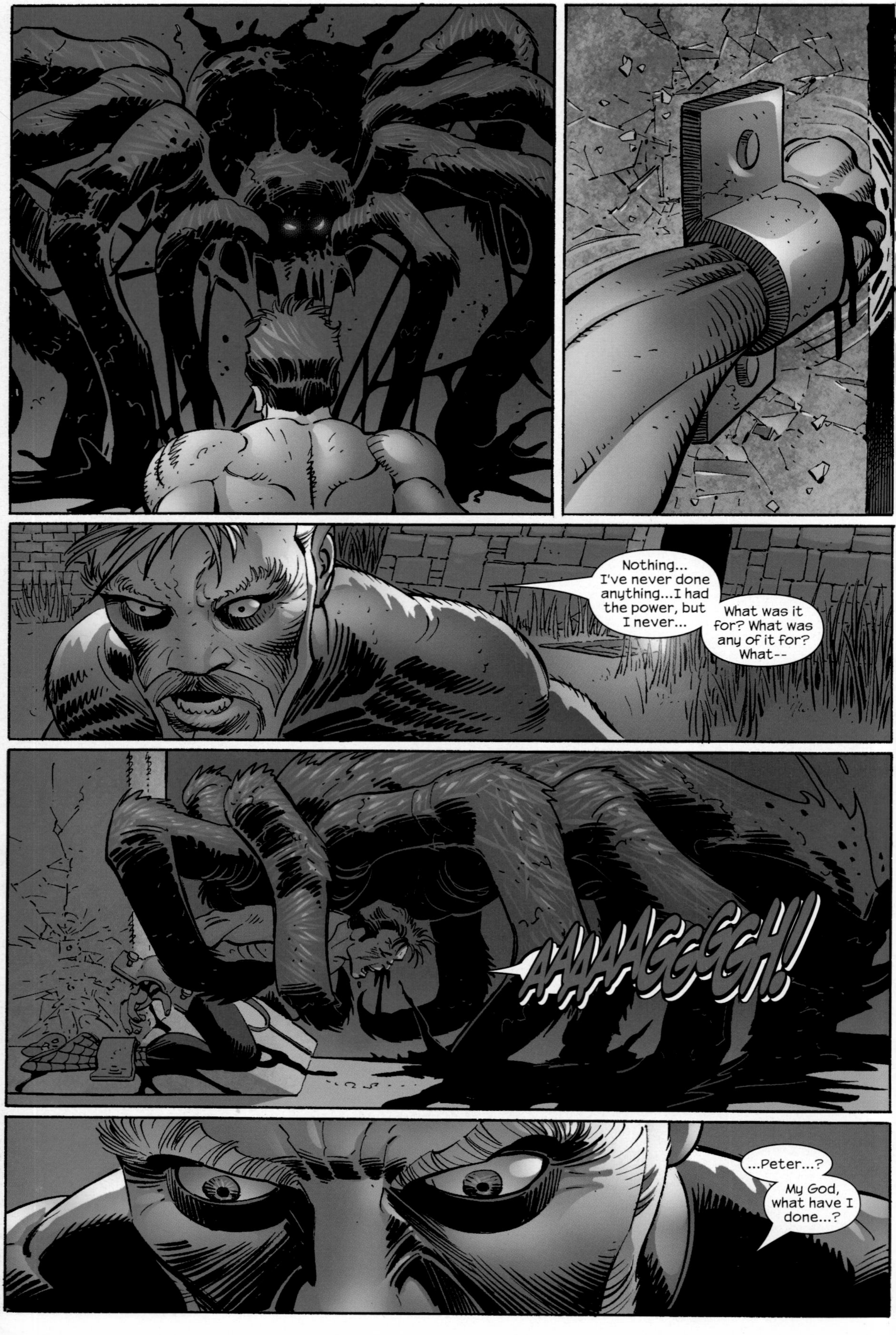
Nothing... I've never done anything...I had the power, but I never...
What was it for? What was any of it for? What--
AAAAAGGGGH!!
...Peter...?
My God, what have I done...?

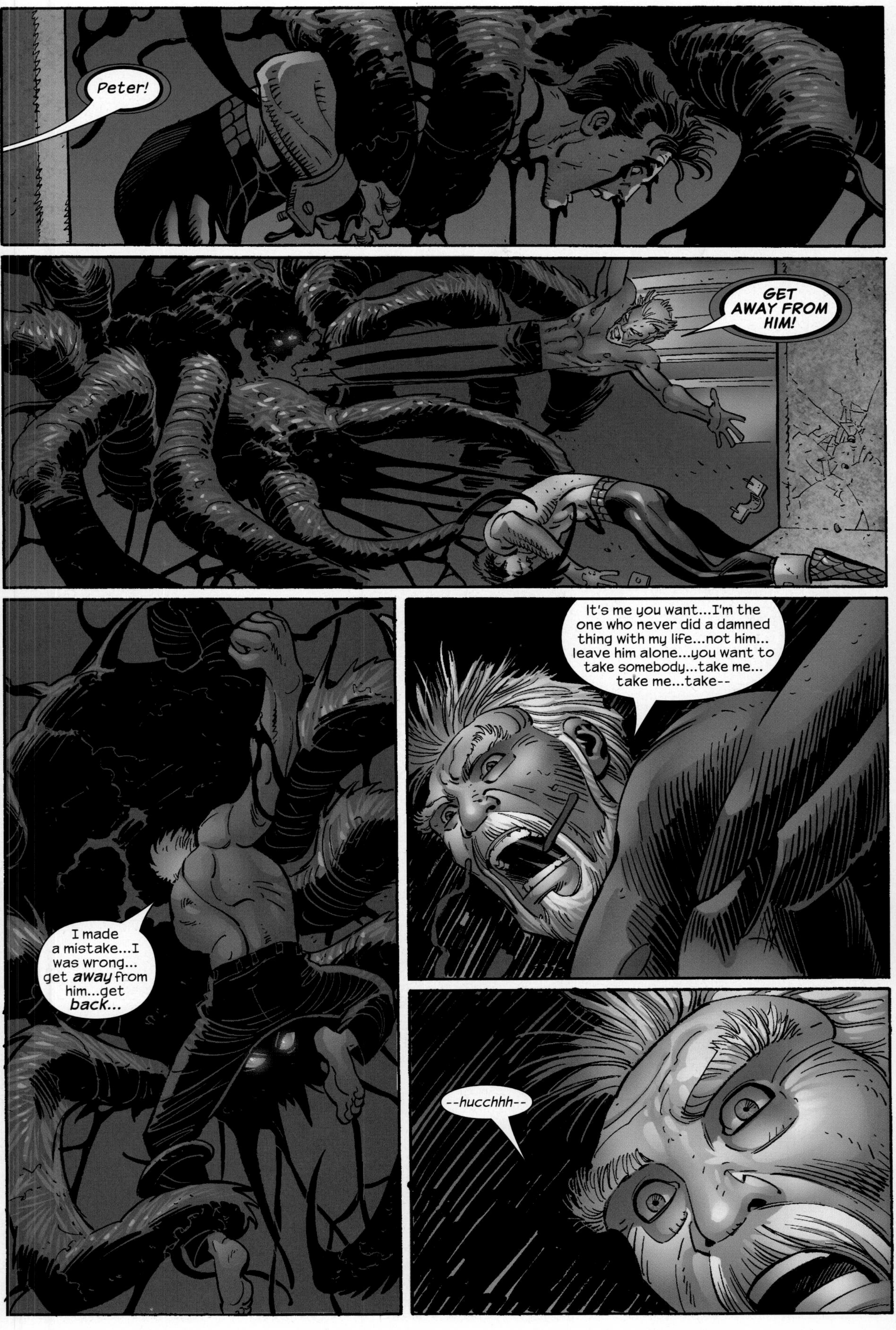
Peter!
GET AWAY FROM HIM!
I made a mistake...I was wrong... get *away* from him...get *back*...
It's me you want...I'm the one who never did a damned thing with my life...not him... leave him alone...you want to take somebody...take me... take me...take--
--hucchhh--

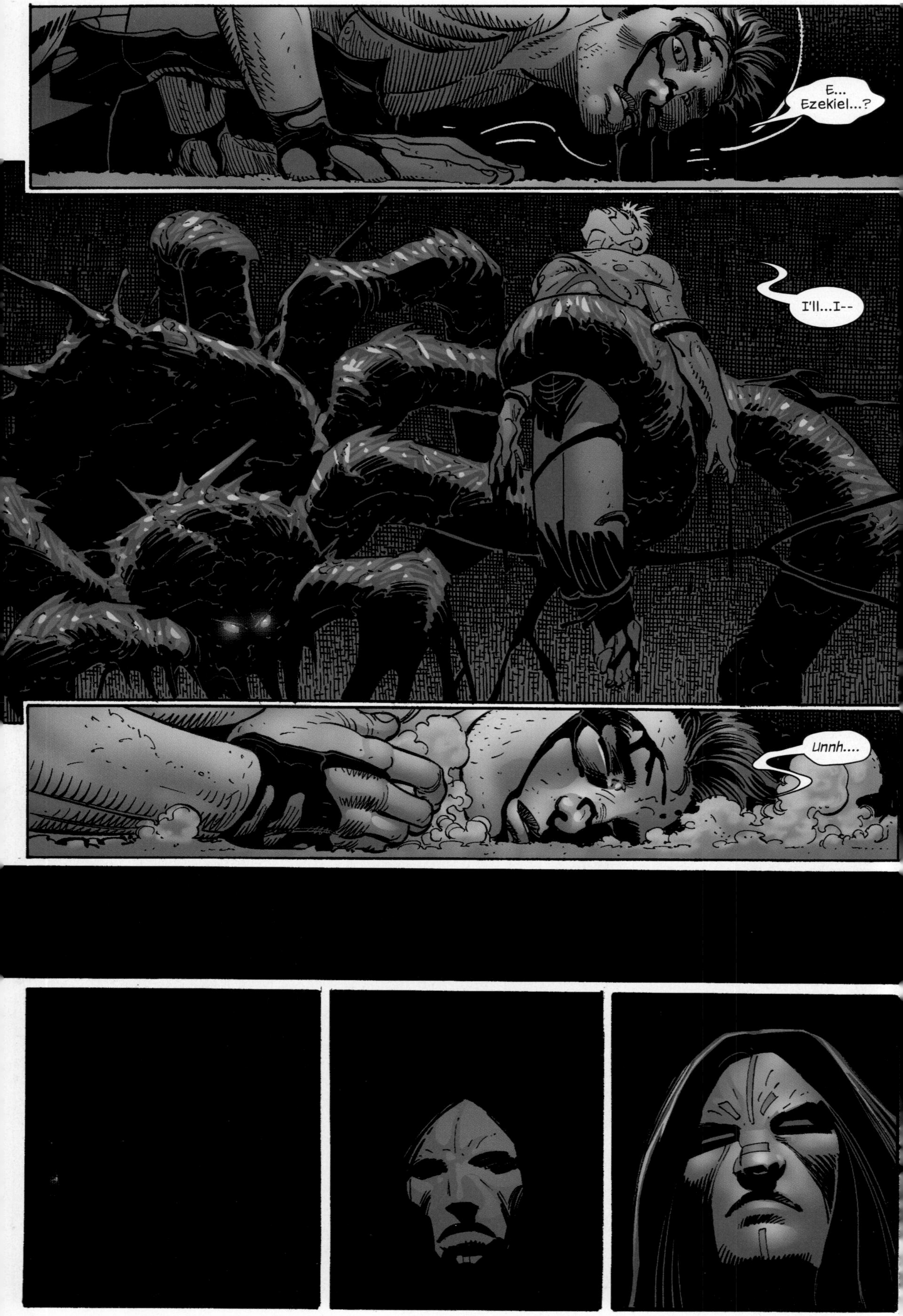
E...
Ezekiel...?
I'll...I--
Unnh....

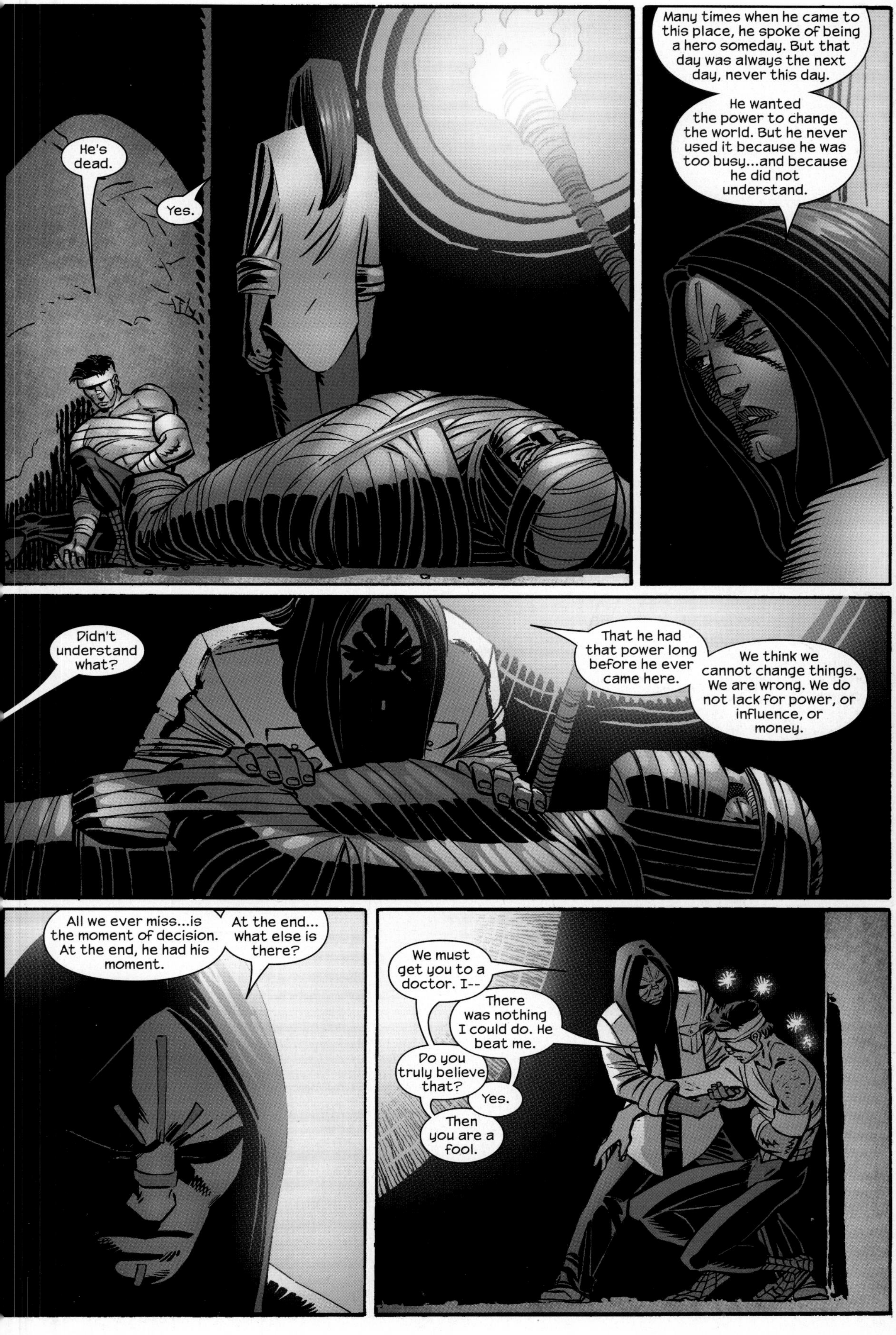
He's dead.
Yes.
Many times when he came to this place, he spoke of being a hero someday. But that day was always the next day, never this day.
He wanted the power to change the world. But he never used it because he was too busy...and because he did not understand.
Didn't understand what?
That he had that power long before he ever came here.
We think we cannot change things. We are wrong. We do not lack for power, or influence, or money.
All we ever miss...is the moment of decision. At the end, he had his moment.
At the end... what else is there?
We must get you to a doctor. I--
There was nothing I could do. He beat me.
Do you truly believe that?
Yes.
Then you are a fool.

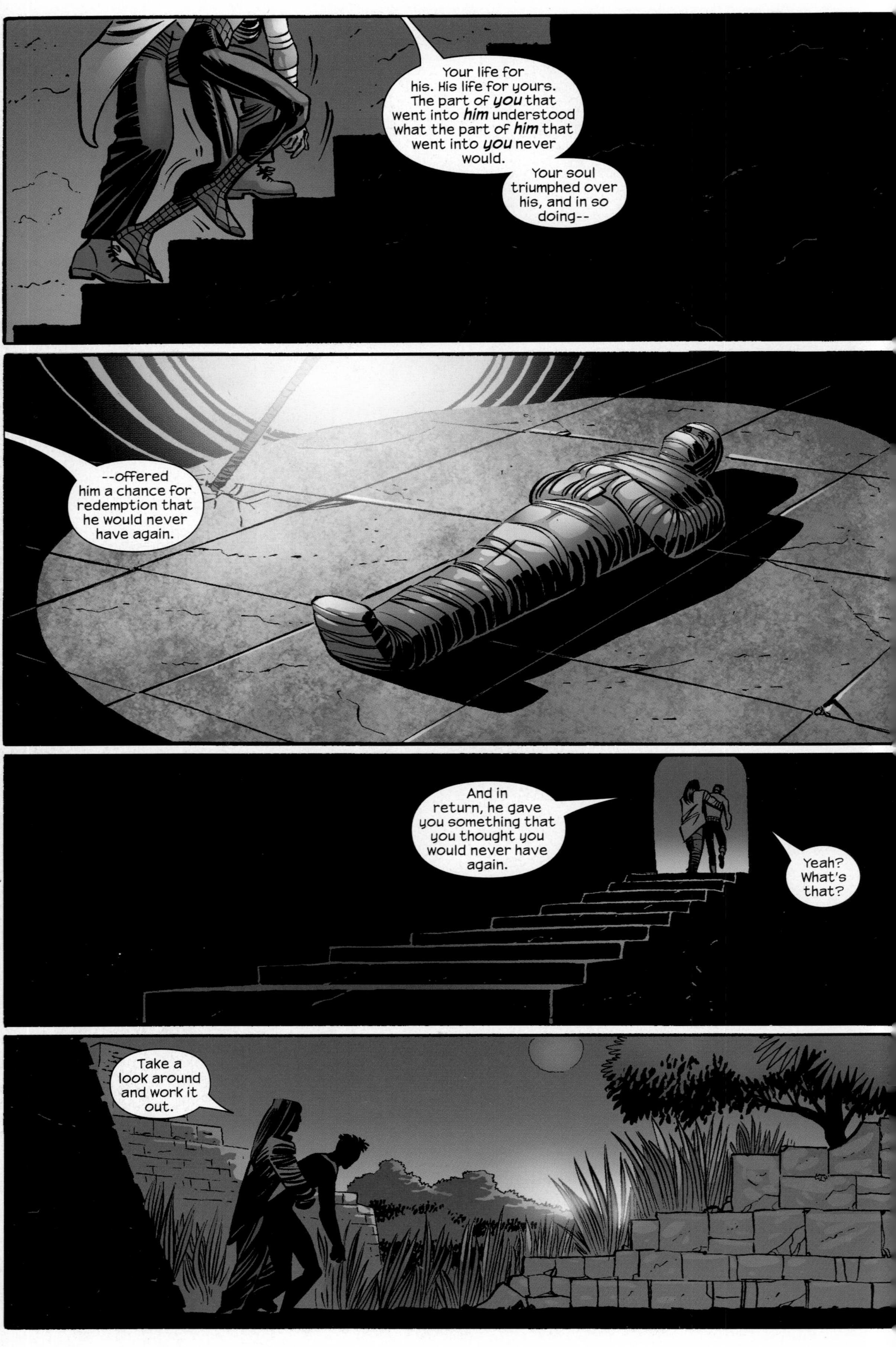
Your life for his. His life for yours. The part of you that went into him understood what the part of him that went into you never would.
Your soul triumphed over his, and in so doing--
--offered him a chance for redemption that he would never have again.
And in return, he gave you something that you thought you would never have again.
Yeah? What's that?
Take a look around and work it out.

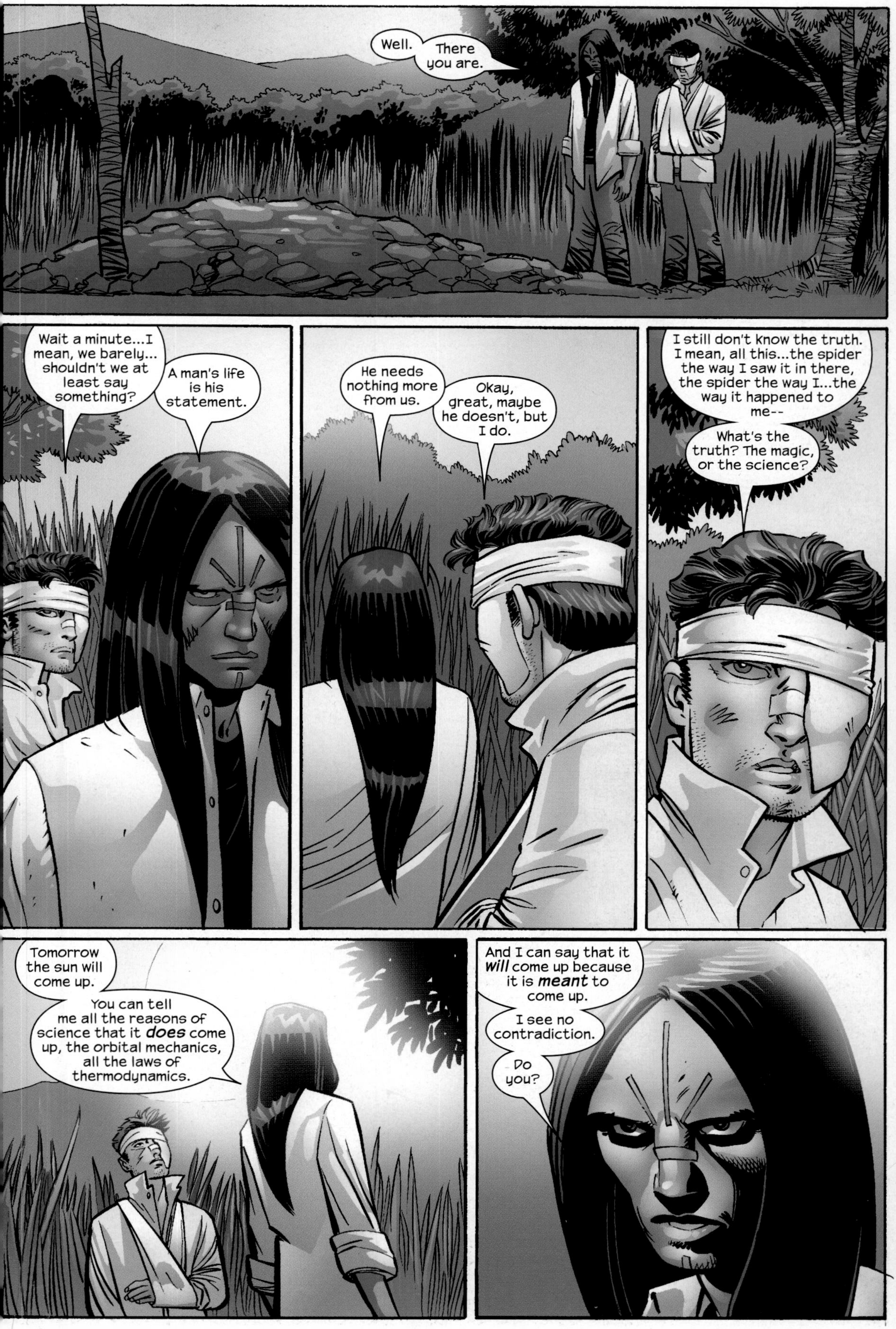
Well.
There you are.
Wait a minute...I mean, we barely... shouldn't we at least say something?
A man's life is his statement.
He needs nothing more from us.
Okay, great, maybe he doesn't, but I do.
I still don't know the truth. I mean, all this...the spider the way I saw it in there, the spider the way I...the way it happened to me--
What's the truth? The magic, or the science?
Tomorrow the sun will come up.
You can tell me all the reasons of science that it *does* come up, the orbital mechanics, all the laws of thermodynamics.
And I can say that it *will* come up because it is *meant* to come up.
I see no contradiction.
Do you?

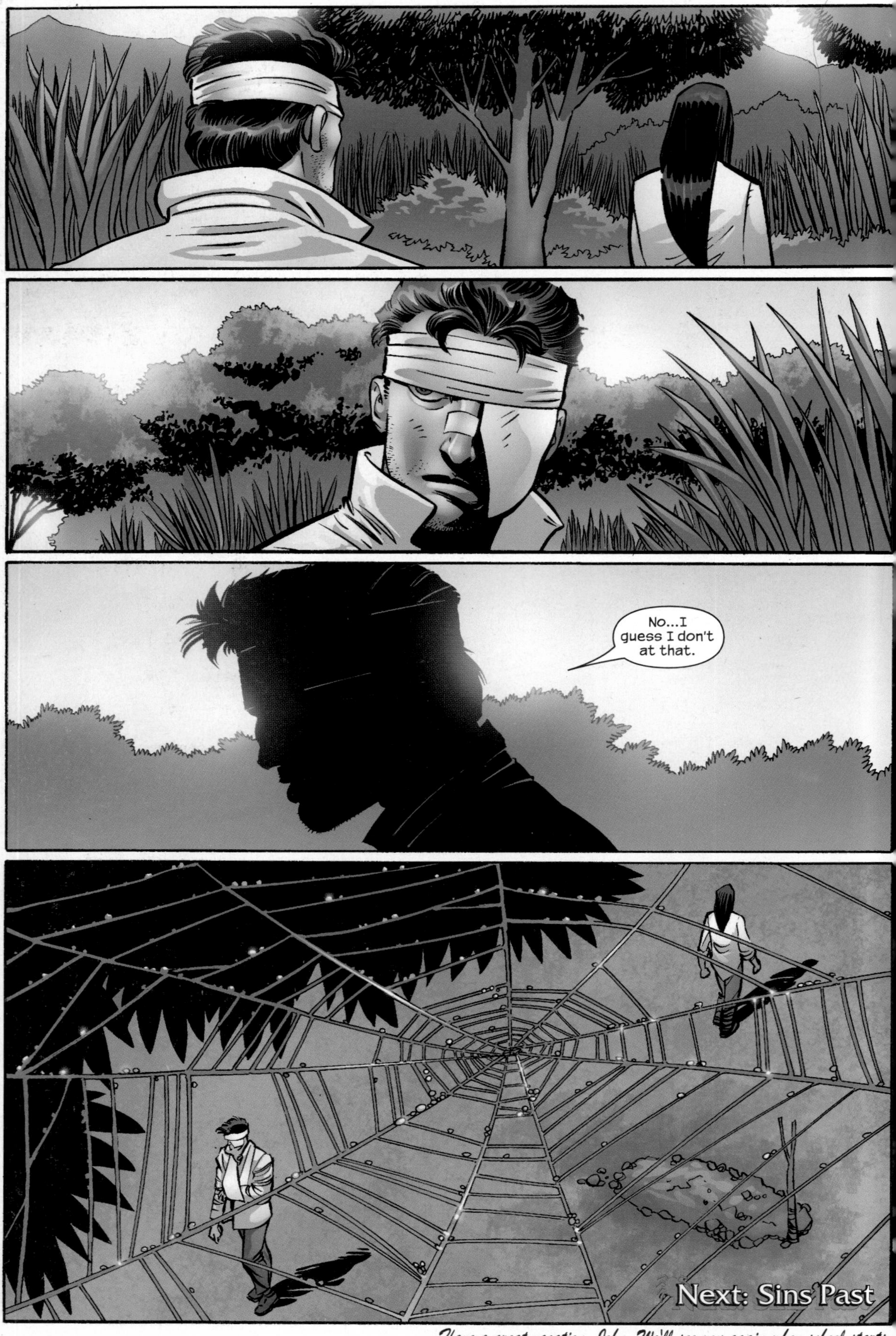
No...I guess I don't at that.
Next: Sins Past

Have a great vacation, John. We'll see you again when school starts.